Atums, 2017

ISBN 1979028893

Origen del documento: Agencia Estatal del Boletín Oficial del Estado

ORGANIC ACT 10/1995, DATED 23RD NOVEMBER, **ON THE CRIMINAL CODE.**

Publication: Official State Gazette number 281 on 24th November 1995

RECITAL OF MOTIVES

If the legal order has been defined as a set of rules that regulate the use of force, one may easily understand the importance of the Criminal Code in any civilised society. The Criminal Code defines criminal and misdemeanours that constitute the cases for application of the supreme action that may be taken by the coercive power of the State, that is, criminal sentencing. Thus, the Criminal Code holds a key place in the Law as a whole, to the extent that, not without reason, it has been considered a sort of "Negative Constitution". The Criminal Code must protect the basic values and principles of our social coexistence. When those values and principles change, it must also change. However, in our country, in spite of profound changes in the social, economic and political orders, the current text dates, as far as its basic core is concerned, from the last century. The need for it to be reformed is thus undeniable.

Based on the different attempts at reform carried out since the establishment of democracy, the Government has prepared a bill submitted for discussion and approval by the both Chambers. Thus, it must explain, even though briefly, the criteria on which it is based, even though these may easily be deduced from reading its text.

The axis of those criteria has been, as is logical, that of positive adaptation of the new Criminal Code to the constitutional values. The changes this bill introduces in that direction are innumerable, although it is worthwhile pointing out some of these.

Firstly, a full reform of the present penalties system, in order for it to achieve the aims of re-socialisation assigned to it by the Constitution. The system proposed partially simplifies regulation of custodial sentences, while extending the possibilities of these being replaced by others that affect less basic legal assets and, on the other, introduces changes in monetary penalties, adopting a day-fine system and adding community service work.

Secondly, the existing antinomy between the principle of minimum intervention and the growing needs for protection in an increasingly more complex society have been dealt with, with a cautious approach to new kinds of offence, although, in turn, eliminating criminal offences that have become obsolete. In the first sense, it is worth pointing out the introduction of offences against the social and economic order, or the new provisions on offences concerning organisation of the territory and natural resources; secondly, the disappearance of the complex figures of robbery with violence and personal threat that, having arisen in the context of combating highway robbery, should disappear, leaving the way to apply the general rules.

Thirdly, special emphasis has been placed on protecting fundamental rights and an attempt has been made to design the punitive instrument with special care wherever the exercise of any of these is at stake: for example, on one hand, specific protection of moral integrity, and on the other, the new regulation of offences against honour. On specifically protecting moral integrity, citizens are granted greater protection against torture, and by defining offences against honour in the manner proposed, freedom of expression is granted the full relevance it may and must be recognised under a democratic regime.

Fourthly, and in keeping with the objective of protecting and respecting fundamental rights, the regime of privilege enjoyed up to present by unlawful interference by civil servants in the rights and liberties of the citizens has been eliminated. Thus, it is proposed that arrests, entering and searching dwellings carried out by authorities or officers outside the cases allowed by the Law be treated as aggravating forms of the relevant common offences, and not as they have been up to present, that is, as special offences that, incomprehensibly and unjustifiably, had been mitigated.

Fifthly, an attempt has been made to advance on the path of real and effective equality, attempting to fulfil the task in that sense that is imposed upon the public powers by the Constitution. Certainly, the Criminal Code is not the most important instrument to carry out such task. However, it may contribute to it by eliminating regulations that are an obstacle to its realisation, or by introducing protective measures to deal with discriminatory situations. In addition to the regulations that grant specific protection against activities that tend toward discrimination, here one must mention the new regulation of offences against sexual freedom. This is aimed at adapting the offences classified to the legal asset protected, which is no longer, as it was historically, a woman's honour, but rather the sexual freedom of all. Protection of a woman's honour hid an intolerable discriminatory situation, which the new laws aim to totally eliminate. The novelty of the punitive techniques used may be surprising, but, in this case, moving away from tradition appears to be the correct thing to do.

Leaving the scope of principles and considering that of preparation techniques, this bill differs from the previous ones in its claim to be universal. The idea formally was that the Criminal Code had to include a complete regulation of the punitive power of the State. The starting point of this idea was already wrong, considering the importance of the powers of penalisation of the Administration in our country; what is more it was both unnecessary and unsettling.

It was unnecessary because the 19th Century option in favour of the Criminal Code and against special laws was based on the undeniable fact that the legislator, in preparing a Code, was constrained, due to external reasons of a social nature, to respect the constitutional principles, something that did not happen, or that happened to a lesser extent, in the case of a special laws. Within the framework of a flexible constitutionalism, this was an especially important argument as the basis to claim an absolutely universal nature of the Code. Nowadays, however, both the Criminal Code as well as the special laws are hierarchically subordinate to the Constitution and submitted thereto, not only due to that hierarchy, but also due to the existence of a jurisdictional control over their constitutionality.

Thus, special laws need not give rise to the caution they historically invoked.

Unsettling because, although it is undeniable that a Code would not deserve that name if it did not contain the majority of the criminal provisions and, of course, the basic principles on which all such provisions are to be based, the fact is that there are matters that it would be difficult to include therein. Now, while a claim to universality is inherent to the idea of a Code, stability and permanence are also goals that befit it, and there are scopes in which, due to the special situation of the rest of the legal order, or the very nature of things, such stability and permanence are impossible. Such is, for example, the case of offences related to exchange controls. In these, the constant changes in the financial conditions and in the legislative context surrounding such offences, makes it advisable, whether one wishes or not, to place the criminal provisions within that setting and to leave them out of the Code. In addition, this is our tradition and there is no lack, in the countries around us, of examples characterised by a similar way of acting.

Thus, in that and other similar cases, it has been decided to refer the criminal regulation of the respective matters to the relevant special laws in their field. The same technique has been applied to the provisions on decriminalisation of abortion. In this case, along with similar reasons to those stated above, one might argue that these are not incriminating laws, but rather laws that regulate cases of non-incrimination. The Constitutional Court of Law has demanded that, in configuring those cases, guarantees be provided that do not seem those of a Criminal Code, but rather those of another kind of regulation.

While preparing the Bill, the parliamentary discussions of 1992, the report by the General Council of the Judiciary, the state of the case law and scientific opinion have been kept very much in mind. It has been carried out based on the deep-rooted idea that the Criminal Code should belong to all and that, thus, all opinions must be heard and the solutions that appear most reasonable adopted, that is, those that everybody should be able to accept.

There is no pretence that this is a perfect work, but rather, simply a useful piece of work. The Government does not have the last word here, but rather only the first. Thus, via this Bill it only expresses its opinion, inviting all political forces and all citizens to collaborate in the task of perfecting it. Only if we all wish to have a better Criminal Code and contribute to achieve this, may an objective whose importance for coexistence and peaceful enjoyment of the rights and liberties the Constitution proclaims, one it is difficult to exaggerate, be attained.

PRELIMINARY TITLE

On penal guarantees and on the application of the Criminal Law

Article 1

1. No action or omission that is not defined as a felony or misdemeanour by Law prior to it being committed shall be punishable.

2. Security measures may only be applied when the cases previously established by the Law concur.

Article 2

1. No felony or misdemeanour shall be punishable by a punishment that is not foreseen by Law prior to it being committed. Likewise, the Laws establishing security measures shall not have retroactive effect.

2. Notwithstanding this, criminal laws that favour the person found guilty shall have retroactive effect, even though final judgement may have been handed down and the convict is serving a prison sentence at the time of them coming into force. When doubt arises in determining the most favourable law, the prisoner shall be heard. However, offences committed while a temporary Law is in force shall be judged pursuant thereto, except for express provisions to the contrary.

Article 3

1. No punishment or security measure may be enforced except by virtue of a final judgement handed down by the competent Judge or Court of Law, pursuant to the procedural laws.

2. Nor may any punishment or security measure be enforced in any way other than that prescribed by the Law and the implementing regulations or with other circumstances or particulars than those stated in its text. Enforcement of a sentence or security measure shall be carried out under control by the competent Judges and Courts of Law.

Article 4

1. Criminal Law shall not apply to cases other than those specifically included therein.

2. Should a Judge or Court of Law, in exercise of the jurisdiction thereof, have knowledge of any action or omission that, without being punishable by law, may be deemed worthy of repression, the Judge or Court shall abstain from all pronouncements thereon and shall submit the reasons why the matter should be subject to criminal penalisation to the Government.

3. The Judge or Court of Law shall likewise resort to the Government, stating whatever deemed appropriate concerning repeal or amendment of the provision, or requesting the exercise of the royal prerogative of mercy, without prejudice to the immediate execution of the sentence, when the rigorous application of the provisions of the Law requires punishment of an action or omission that, in the opinion of the Judge or Court of Law, should not the case, or when the punishment is notably excessive, in view of the harm caused by the offence and the personal circumstances of the person found guilty.

4. Should there be a petition for the royal pardon and the Judge or Court of Law has noted in a duly grounded resolution that fulfilment of the sentence might have caused a right to a process without undue delay to have been infringed, he shall suspend its execution until resolving the petition filed.

The Judge or Court of Law may also suspend execution of the sentence until resolution of the petition for the royal pardon when, if the sentence were to be executed, the royal pardon would be ineffective even if granted

Article 5

No punishment whatsoever shall be imposed in the absence of either mens rea or negligence.

Article 6

1. Security measures shall be based on the criminal risk of the subject on whom they are imposed involves, exteriorised by committing an act defined as a felony.

2. Security measures may not be more onerous, nor last longer than the punishment abstractly applicable to the act committed, nor exceed the limit necessary to prevent the principal being dangerous.

Article 7

In order to determine the Criminal Law applicable thereto, felonies and misdemeanours shall be deemed to have been committed at the moment when the subject perpetrates the action, or omits the act he was obliged to perpetrate.

Article 8

Acts liable to be defined pursuant to two or more provisions of this Code and not included in Articles 73 to 77 shall be punishable by observing the following rules:

1. A special provision shall have preferential application rather than a general one;

2. A subsidiary provision shall be applied only if the principal one is not, whether such a subsidiary nature is specifically declared or when it may tacitly be deduced.

3. The most ample or complex penal provision shall absorb those that punish offences committed therein.

4. Failing the preceding criteria, the most serious criminal provision shall exclude those punishing the act with a minor punishment.

Article 9

The provisions of this Title shall be applied to the felonies and misdemeanours that are punishable by special laws. The remaining provisions of this Code shall be applied to supplement everything not specifically foreseen therein.

BOOK I

General provisions on felonies and misdemeanours, the persons responsible, the penalties, security measures and other consequences of criminal offences

TITLE I

On felonies and misdemeanours

CHAPTER I

On felonies and misdemeanours

Article 10

Felonies or misdemeanours are intentional or negligent actions or omissions punishable by Law.

Article 11

Felonies or misdemeanours that consist of production of a result shall only be construed to be committed by omission when not avoiding the result thereof, by infringing a special legal duty of the principal, is equivalent, pursuant to the sense of the wording of the Law, to its cause. To such end, an action shall be equivalent to an omission:

a) If there is a specific legal or contractual obligation to act;

b) If the party omitting has created an occasion of for risk to the right protected by law, by means of a preceding action or omission.

Article 12

Negligent actions or omissions shall only be punished when specifically provided by the Law.

Article 13

1. Serious felonies are offences that the Law punishes with serious penalties.

2. Less serious felonies are offences that the Law punishes with less serious penalties.

3. Misdemeanours are those the Law punishes with minor penalties.

4. When the punishment, due to its scope, may be included simultaneously among those mentioned in the first two Sections of this Article, the offence shall be deemed as a serious felony in all cases.

Article 14

1. An essential error related to the event constituting the offence shall preclude criminal accountability. If the error, considering the circumstances of the case and the personal ones of the principal, could have been overcome, the offence shall be punishable, in that event, due to negligence.

2. Error as to a fact that classifies the offence, or regarding an aggravating circumstance, shall prevent its appreciation.

3. An essential error concerning the unlawfulness of the fact constituting the criminal offences precludes criminal accountability. Should it have been possible to overcome the error, the punishment lower by one or two degrees shall be applied.

Article 15

1. Both a consummated offence and an attempted offence are punishable.

2. Misdemeanours shall only be punishable when consummated, except those attempted against persons or properties.

Article 16

1. An attempted offence takes place when a person begins to perpetrate an offence by direct action, perpetrating all or part of the acts that objectively should produce the intended result, and notwithstanding this, such is not attained due to causes beyond the control of the principal.

2. Whoever voluntarily avoids the offence being consummated, either by going no further with its commission when already commenced, or by preventing the result from taking place, shall be exempt from criminal accountability, without prejudice to the accountability he may have incurred for the acts perpetrated, should these already have constituted another felony or misdemeanour.

3. When various subjects intervene in an act, the one or those who desist from execution thereof once already commenced, and who prevent or attempt to prevent consummation, in a serious, firm manner, shall be exempt from criminal accountability, without prejudice to accountability they may have incurred for the acts perpetrated, should these already have constituted another felony or misdemeanour.

Article 17

1. A conspiracy exists when one or more persons collude to commit a crime and decide to carry it out.

2. A proposition exists when he who has resolved to commit a crime invites another or other persons to commit it.

3. Conspiracy and solicitation to perpetrate an offence shall only be punishable in the cases specifically foreseen in the Law.

Article 18

1. Provocation exists when a direct incitation is present by means of the printing press, radio broadcasting or any other means with a similar effectiveness, affording publicity, or when persons have gathered, inciting the perpetration of a crime.

Conniving at a criminal act by expressing approval thereof, for the purposes of this Code, is presentation, before an assembly of persons, or by any means of diffusion, of ideas or doctrines that defend the offence or praise the principal. Connivance at a criminal act by expressing approval thereof shall only be criminal as a form of provocation and if, due to its nature and circumstances, it constitutes a direct incitement to commit a crime.

2. Provocation shall be punished exclusively in cases in which the Law foresees this.

If the provocation has been followed by perpetration of the offence, it shall be punished as induction.

CHAPTER II

On the causes of exclusion from criminal accountability

Article 19

Those under the age of eighteen years shall not be criminally accountable pursuant to this Code. When a minor under that age commits an offence, he shall be held accountable pursuant to the terms set forth in the law regulating the criminal accountability of minors.

Article 20

The following persons shall not be criminally accountable:

1. Those who, at the time of committing a crime, due to any mental anomaly or alteration, cannot comprehend the unlawful nature of the act, or to act in line with that comprehension.

A transitory mental disorder shall not cause exoneration from the punishment when provoked by the subject in order to commit the offence, or when he would or should have foreseen that it would be committed.

2. Whoever, at the time of committing a felony or misdemeanour, is in a state of absolute intoxication due to consumption of alcoholic beverages, toxic and narcotic drugs, psychotropic substances or others that cause similar effects, as long as such state have not been sought for the purpose of committing it, or when he would or should have foreseen that it would be committed, or when under the influence of a withdrawal syndrome, due to his dependence on such substances, that prevents him from comprehending the unlawfulness of the act, or acting in keeping with such comprehension.

3. Whoever, due to suffering alterations in perception from the time of birth, or from childhood, has a seriously altered his awareness of reality.

4. Whoever is acting in defence of his person or his own rights or those of others, as long as the following requisites are fulfilled:

One. Unlawful aggression. In the case of defence of goods, unlawful aggression shall be deemed as an attack on these that constitutes a felony or misdemeanour and that places them in serious danger of deterioration or imminent loss. In the case of defence of the dwelling or its premises, trespassing the former or latter shall be deemed unlawful aggression.

Two. Rational need for the means employed to prevent or repel it.

Three. Lack of sufficient provocation on the part of the defending

person.

5. Whoever, in a state of necessity, in order to avoid damage to himself or others, causes damage to another's legally protected interest or fails to perpetrate a duty, as long as the following requisites concur:

One. The damage caused is not greater than the damage sought to be prevented;

Two. That the situation of necessity has not been intentionally provoked by the

subject;

Three. That the person is need is not bound, due to his office or occupation, the obligation to sacrifice himself.

6. Whoever acts driven by insurmountable fear.

7. Any person who acts in carrying out of a duty or in the lawful exercise of a right, authority or office.
In the cases of the first three Sections, the security measures foreseen in this Code shall be applied.

CHAPTER III

On the circumstances that mitigate criminal accountability

Article 21

The following are mitigating circumstances:

1. The causes stated in the preceding Chapter, when not all the necessary requisites to exclude accountability in the respective cases concur.

2. The convict acting due to his serious addiction to the substances mentioned in Section 2 of the preceding Article.

3. The convict acting due to causes or stimuli so overpowering that they produced fury, obstinacy or another similar state of mind.

4. The convict having proceeded to confess his crime to the authorities before having knowledge of the judicial proceedings brought against him.

5. The convict having compensated the victim for the damages caused or having lessened the effects thereof, at some phase of the procedure and prior to the trial taking place.

6. Extraordinary or undue drawing out of the formalities of the proceedings, as long as this is not due to the convict, such prolongation being disproportionate to the complexity of the cause.

7. Any other circumstance of a similar importance to the aforesaid.

CHAPTER IV

On the circumstances that aggravate criminal accountability

Article 22

The following are aggravating circumstances:

1. Perpetrating the act with premeditation.

There is premeditation when the convict commits any of the offences against persons using means or ways to do so that tend directly or especially to assure them, without risk to his person that might arise from defence by the victim.

2. Perpetrating the act using a disguise, abuse of superiority, or taking advantage of the circumstances of the place, time or aid from other persons that weaken the defence of the victim or facilitate impunity of the convict.

3. Perpetrating the act for a price, reward or promise.

4. Committing the offence for racist or anti-Semitic reasons, or another kind of discrimination related to ideology, religion or belief of the victim, ethnicity, race or nation to which he belongs, his gender, sexual orientation or identity, illness suffered or disability.

5. To deliberately and inhumanely increase victim's suffering, causing unnecessary suffering while committing the crime.

6. Acting with abuse of confidence.

7. When the convict avails himself of his public status.

8. Having a criminal record.

There is recidivism when, when committing the crime, the convict has been sentenced by final judgement for a felony under the same category in this Code, as long as it is of the same nature.

For the purposes of this Section, a cancelled criminal record or one that should be cancelled shall not be counted.

CHAPTER V

On the mixed circumstance of kinship

Article 23

A circumstance that may mitigate or aggravate accountability, according to the nature, motives and effects of the crime, is when the victim is or has been the spouse or person with whom the convict has had a stable emotional relationship, or being the ascendant, descendant or biological or adoptive sibling of the offender or spouse or cohabitating partner thereof.

CHAPTER VI

General provisions

Article 24

1. For criminal purposes, status of authority shall be deemed to be held by persons who, alone, or as a member of any corporation, board or collegiate body, have a commanding post or exercise jurisdiction pertaining thereto. In all cases, members of the Congress of Deputies, of the Senate, of the Legislative Assemblies of the Autonomous Communities and the European Parliament shall be deemed authorities. The officers of the Public Prosecutor's Office shall also be deemed authorities.

2. Civil servant status shall also be deemed to be held by all those who, by immediate provision of the Law, or by election or appointment by the authority with relevant powers, participate in the exercise of public duties.

Article 25

For the purposes of this Code, all persons who suffer an illness of a persistent nature that prevents them from controlling their person or assets themselves shall be deemed incapable, whether or not their incapacity has been declared.

Article 26

For the purposes of this Code, a document shall be deemed any material medium that expresses or includes data, facts or narrations that are effective as evidence, or of any other kind of legal importance.

TITLE II

On persons criminally responsible for felonies and misdemeanours

Article 27

Those criminally responsible for felonies and misdemeanours are the principals and their accessories.

Article 28

Principals are those who perpetrate the act themselves, alone, jointly, or by means of another used to aid and abet.

The following shall also be deemed principals:

a) Whoever directly induces another or others to commit a crime;

b) Whoever co-operates in the commission thereof by an act without which a crime could not have been committed.

Article 29

Accessories are those who, not being included in the preceding Article, co-operate in carrying out the offence with prior or simultaneous acts.

Article 30

1. In felonies and misdemeanours that are committed using media or supports of mechanical diffusion, neither the accessories, nor those who have personally or actually favoured these shall be held criminally accountable.

2. The principals to which Article 28 refers shall be held accountable in a progressive, excluding and subsidiary manner, in the following order:

1º. Those who materially drafted the text or produced the sign concerned, and those who induced others to perpetrate the act;

2º. The directors of the publication or programme in which it is disseminated;

3º. The directors of the printing, broadcasting or distribution company;

4º. The directors of the recording, playing or printing company;

3. When, for any reason other than extinction of criminal accountability, or for declaration of contempt of court or not residing in Spain, any of the persons included in any of the Sub-Sections of the preceding Section may be prosecuted, proceedings shall be taken against those mentioned in the Sub-Section immediately following.

Article 31

1. Whoever acts as *de facto* or *de jure* administrator of a legal person, or on behalf or in legal or voluntary representation of another, shall be held personally accountable, even though he does not fulfil the conditions, qualities or relationship that the relevant definition of felony or misdemeanour requires to be an active subject thereof, if such circumstances concur in the entity or person in whose name or on behalf of whom he so acts.

2 (Suppressed)

Article 31 bis[1]

1. In the circumstances provided for in this Code, legal entities shall be criminally liable for offences committed in their name or on their behalf, and for their benefit, by their legal representatives and administrators, whether de facto or de jure.

In the same circumstances, legal entities shall be criminally liable for offences committed, in the course of their business and on their behalf and for their benefit, by those who, being subject to the authority of the individuals referred to in the preceding paragraph, may have committed the acts on account of not having exercised due control over them, given the specific circumstances of the case.

---

[1] The first paragraph of section 5 is amended by single art. 1 of Organic Law 7/2012 of 27 December.

2. The criminal liability of legal entities shall be enforceable provided that it can be established that an offence has been committed, which must have been committed by an individual holding or carrying out any of the posts or duties referred to in the preceding section, even when the specific individual responsible has not been singled out or it has not been possible to bring proceedings against him. Where, as a result of the same circumstances, a fine is imposed on both parties, the judges or courts shall modulate the respective amounts, such that the resulting total is not disproportionate to the seriousness of the offence.

3. Neither the fact of the circumstances in which the individuals that committed the acts, or made them possible on account of not exercising due control, affect or aggravate the liability of the accused, nor the fact that those individuals have died or absconded, shall preclude or alter the criminal liability of legal entities, without prejudice to the provisions of the following section.

4. Extenuating circumstances in relation to the criminal liability of legal entities shall only be deemed to exist, if, subsequent to the offence being committed and through their legal representatives, they have:

a) Confessed the offence to the authorities, before learning that legal proceedings were being brought against them.

b) Collaborated with the investigation into the matter, providing evidence, at any point in the proceedings, that was new and decisive in relation to clarifying the criminal liability arising from the facts.

c) Repaired or diminished the damage caused by the offence, at any point in the proceedings and prior to evidence being heard.

d) Established, prior to the hearing of evidence, effective measures to prevent and detect offences that may be committed in the future with the means or under the cover of the legal entity.

5. Provisions relating to the criminal liability of legal entities shall not apply to the state, to regional or institutional public authorities, to regulatory bodies, to public business agencies or entities, to international public law organisations, or to such others as exercise powers of sovereignty or government, conferred by public authority; nor shall such provisions apply to state companies that implement public policy or provide services of general economic interest.

In such cases, the courts may pronounce criminal liability in the event that they find the entity in question is a legal form created by its promoters, founders, administrators or representatives in order to avoid possible criminal liability.

TITLE III

On penalties

CHAPTER I

On punishments, their types and effects

SUBCHAPTER 1. ON PUNISHMENTS AND THEIR TYPES

Article 32

Penalties that may be imposed pursuant to this Code, either under principal or accessory terms, include deprivation of freedom, of other rights and fines.

Article 33

1. Pursuant to their nature and duration, the punishments shall be classified as serious, less serious and minor:

2. Severe penalties include:

a) Imprisonment exceeding five years;

b) Absolute barring;

c) Special barring for a term exceeding five years;

d) Suspension from public employment and office for a term exceeding five years;

e) Deprivation of the right to drive motor vehicles and mopeds for a term exceeding eight years;

f) Deprivation of the right to own and carry weapons for a term exceeding eight years;

g) Deprivation of the right to reside in specific places or to visit them, for a term exceeding five years;

h) Prohibition to approach the victim or those of his relatives or other persons determined by the Judge or Court of Law, for a term exceeding five years;

i) Prohibition to communicate with the victim or with those of his relatives or other persons determined by the Judge or Court of Law, for a term exceeding five years;

j) Deprivation of parental rights.

3. Less serious penalties include:

a) Imprisonment from three months to five years;

b) Special barring up to five years;

c) Suspension from public employment and office up to five years;

d) Deprivation of the right to drive motor vehicles and mopeds from a year and a day to eight years;

e) Deprivation of right to own and carry weapons from a year and a day to eight years;

f) Deprivation of right to reside in specific places or to visit them, for a term of six months to five years;

g) Prohibition to approach the victim or those of his relatives or other persons determined by the Judge or Court of Law, for a term of six months to five years;

h) Prohibition to communicate with the victim or with those of his relatives or other persons determined by the Judge or Court of Law, for a term of six months to five years;

i) Fine of more than two months;

j) The proportional fine, whatever its amount, except as provided in Section 7 of this Article.

k) Community service, from thirty-one to 180 days;

l) Permanent location from three months and a day to six months;

m) Loss of the possibility of obtaining public subsidies or aid and the right to enjoy tax or Social Security benefits or incentives, whatever their duration.

4. Minor penalties include:

a) Deprivation of the right to drive motor vehicles and mopeds from three months to a year;

b) Deprivation of right to own and carry weapons from three months to a year;

c) Deprivation of right to reside in specific places or to visit them, for a term under six months;

d) Prohibition to approach the victim or his relatives or other persons determined the Judge or Court of Law, for a term of one month to less than six months;

e) Prohibition to communicate with the victim or with his relatives or other persons determined by the Judge or Court of Law, for a term of one month to less than six months;

f) A fine from ten days to two months;

g) Permanent traceability from one day to three months;

h) Community service, from one to 30 days.

5. Personal subsidiary liability for failure to pay the fine shall have a more or less serious nature, according to the punishment it substitutes.

6. Accessory penalties shall have the respective duration of the principal punishment, except if specifically provided otherwise in other provisions of this Code.

7. Penalties applicable to legal persons, that are all deemed serious, are as follows:

a) Fine by quotas or proportional;

b) Dissolution of the legal person. The dissolution shall cause definitive loss of its legal personality, as well as of its capacity to act in any way in legal transactions, or to carry out any kind of activity, even if lawful.

c) Suspension of its activities for a term that may exceed five years;

d) Closure of its premises and establishments for a term that may not exceed five years;

e) Prohibition to carry out the activities through which it has committed, favoured or concealed the felony in the future. Such prohibition may be temporary or definitive. If temporary, the term may not exceed fifteen years;

f) Barring from obtaining public subsidies and aid, to enter into contracts with the public sector and to enjoy tax or Social Security benefits and incentives, for a term that may not exceed fifteen years;

g) Judicial intervention to safeguard the rights of the workers or creditors for the time deemed necessary, which may not exceed five years.

The intervention may affect the whole of the organisation or be limited to some of its premises, sections or business units. The Judge or Court of Law shall determine exactly the content of the intervention and shall determine who shall take charge of the intervention and within which regularity monitoring reports must be submitted to the judicial body, in the sentence, or subsequently by ruling. The intervention may be amended or suspended at any times, following a report by the receiver and the Public Prosecutor. The receiver shall be entitled to access all the installations and premises of the company or legal person and to receive as much information as he may deem necessary to exercise his duties. The implementing regulations shall determine the aspects related to the exercise of the duties of the receiver, as well as his remuneration or necessary qualifications.

Temporary closure of premises or establishments, suspension of corporate activities and judicial intervention may also be agreed by the Investigating Judge as a precautionary measure during investigation of the case.

Article 34

The following shall not be deemed penalties:

1. Preventive detention and custody and other precautionary measures of a penal nature;

2. Fines and other correctives imposed on subordinates or those administered in use of governmental or disciplinary attributions;

3. Deprivation of rights and reparatory penalties established in the civil or administrative laws.

SUBCHAPTER 2. ON PUNISHMENTS DEPRIVING OF FREEDOM

Article 35

Sentences depriving of freedom shall de deemed to include imprisonment, permanent traceability and personal subsidiary accountability for failure to pay fines.

Article 36

1. Imprisonment shall have a minimum duration of three months and a maximum of twenty years, apart from the exceptional terms provided in other provisions of this Code.

Its fulfilment, as well as penitentiary benefits involving shortening of the sentence, shall be applied pursuant to the terms of the laws and this of Code.

2. When the term of the prison sentence handed down exceeds five years, the Judge or Court of Law may order that classification of the prisoner in pre-release penitentiary treatment not take place until half of the sentence handed down has been served.

In any event, when the term of the prison sentence handed down exceeds five years and it is for a felony of those listed below, classification of the convict in pre-release penitentiary treatment may not take place until half the sentence has been served:

a) A felony related to terrorist organisations and groups and felonies of terrorism under Chapter VII of Title XXII of Book II of this Code;

b) A felony committed within a criminal organisation or group;

c) A felony under Article 183;

d) A felony under Chapter V of Title VIII of Book II of this Code, when the victim is under thirteen years old.

The Parole Board Judge, following an individual assessment that favours social reinsertion, and evaluating the personal circumstances of the prisoner and evolution of the re-education treatment, as appropriate, may issue a reasoned ruling, having heard the Public Prosecutor, the Directorate-General for Penitentiary Institutions and the other parties, to apply the general regime of serving sentence, except in the cases set forth in the preceding Section.

Article 37

1. Permanent traceability shall last up to six months. Its serving binds the convict to remain under house arrest, or at a specific place set by the Judge in the sentence, or subsequently in a reasoned ruling.

However, in cases in which permanent traceability is foreseen as the main punishment, due to repetition of the offence committed, and whenever specifically provided by the applicable specific provision, the Judge may order in the sentence that the punishment of permanent traceability be served on Saturdays, Sundays and holidays, at the penitentiary centre nearest to the convict's dwelling.

2. On application by the convict, and if the circumstances make this advisable, having heard the Public Prosecutor, the Judge or Court of Law sentencing may resolve that the sentence be served on Saturdays and Sundays, or non continuously.

3. Should the convict fail to serve the sentence, the Judge or Court of Law sentencing shall draw up an attestation to proceed against him pursuant to the terms set forth in Article 468.

4. In order to guarantee effective serving, the Judge or Court of Law may order use of mechanical or electronic resources to allow the convict to be located.

Article 38

1. The duration of sentences shall begin to be counted from the day on which the sentence finding guilty is final, if the convict is already in prison.

2. When the convict is not in prison, the duration of the sentence shall begin to be counted from him being admitted to the appropriate establishment where it is to be served.

SUBCHAPTER 3. ON PENALTIES OF DEPRIVATION OF RIGHTS

Article 39

The following are penalties of deprivation of rights:

a) Absolute barring;

b) Those of special barring from public employment and office, profession, trade, industry or commerce, or other activities determined in this Code, or of parental rights, those of fostership, guardianship or care, right to passive suffrage or any other right;

c) Suspension from public employment and office;

d) Deprivation of right to drive motor vehicles and mopeds;

e) Deprivation of right to own and carry weapons;

f) Deprivation of right to reside in specific places or to visit them;

g) Prohibition to approach the victim or of his relatives or other persons determined by the Judge or Court of Law;

h) Prohibition to communicate with the victim or his relatives or other persons determined by the Judge or Court of Law.

i) Community service;

j) Deprivation of parental rights

Article 40

1. The punishment of absolute barring shall have a term of six to twenty years; those of special barring, from three months to twenty years, and that of suspension from public employment and office, from three months to six years.

2. The punishment of deprivation of the right to drive motor vehicles and mopeds, and that of deprivation of the right to own and carry weapons, shall have a term from three months to ten years.

3. The punishment of deprivation of the right to reside in specific places or to visit them shall have a term of up to ten years. Prohibition to approach the victim or his relatives or other persons, or to communicate with them, shall have a term from one month to ten years.

4. The punishment of community service shall have a term of one day to a year.

5. The term of each one of these penalties shall be that foreseen in the preceding Sections, apart from where exceptionally provided by other provisions of this Code.

Article 41

The punishment of absolute barring leads to definitive deprivation of all honours, public employment and posts the convict has, including those to which he has been elected. It also causes incapacity to obtain these or any other honours, posts or public employment, and to be elected to public office, during the term of the sentence.

Article 42

The punishment of special barring from public employment and office causes definitive deprivation of the employment or office it befalls, even if elected thereto, and of the honours related thereto.

It also causes incapacity to obtain the same or others of the same kind during the term of the sentence. The sentence must specify the employment, posts and honours the barring affects.

Article 43

Suspension from public employment and office shall cause the convict to be deprived of exercise thereof during the whole term of the sentence.

Article 44

Special barring from the right of passive suffrage deprives the convict, during the term of the sentence, of the right to be elected to public office.

Article 45

Special barring from a profession, trade, industry or commerce, or any other right, that must be duly reasoned and specified in the sentence, deprives the convict of the right to exercise these during the term of the sentence.

Article 46

Special barring from exercise of parental rights, guardianship, care, safekeeping or fostership, deprives the convict the rights inherent to the former, and brings about extinction of the others, as well as incapacity to obtain appointment to such offices during the term of the sentence. The punishment of deprivation of parental rights implies the loss of entitlement thereof, while the rights the offspring has with regard to the convict shall subsist. The Judge or Court of Law may order these penalties regarding all or some of the minors or incapacitated parties under the charge of the convict, in view of the circumstances of the case.

For the purposes of this Article, parental rights include those regulated by the Civil Code, even if prorogued, as well as similar institutions foreseen in the civil legislation of the Autonomous Communities.

Article 47

Handing down a punishment of deprivation of the right to drive motor vehicles and mopeds shall bar the convict from exercising both rights for the term set in the judgement. Handing down a punishment of deprivation of the right to own and carry weapons shall bar the convict from exercising that right for the term set in the judgement.

When the punishment imposed is for a term exceeding two years, it shall involve loss of the currency of the permit or licence that enables the person to drive, or to hold and carry, respectively.

Article 48

1. Deprivation of right to reside in specific places or to visit them shall prevent the convict from residing in or going to the place where he has committed the felony or misdemeanour, or that where the victim or his family lives, if different.

2. Prohibition to approach the victim, or his relatives or other persons determined by the Judge or Court of Law, shall prevent the convict from approaching them, wherever they may be, as well as approaching their dwelling, their places of work, and any other regularly visited by them, with suspension of visitation, communication and overnight stay rights with regard to offspring that, if appropriate, might have been recognised by a civil judgement, until total fulfilment of the sentence concerned.

3. Prohibition to communicate with the victim, or with his relatives or other persons determined by the Judge or Court of Law, shall prevent the convict from establishing contact with them by any means of communication computer, telematic, written, verbal or visual means.

4. The Judge or Court of Law may resolve that control of these measures be exercised through the electronic means so permitting.

Article 49

Community service, which may not be imposed without the consent of the convict, shall oblige him to provide his non-remunerated co-operation in specific activities of public utility, that may consist, in relation to offences of a similar nature to that committed by the convict, of tasks to repair the damage caused, or support or assistance for victims, as well as participation by the convict in workshops or training or re-education programmes on labour, cultural, traffic education, sexual and other similar matters. The daily duration may not exceed eight hours and its conditions shall be as follows:

1. Its carrying out shall be conducted under control by the Penitentiary Parole Board Judge, who shall require reports to be prepared for that purpose, on carrying out of work for the Administration, public entity or association of general interest for which the services are provided.

2. It shall not be against the dignity of the convict.

3. The social services tasks shall be provided by the Administration, which may enter into the appropriate arrangements for such purposes.

4. It shall enjoy the protection convicts are afforded by the penitentiary laws on Social Security matters.

5. It shall not be subject to attainment of economic interests.

6. Once the penitentiary social services have carried out the necessary verifications, they shall notify the Penitentiary Parole Board Judge of the relevant incidents in execution of the punishment and, in all cases, if the convict:

- a) Is absent from the work for at least two working days, as long as it involves voluntary refusal by him to serve the sentence;

- b) In spite of demands by the person in charge of the work centre, his performance is considerably lower than the required minimum;

- c) Were to repeatedly and manifestly oppose or fail to abide by the instructions he is given by the manager of the occupation, related to its carrying out thereof;

- d) For any other reason, his conduct were to cause the work manager to refuse to keep him at the centre any longer.

Once the report is appraised, the Penitentiary Parole Board Judge may order its conclusions to be enforced by the centre itself, to send the convict to conclude execution thereof at another centre, or to deem that the convict has failed to serve the sentence.

In the event of breach thereof, an attestation shall be issued to proceed against him, pursuant to Article 468.

7. Should the convict be missing from work for a justified reason, he shall not be deemed to have abandoned the activity. However, the work missed shall not be included in the calculation of serving the sentence; such calculation shall include the days or working time effectively worked from the total to which he has been sentenced.

SUBCHAPTER 4. ON PUNISHMENT BY FINE

Article 50

1. Punishment by fine shall consist in sentencing the convict to pay a pecuniary punishment.

2. Punishment by fine shall be imposed, except if the Law states otherwise, by the day-fine system.

3. The minimum length shall be ten days and the maximum two years. Fine penalties against legal persons shall have a maximum length of five years.

4. The daily quota shall be a minimum of two and a maximum of four hundred euros, except in the case of fines imposed on legal persons, in which the daily quota shall have a minimum of 30 and a maximum of 5,000 euros. For the purposes of calculation, when the term is set by months or years, it shall be construed that months are of thirty days and years of three hundred and sixty days.

5. Judges or Courts of Law shall duly determine the extent of the punishment within the limits established for each offence and pursuant to the rules of Chapter II of this Title. They shall also set the amount of these quotas in the judgement, for which they shall only take into account the financial situation of the convict, deducting, revenue, family obligations and charges and his other personal circumstances from his assets.

6. When justified, the Court of Law may authorise payment of the fine within a term that does not exceed two years from the final judgement, either as a lump sum, or in the instalments.

In such case, failure to pay two such instalments shall give rise to maturity of the remaining sums.

Article 51

If the financial status of the convict were to change after sentencing, the Judge or Court of Law, exceptionally, and after duly investigating the situation, may amend both the amount of the instalments, as well as the terms for payment thereof.

Article 52

1. Notwithstanding the terms set forth in the preceding Articles and when the Code so determines, the fine shall be established in proportion to the damage caused, the value of the object of the offence, or the profit obtained from it.

2. In such cases, the Judges and Courts of Law shall establish the fine within the limits set for each offence, considering not only the mitigating and aggravating circumstances of the fact to determine the amount in each case, but mainly the financial situation of the offender.

3. Should the financial situation of the convict worsen after sentencing, the Judge or Court of Law, exceptionally and after due investigation of the situation, may reduce the amount of the fine within the limits set by the law for the offence concerned, or authorise its payment subject to the terms to be determined.

4. In cases in which this Code foresees punishment by fine for legal persons in proportion to the profit obtained or facilitated, to the damage caused, to the value of the object, or to the sum obtained unduly or by fraud, if it is not possible to calculate such on the basis of those items, the Judge or Court of Law shall justify the impossibility to proceed to that calculation and the fines foreseen shall be replaced by the following ones:

a) Fine of two to five years, if the offence committed by a natural person has a prison sentence established in more than five years;

b) Fine of one to three years, if the offence committed by a natural person has a prison sentence established in more than two years, not included in the preceding Section;

c) Fine of six months to two years, in the rest of cases.

Article 53

1. Should the convict not pay the fine set, voluntarily or by enforcement, he shall be subject to a subsidiary personal liability of one day of custodial sentence for every two daily quotas not paid that, if a misdemeanour is involved, may be fulfilled by means of permanent traceability. In such case, the limitation on duration established in Article 37.1 of this Code shall not apply.

The Judge or Court of Law may also, with the convict's prior approval, order that the subsidiary accountability be served by community service. In such case, each day of custodial sentence shall be equivalent to one day of work.

2. In cases of proportional fines, the Judges and Courts of Law shall establish the appropriate personal subsidiary liability at their own discretion, which may not exceed one year in duration, in any case. The Judge or Court of Law may also order community service to be done, when previously agreed with the convict.

3. Such subsidiary liability shall not be imposed on convicts imprisoned for more than five years.

4. Settlement of the subsidiary liability extinguishes the obligation to pay the fine, even though the convict's financial situation were to improve.

5. The fine imposed on a legal person may be paid by instalments over a period of up to five years, when its amount is proven to endanger the survival thereof, or maintenance of the jobs existing thereat, or when this is advisable in the general interest.

Should the legal person convicted not pay the fine imposed within the term set, voluntarily or by enforcement, the Court of Law may order it to be intervened until it is fully paid.

SUBCHAPTER 5. ON ACCESSORY PENALTIES

Article 54

Penalties of barring are accessory in cases in which such punishment is not especially imposed but the Law declares that other penalties involve the former.

Article 55

The punishment of imprisonment equal to or exceeding ten years shall bear with it absolute barring during the term of the sentence, except if that is already foreseen as a main punishment in the case concerned. The Judge may also order special barring from exercise of parental rights, guardianship, care, safekeeping or fostership, or la deprivation of parental rights, when these rights have a direct relation to the felony committed. Such relationship must specifically be determined in the judgement.

Article 56

1. In prison sentences under ten years, the Judges or Courts of Law shall impose any one or number of the following, in view of the severity of the offence:

1º. Suspension from public employment and office;

2º. Special barring from the right of passive suffrage during the term of the sentence;

3º. Special barring from public employment and office, profession, trade, industry, commerce, exercise of parental rights, guardianship, care, safekeeping or fostership or any other right, deprivation of parental rights, if these rights were directly related to the felony committed, such relationship being specifically determined in the judgement, without prejudice to application of the provisions contained in Article 579 of this Code.

2. What is set forth in this Article shall be construed to be without prejudice to application of the terms set forth in other provisions of this Code, with regard to imposing these penalties.

Article 57

1. In felonies of unlawful killing, abortion, injuries, against liberty, of torture and against moral integrity, sexual freedom and indemnity, privacy, the right to personal dignity and the inviolability of the dwelling, honour, property and the social-economic order, in view of the severity of the facts or the danger posed by the convict, the Judge or Court of Law may impose in their judgements one or several of the prohibitions foreseen in Article 48, for a time that shall not exceed ten years, if the felony is serious, or of five if less serious.

Notwithstanding the foregoing, should the convict be sentenced to imprisonment and the Judge or Court of Law imposes one or several of those prohibitions, he shall do so for a time exceeding the imprisonment imposed in a sentence of between one and ten years if the offence is serious, and between one and five years, if less serious. In such case, the punishment of imprisonment and the aforesaid prohibitions must be served simultaneously by the convict.

2. In cases of the felonies mentioned in the first Section of Section 1 of this Article, committed against a former spouse, or against a person who has been bound to the convict by a similar emotional relationship, even without cohabitation, or against the descendents, ascendants or biological, adopted or fostered siblings, of that person or of the spouse or cohabitating partner, or against minors or the incapacitated cohabitating with them, or subject to the parental rights, guardianship, care, fostership or *de facto* safekeeping of the spouse or cohabitating partner, or against a person protected by any other relationship arising within the core family cohabitation, as well as against persons who, due to their special vulnerability, are subject to their custody or safekeeping at public or private centres, the punishment foreseen in Section 2 of Article 48 shall be imposed in all cases for a time that shall not exceed ten years if the felony is serious, or five if less serious, without prejudice to the terms set forth in Section Two of the preceding Section.

3. The prohibitions established in Article 48 may also be imposed for a period of time that shall not exceed six months if commission of an offence classified as a felony against persons under Articles 617 and 620 is involved.

SUBCHAPTER 6. COMMON PROVISIONS

Article 58

1. The term of pre-trial custody shall be fully credited by the Judge or Court of Law sentencing to serving the punishment or penalties imposed in the case concerning that for which such custody was ordered, except when it has coincided with a custodial sentence imposed on the convict in another case, which has been settled, or is due to be settled thereon. In no event may the same period of pre-trial custody be credited to more than one case.

2. Crediting pre-trial custody in a case other than the one for which it was decreed shall be ordered at the Court's own motion or at the request of the convict and following verification that it has not been credited to any other case, carried out by the Penitentiary Parole Board Judge of the jurisdiction to which the penitentiary centre where the convict is located is assigned, after hearing the Public Prosecutor.

3. Crediting pre-trial custody served in another case shall only be appropriate when that preventive measure is subsequent to the criminal acts that caused the punishment intended to be settled.

4. The preceding rules shall also be applied regarding deprivation of rights ordered on a preventive basis.

Article 59

When the preventive measures suffered and the punishment imposed are different in nature, the Judge or Court of Law shall deem the punishment imposed to have been served in the part deemed to have been compensated.

Article 60

1. When, after having pronounced the final judgement, a convict is found to suffer a lasting situation of serious mental disorder that prevents him from being aware of the sense of the punishment, the Penitentiary Parole Board Judge shall suspend execution of the custodial sentence imposed on him, guaranteeing that he receives the necessary medical care, for which he may order that a security measure of custodial sentence be imposed of those foreseen in this Code, that may not be, in any case, more onerous than the punishment substituted. If a punishment of a different nature, the Penitentiary Parole Board Judge shall appraise whether the situation of the convict allows him to be aware of the sense of the punishment and, if appropriate, shall suspend execution thereof, imposing the security measures he may deem necessary.

The Parole Board Judge shall notify the Public Prosecutor, sufficiently in advance, of the upcoming extinction of the punishment or security measure imposed, for the purposes foreseen by Additional Provision One of this Code.

2. Once the convict regains his mental health, he shall serve the sentence, if the punishment has not prescribed, without prejudice to the Judge or Court of Law being able to deem the sentence extinguished, or to reduce its term, for reasons of equity, to the extent that serving the punishment may be unnecessary or counter-productive.

CHAPTER II

On application of penalties

SUBCHAPTER 1. GENERAL RULES ON APPLICATION OF PENALTIES

Article 61

When the Law establishes a punishment, it shall be construed that it is imposed on the principals of the consummated crime.

Article 62

Principals of an attempted crime shall have a punishment imposed that is lower by one or two degrees to that set by Law for the consummated crime, to the extent deemed appropriate, in view of the danger inherent to the attempt and to the degree of execution achieved.

Article 63

Accessories of a consummated or attempted crime shall be sentenced to a lower degree of punishment to that set by Law for the principals of the same offence.

Article 64

The above rules shall not be applicable in cases in which attempt and complicity are especially punishable by Law.

Article 65

1. Aggravating or mitigating circumstances consisting of any cause of a personal nature shall only aggravate or mitigate the accountability of those fulfilling those circumstances.

2. Those that involve the material execution of the act, or the means used to perpetrate it, shall only be of use to aggravate or mitigate the accountability of those who have had knowledge of thereof at the moment of the action, or of their co-operation in the crime.

3. When the inducer or the necessary co-operator do not fulfil the conditions, qualities or personal relations that are the basis for the convict being guilty, the Judges or Courts of Law may impose a lower degree of punishment to that stated by Law for the crime concerned.

Article 66

1. In application of the punishment, in the case of malicious offences, the Judges or Courts of Law shall abide by the following rules, according to whether or not there are mitigating or aggravating circumstances:

   1. When only one mitigating circumstance concurs, the lower half of the punishment the Law sets for the offence shall be applied.

   2. When two or more mitigating circumstances concur, or one or several highly qualified ones, and there are no aggravating ones whatsoever, they shall apply the punishment that is lower by one or two degrees to that established by Law, in view of the number and entity of those mitigating circumstances.

   3. When only one or two aggravating circumstances concur, they shall apply the punishment from the top half of that set by Law for the offence.

   4. When there are more than two aggravating circumstances and no mitigating ones whatsoever, the higher degree of punishment to that established by Law, in its lower half, may be imposed.

   5. When the aggravating circumstance of recidivism concurs, with the qualification that the offender was a convicted offender by final judgement at the time, of at least three felonies under the same title of this Code, as long as of the same nature, the higher degree of punishment to that foreseen by Law for the felony concerned may be applied, taking preceding convictions into account, as well as the severity of the new felony committed. For the purposes of this rule, criminal records that are cancelled, or that should be, shall not be taken into account.

   6. When there are no mitigating or aggravating circumstances, the punishment established by Law for the offence committed shall be applied, to the extent deemed appropriate, in view of the personal circumstances of the criminal and to the greater or lesser severity of the fact.

   7. When mitigating and aggravating circumstances concur, these shall be valued and compensated rationally to individualise the punishment. In the event of a qualified ground of attenuation persisting, the lower degree of punishment shall be applied. If a qualified ground of aggravation is maintained, the upper half of the punishment shall be applied.

8. When Judges or Courts of Law apply a punishment that is more than one degree lower, they may do so to its full extent.

2. In felonies involving negligence, the Judges or Courts of Law shall apply the penalties at their prudent discretion, without being subject to the rules set forth in the preceding Section.

Article 66 bis

In application of the penalties imposed on legal persons, the terms set forth in rules 1. to 4 and 6 to 8 of the First Section of Article 66 shall apply, as well as the following:

1. In the cases that are established by the provisions of Book II, to decide on imposition and the extent of the penalties foreseen under Sub-Sections b) to g) of Section 7 of Article 33, the following must be taken into account:

a) Their need to prevent continuity of the criminal activity or its effects:

b) Their economic and social consequences, and especially the effects on workers;

c) The post in the structure of the legal person held by the natural person or body that failed in its duty to control.

2. When the penalties foreseen under Sub-Sections c) to g) of Section 7 of Article 33 are imposed with a limited duration, the latter may not exceed the maximum term of a sentence of imprisonment foreseen in the event of the felony being committed by a natural person.

In order to impose the penalties foreseen in Sub-Sections c) to g) for a term exceeding two years it shall be necessary for any of the following two circumstances to concur:

a) For the legal person to be a repeat offender;

b) For the legal person to be used instrumentally to commit criminal offences. The latter case shall be deemed to arise whenever the lawful activity of the legal person is less important than its unlawful activity.

For permanent imposition of the penalties foreseen in Sub-Sections b) and e), and to hand down a term exceeding five years of those foreseen in Sub-Sections e) and f) of Section 7 of Article 33, it shall be necessary for any of the following two circumstances to concur:

a) For it to be a case of fact foreseen under rule 5 of Section 1 of Article 66;

b) For the legal person to be used instrumentally to commit crimes. The latter case shall be deemed to arise whenever the lawful activity of the legal person is less important than its unlawful activity.

Article 67

The rules of the preceding Article shall not be applied to the aggravating or mitigating circumstances that the Law has taken into account in describing or penalising an offence, or those that are thus inherent to the offence, without concurrence of which it could not have been committed.

Article 68

In the cases foreseen in circumstance one of Article 21, the Judges or Courts of Law shall impose a lower punishment in one or two degrees to that stated in the Law, considering the number and entity of the requisites absent or concurring, and the personal circumstances of their principal, without prejudice to application of Article 66 of this Code.

Article 69

Those over eighteen and under twenty one years of age who commit an offence may have the provisions of the Law regulating the criminal accountability of minors applied to them in the cases and with the requisites set forth therein.

Article 70

1. The higher and lower degree of punishment to that foreseen by Law for any offence shall have the extent resulting from application of the following rules:

   1. The higher degree of punishment shall be formed based on the maximum figure set by the Law for the felony concerned and increasing that by half its amount, the resulting sum being its maximum limit. The minimum limit to the upper degree of punishment shall be the maximum punishment set by Law for the felony concerned, increased by one day, or by a day-fine, in view of the nature of the punishment to be imposed.

   2. The lower degree of punishment shall be formed on the basis of the minimum figure set for the felony concerned and deducting that half from its amount, the result of that deduction being its minimum limit. The maximum limit of the lower degree of punishment shall be the minimum of the punishment set by Law for the felony concerned, reduced by a day, or by a day-fine, in view of the nature of the punishment to be imposed.

2. For the purposes of determining the upper or lower half of the punishment or of specifying the upper or lower degree of punishment, the day or day-fine are deemed indivisible and shall act as upward or downward units of penalisation, according to the cases concerned.

3. When, in application of rule 1 of Section 1 of this Article, the higher degree punishment exceeds the maximum limits set for each punishment in this Code, they shall be deemed those immediately above, to wit:

   1. If the punishment determined is that of imprisonment, the same punishment, with the condition that its maximum term shall be thirty years.

   2. If absolute or special barring, the same punishment, with the condition that its maximum duration shall be thirty years.

   3. If suspension from public employment and office, the same punishment, with the condition that its maximum duration shall be eight years.

   4. If deprivation of the right to drive motor vehicles and mopeds, the same punishment, with the condition that its maximum duration shall be fifteen years.

   5. If deprivation of the right to own and carry weapons, the same punishment, with the condition that its maximum duration shall be twenty years.

   6. If deprivation of the right to reside in specific places or to visit them, the same punishment, with the condition that its maximum duration shall be twenty years.

   7. If prohibition to approach the victim or his relatives or other persons determined by the Judge or Court of Law, the same punishment, with the condition that its maximum duration shall be twenty years.

   8. If prohibition to communicate with the victim or with his relatives or other persons determined by the Judge or Court of Law, the same punishment, with the condition that its maximum duration shall be twenty years.

   9. If a fine, the same punishment, with the condition that its maximum duration shall be thirty months.

Article 71

1. When determining the punishment that is lower by one degree, the Judges or Courts of Law shall not be limited by the minimum amounts stated in the Law for each class of punishment, but rather they may reduce them in the manner arising from application of the relevant rule, without this amounting to this being demoted to a misdemeanour.

2. However, when, due to application of the above rules, it is appropriate to hand down a sentence of imprisonment under three months, this shall be substituted in all cases, pursuant to the terms of Section 2 of Chapter III of this Title, without prejudice to suspension of execution of the punishment in the appropriate cases.

Article 72

In application of the punishment, the Judges or Courts of Law, pursuant to the rules this Chapter contains, shall reason the specific degree and extent of that handed down in their judgement.

SUBCHAPTER 2. SPECIAL RULES FOR APPLICATION OF PENALTIES

Article 73

Whoever is responsible for two or more felonies or misdemeanours shall have all the relevant penalties imposed on him for the diverse offences for their simultaneous fulfilment, if possible, due to the nature and effects thereof.

Article 74

1. Notwithstanding what is set forth in the preceding Article, whoever perpetrates multiple actions or omissions, in the execution of a preconceived plan or taking advantage of an identical occasion, that offend one or several subjects and infringe the same criminal provision or provisions that are equal to or of a similar nature, shall be punished as the principal of a continued felony or misdemeanour with the punishment stated for the most serious offence, that shall be imposed in its upper half, it being possible to reach the lower half of the higher degree of punishment.

2. In the case of crimes against property, the punishment shall be imposed taking into account the full damage caused. In these crimes, the Judge or Court of Law shall justify imposition of the punishment raised by one or two degrees, to the extent deemed convenient, if the fact were to be evidently serious and were to have damaged persons at large.

3. What is set forth in the previous Sections does not include offences against eminently personal property, except those constituting offences against honour and sexual freedom and indemnity that affect the same victim. In these cases, the nature of the fact and the provision infringed shall be deemed to apply criminal continuity or not.

Article 75

When some or all of the penalties for the diverse offences cannot be served simultaneously by a convict, the order of their respective severity shall be followed for their successive fulfilment, whenever possible.

Article 76

1. Notwithstanding what is set forth in the preceding Article, the maximum effective sentence to be served by a convict may not exceed triple the time imposed for the most serious of the penalties incurred, declaring the others to be extinguished from when those already imposed cover that maximum, which may not exceed twenty years. Exceptionally, such maximum limit shall be:

   a) Of twenty- five- years, when a convict has been found guilty of two or more felonies and one of them is punished with Law with a prison sentence of up to twenty years;

   b) Of thirty years, when a convict has been found guilty of two or more felonies and one of them is punishable by Law with a prison sentence exceeding twenty years;

   c) Of forty years, when a convict has been found guilty of two or more felonies and at least two of them are punishable by Law with a prison sentence exceeding twenty years;

d) Of forty years, when a convict has been found guilty of two or more felonies elated to terrorist organisations and groups and offences of terrorism under Section two of Chapter VII of Title XXII of Book II of this Code and any of them is punishable by Law with a prison sentence exceeding twenty years.

2. The limitation shall be applied, even though the penalties have been imposed in different proceedings, if the facts, due to their connection or the moment when committed, could have been tried as a single case.

Article 77

1. What is set forth in the preceding two Articles is not applicable in the event of a sole fact constituting two or more crimes, or when one of them is the necessary means to commit the other.

2. In these cases, the upper half of the punishment foreseen for the most serious crime shall be applied, without exceeding the aggregate punishment that would be applicable if the crimes were punished separately.

3. When the punishment thus calculated exceeds such limit, the crimes shall be punished separately.

Article 78

1. If, due to the limitations established in Section 1 of Article 76, the punishment to be served were to be lower than half the aggregate sum of those imposed, the Judge or Court of Law sentencing may order that penitentiary benefits, term-release permits, pre-release classification and calculation of the time to be served prior to probation shall refer to the total penalties imposed in the sentences.

2. Such a resolution shall be mandatory in the cases foreseen in Sections a), b), c) and d) of Section 1 of Article 76 of this Code, as long as the punishment to be served is lower than half the aggregated sum of those imposed.

3. In these cases, the Parole Board Judge, following individual assessment in favour of social reinsertion and evaluating the personal circumstances of the convict and evolution of the re-education treatment as appropriate, may hand down a reasoned resolution, having heard the Public Prosecutor, the Directorate-General for Penitentiary Institutions and the other parties, on application of the general regime of serving sentences. In the case of felonies related to terrorist organisations and groups and offences of terrorism under Section two of Chapter VII of Title XXII of Book II of this Code, or committed within criminal organisations, and according to the aggregate sum of penalties imposed, the preceding possibility shall only be applicable:

a) To pre-release, when a fifth of the maximum limit of serving of the sentence is left to be served;

b) To probation, when an eighth of the maximum limit of serving of the sentence is left to be served.

Article 79

Whenever the Judges or Courts of Law impose a sentence involving ancillary penalties, they shall also specifically condemn the convict to the latter.

CHAPTER III

On substitute forms of execution of sentences depriving of freedom and on probation

SUBCHAPTER 1. ON SUSPENSION OF EXECUTION OF SENTENCES OF IMPRISONMENT

Article 80

1. Judges or Courts of Law may suspend execution of custodial sentences not exceeding two years, by reasoned resolution.

Such resolution shall fundamentally consider the criminal hazard posed by the convict, as well as the existence of other criminal proceedings against him.

2. The term of suspension shall be two to five years for custodial sentences under two years, and from three months to a year for lower penalties, and shall be set by the Judges or Courts of Law, following a hearing of the parties, in view of the personal circumstances of the criminal, the characteristics of the act and the term of the sentence.

3. Suspension of the sentence execution shall not include the civil liability arising from the felony or misdemeanour punished.

4. Judges and Courts of Law sentencing may grant suspension of any sentence handed down without this being subject to any requisite whatsoever, in the event of the convict suffering a very serious disease with incurable consequences, except if he had another sentence suspended for the same reason at the time of committing the felony.

Article 81

The following shall be the necessary conditions to suspend execution of a sentence:

1. For the convict to have offended for the first time. To that end, former convictions for felonies due to negligence or criminal records that are or should be cancelled, shall not be taken into account, pursuant to the terms set forth in Article 136 of this Code.

2. That the sentence or sentences handed down, or the sum of those handed down, do not exceed two years, without such calculation including that arising from failure to pay the fine.

3. For the civil liabilities arising to have been paid, except if the Judge or Court of Law sentencing, after hearing the parties concerned and the Public Prosecutor, declares that it is fully or partially impossible for the convict to honour these.

Article 82

Having declared the judgement final and the requisites established in the preceding Article having being accredited, the Judges or Courts of Law shall most urgently pronounce themselves on whether or not suspension of the sentence execution shall be granted.

Article 83

1. Suspension of the sentence execution shall always depend on the convict not offending during the term set by the Judge or Court of Law, pursuant to Article 80.2 of this Code. In the case of the suspended sentence being one of imprisonment, if deemed necessary, the Judge or Court of Law sentencing may also grant suspension on condition that the obligations or duties set among the following are fulfilled:

1. Prohibition to visit certain places;

2. Prohibition to approach the victim, or his relatives or other persons determined by the Judge or Court of Law, or to communicate with them;

3. Prohibition to leave his place of residence without authorisation from the Judge or Court of Law;

4. Personal appearance before the Court of Law or Tribunal, or the service of the Administration these appoint to report on and justify his activities;

5. Participation in training, labour, cultural, traffic education, sexual and environmental defence training programmes, those on protection of animals and other similar ones;

6. Fulfilling the other duties the Judge or Court of Law may deem convenient for social reinstatement of the convict, with his approval, as long as these are not contrary to his personal dignity.

In the case of offences of gender- related violence, the Judge or Court of Law shall condition suspension, in all cases, to fulfilment of the obligations or duties foreseen in rules 1, 2 and 5 of this Section.

2. The relevant services of the competent Administration shall report to the Judge or Court of Law sentencing, at least every three months, on fulfilment of the rules of conduct imposed.

Article 84

1. Should the subject offend during the term of suspension set, the Judge or Court of Law shall revoke the suspension of the sentence execution.

2. Should the subject fail to fulfil the obligations or duties imposed during the term of suspension, the Judge or Court of Law may, after hearing the parties, as appropriate:

a) Replace the rule of conduct imposed with another one;

b) Extend the term of suspension, without such term exceeding five years in any event;

c) Revoke suspension of the sentence execution, if the breach is repeated.

3. In the event of the punishment suspended being one of imprisonment for committing offences of gender-related violence, breach by the convict of the obligations or duties foreseen in rules 1, 2 and 5 of Section 1 of Article 83 shall lead to revocation of suspension of the sentence execution.

Article 85

1. When suspension is revoked, execution of the sentence shall be ordered.

2. Once the term of suspension set has elapsed without the subject having offended and having abided by the appropriate rules of conduct set, the Judge or Court of Law shall order remission of the sentence.

Article 86

In offences that may only be pursued following accusation or private criminal prosecution by the victim, the Judges and Courts of Law shall hear that party, or the representative when appropriate, prior to granting the benefits of suspension of sentence execution.

Article 87

1. Even when conditions 1 and 2 foreseen in Article 81 are not met, the Judge or Court of Law, after hearing the parties, may order suspension of execution of custodial sentences not exceeding five years for convicts who have committed the criminal act due to their dependence on the substances stated in Section 2 of Article 20, as long as this is sufficiently certified by a duly accredited or endorsed public or private centre or service that the convict has overcome the addition or is subject to treatment for that purpose at the moment of deciding on the suspension.

In all cases, the Judge or Court of Law shall request a Forensic Doctor's report on the above particulars.

2. Should the convict be a repeat offender, the Judge or Court of Law shall evaluate, in a reasoned resolution, whether or not it is appropriate to grant the benefit of suspension of sentence execution, in view of the circumstances of the case and of the convict.

3. Suspension of sentence execution shall always be on condition the convict does not offend during the period set, which shall from three to five years.

4. Should the convict be under treatment for drug addiction, suspension of the sentence execution shall also be on condition he does not abandon the treatment until its conclusion. The centres or services responsible for the treatment shall be bound to provide the Court of Law or Tribunal sentencing the necessary information to check this has commenced, within the terms set, and never exceeding one year in frequency, as well as to periodically ascertain the evolution, the changes to be undergone and the conclusion thereof.

5. The Judge or Court of Law shall revoke suspension of the sentence execution if the convict were to breach any of the conditions set.
Once the term of suspension has elapsed without the subject having offended, the Judge or Court of Law shall order remission of the sentence if the convict is proven to have overcome addiction or to continue in treatment. If this is not so, the Judge or Court of Law shall order serving thereof except if, having scrutinised the relevant reports, the Judge or Court of Law deems it necessary to continue treatment; in which case, by reasoned ruling, grant an extension of the term of suspension for a term not exceeding two years may be granted.

SUBCHAPTER 2. ON SUBSTITUTION OF PUNISHMENTS DEPRIVING OF FREEDOM

Article 88

1. After hearing of parties, in the judgement or subsequently in a reasoned ruling, prior to execution thereof commencing, the Judge or Court of Law may substitute a prison sentence that does not exceed one year with a fine or community service, and in cases of a prison sentence that do not exceed six months, also with permanent traceability, although the Law does not foresee these penalties for the felony concerned when the personal circumstances of the convict, the nature of the act, his conduct and, in particular, the effort to repair the damage caused, make this advisable, as long as he is not an habitual offender, substituting one day of imprisonment with two fine quotas or one day of work, or for one day of permanent traceability. In these cases, the Judge or Court of Law may also order the convict to observe one or several obligations or duties foreseen in Article 83 of this Code, if they have not been established as penalties in the judgement, for a term that may not exceed the term of the sentence substituted.

Exceptionally, a Judge or Court of Law may substitute prison sentences not exceeding two years with a fine, or with a fine and community service, for convicts who are not habitual offenders, when the circumstances of case and the offender mean that serving it would thwart the ends of prevention and social reinstatement. In these cases, the replacement shall be carried out with the same requisites and under the same terms and conversion modules as established in the preceding Section when sentenced to pay a fine.

In the event of the prisoner having been convicted of a gender- violence related offence, a sentence of imprisonment may only be substituted by that of community service or permanent traceability in a different location, away from the victim's dwelling. In such case, the Judge or Court of Law shall also order observance of the obligations or duties foreseen in rules 1 and 2 of Section 1 of Article 83 of this Code, in addition to attending specific re-education and psychological treatment programmes.

2. In the event of breach of all or part of the substitution punishment, a sentence of imprisonment initially handed down shall be executed discounting, when appropriate, the part of time equivalent to the quotas paid, pursuant to the conversion rule established in the preceding Section.

3. Under no circumstances whatsoever may penalties that substitute others be substituted in turn.

Article 89

1. Custodial sentences under six years handed down to an alien who is not legally resident in Spain shall be substituted in the judgement by his deportation, except if the Judge or Court of Law, after hearing the convict, the Public Prosecutor and the parties appearing, were to appreciate and give reasons to justify the sentence being served at a penitentiary centre in Spain.

Deportation may also be provided for in a subsequent reasoned court ruling, following hearing the convict, the Public Prosecutor and the other parties appearing.

2. The alien may not return to Spain within the term of ten years, as from the date of deportation, pursuant to the term of the sentence substituted and the personal circumstances of the convict.

3. Deportation shall halt all administrative proceedings being processed for a permit to reside or work in Spain.

4. Should the deported alien return to Spain before the term established by the court, he shall serve the sentences substituted. However, if caught at the border, he shall be directly expelled by the governmental authority and the term of prohibition to enter the country shall then begin to be counted again in full as from that moment.

5. A Judge or Court of Law, at the request of the Public Prosecutor and following hearing of the convict and the parties appearing, shall resolve in the sentence, or in the execution thereof, whether to deport the alien who is not legally resident in Spain, who must serve, or is serving any custodial sentence, in the event of him having attained the pre-release or served three quarters of the sentence, except if, following hearing of the Public Prosecutor and giving the reasons, the Judge or Court considers there are reasons for it to be served in Spain.

6. When, on ordering deportation in any of the manners foreseen in this Article, the alien is not found or is not effectively in custody serving the sentence handed down, the Judge or Court of Law may order him to be detained in an alien internment centre to effectively assure deportation, under the terms and with the limits and guarantees foreseen in the Law for governmental deportation.

In all cases, if deportation cannot take place once this is ordered to substitute imprisonment, execution of the sentence originally handed down shall be carried out, or the period of sentence pending, or application, when appropriate, of suspension of its execution, or substitution under the terms of Article 88 of this Code.

7. The provisions established in the preceding Sections shall not be applicable to aliens convicted of committing the offences referred to in Articles 31.2, 31.3 and 31.8 bis of this Code.

SUBCHAPTER 3. ON PROBATION

Article 90

1. Probation shall be established in sentences of imprisonment for convicts who fulfil the following circumstances:

a) Who have attained pre-release penitentiary treatment;

b) Who have served three quarters of the sentence handed down;

c) Who have a record of good conduct and when the convicts have an individual favourable assessment of social reinstatement, issued in the final report foreseen in Article 67 of the General Penitentiary Organic Act.

The preceding circumstance shall not be deemed to have been fulfilled if the convict has not paid the civil liability arising from the felony, in the cases and pursuant to the criteria established under Article 72.5 and 6 of the General Penitentiary Organic Act.

Likewise, in the case of persons found guilty of felonies related to terrorist organisations and groups and offences of terrorism under Section two of Chapter VII of Title XXII of Book II of this Code, or for felonies committed within criminal organisations, it shall be construed that there is an assessment of social reinstatement when a convict shows unequivocal signs of having abandoned the ends and means of the terrorist activity and has also actively collaborated with the authorities, either to prevent other offences being committed by the armed gang, organisation or terrorist group, or to mitigate the effects of the felony, or to identify, capture and prosecute those responsible for terrorist offences, to obtain evidence, or to prevent the activities or development of the organisations or associations to which he has belonged or with which he has collaborated, which may be accredited by a specific declaration of disavowal of their criminal activities and abandoning violence, and specifically apologising to the victims of his offence, as well as by means of technical reports that accredit that the convict has really cut off ties with the terrorist organisation and the environment and activities of unlawful assemblies and groups that surround these, and that he has collaborated with the authorities.

2. When decreeing probation for convicts, the Parole Board Judge may, by reasoned opinion, order them to observe one or several of the rules of conduct or measures foreseen in Articles 83 and 96.3 of this Code.

Article 91

1. Exceptionally, when the circumstances of Sections a) and c) of Section 1 of the preceding Article are fulfilled, and as long as felonies related to terrorist organisations and groups and offences of terrorism under Section two of Chapter VII of Title XXII of Book II of this Code, or committed within criminal organisations are not involved, the Parole Board Judge, following a report by the Public Prosecutor, the Directorate-General for Penitentiary Institutions and the other parties, may grant those sentenced to custodial sentences who have served two thirds of their sentence probation, as long as they deserve such benefit due to having continually worked or having performed cultural or occupational activities.

2. At the proposal of the Directorate-General for Penitentiary Institutions and following a report by the Public Prosecutor and the other parties, having fulfilled the circumstances of Sections a) and c) of Section 1 of the preceding Article, the Parole Board Judge may anticipate the granting probation, once half the sentence has been served, in relation to the term foreseen in the preceding Section, up to a maximum of ninety days for each year elapsed of effective serving of the sentence, as long as these are not felonies related to terrorist organisations and groups and the offences of terrorism under Section two of Chapter VII of Title XXII or committed within criminal organisations. Such measure shall require the convict to have continuously performed the activities indicated in the preceding Section and to evidence, in addition, effective and fruitful participation in programmes to compensate victims, or treatment or detoxification programmes, as appropriate.

Article 92

1. Notwithstanding what is set forth in previous Articles, convicts who have reached the age of seventy years, or those who reach that age while serving their sentence, and who fulfil the established requisites, except that of having served three quarters thereof or, when appropriate, two thirds, may be granted probation.

The same criterion shall be applied when, in view of a medical report, a convict is seriously ill with an incurable disease.

2. Should the Penitentiary Administration be aware that the convict fulfils any of the cases foreseen in the preceding Sections, it shall bring probation proceedings before the Penitentiary Parole Board Judge with the required urgency and, when resolving thereon, he shall evaluate, along with the personal circumstances, the difficulty to offend and the scant danger the convict entails.

3. Should hazard to the life of the convict be patent, due to illness or old age, evidenced by the opinion of a Forensic Doctor and of the medical services of the penitentiary institution the Penitentiary Parole Board Judge may, following appropriate status reclassification, authorise probation with no further formality than requiring the penitentiary centre to report on the final prognosis in order to be able to carry out the assessment referred to in the preceding Section, all without prejudice to the monitoring and control foreseen in Article 75 of the General Penitentiary Organic Act.

Article 93

1. The probation period shall last the whole of the remaining period of the sentence to be served by the convict. Should the convict offend or fail to abide by the rules of conduct imposed during that period, the Penitentiary Parole Board Judge shall revoke the probation granted, and the convict shall return to prison for the term remaining or to the relevant penitentiary degree, without prejudice to calculation of the time spent on probation.

2. In the case of convicts for felonies related to terrorist organisations and groups and felonies of terrorism under Section two of Chapter VII of Title XXII of Book II of this Code, the Parole Board Judge may request reports to evidence whether the conditions that allowed probation subsist. Should the convict offend or fail to abide by the conditions that allowed him to obtain probation during that period, the Parole Board Judge shall revoke the parole granted and the convict shall return to prison for the term remaining or to the relevant penitentiary degree.

3. In the case foreseen in the preceding Section, the convict shall serve the remaining time until complete serving of the sentence, with loss of the time spent on probation.

SUBCHAPTER 4. COMMON PROVISIONS

Article 94

For the purposes foreseen in Section 2 of this Chapter, habitual offenders are deemed to be those who have committed three or more offences under a same heading within a term not exceeding five years and who have been convicted thereof.

In order to carry out such calculation, on one hand, the moment of possible suspension or substitution of the sentence pursuant to Article 88 shall be considered and, on the other hand, the date on which the offences taken as the basis to appraise the habitual nature thereof were committed.

TITLE IV

On security measures

CHAPTER I

On security measures in general

Article 95

1. Security measures shall be applied by the Judge or Court of Law, following the reports deemed convenient, on persons in the cases foreseen in the following Chapter of this Code, provided the following circumstances concur:

   1. That the subject has committed an act deemed a felony;

   2. That the act and personal circumstances of the subject may lead to believe that further felonies may probably be committed in future.

2. When the punishment that may have been handed down for the felony committed is not one of imprisonment, the Judge or Court of Law sentencing may only order one or some of the measures foreseen in Article 96.3.

Article 96

1. The security measures that may be imposed under this Code may involve or not deprivation of freedom.

2. The following are measures involving deprivation of freedom:

   1. Internment in a psychiatric institution;

   2. Internment in a detoxification centre;

   3. Internment in a special education centre;

3. The following are measures not involving deprivation of freedom:

   1.) Barring from a profession;

   2.) Deportation of aliens not legally resident in Spain;

   3.) Probation;

   4.) Family custody. The person subject to this measure shall be subject to care and surveillance by a relative so appointed, who accepts custody, who shall implement this in liaison with the Penitentiary Parole Board Judge and without detriment to the schooling or working activities of the individual under custody;

   5.) Deprivation of right to drive motor vehicles and mopeds;

   6.) Deprivation of right to own and carry weapons.

Article 97

During execution of the sentence, the Judge or Court of Law sentencing shall adopt any of the following decisions by the procedure established in the following Article:

   a) Maintaining implementation of the security measure imposed.

   b) Decreeing cessation of any security measure imposed when the subject ceases to involve a criminal risk.

   c) Substitution of a security measure with another deemed more adequate, among those foreseen in the case concerned. Should substitution be ordered and the subject evolves negatively, the substitution shall be left without effect and the measure substituted reapplied.

   d) Suspending execution of the measure in view of the result already obtained from its implementation, for a term not exceeding that remaining, up to the maximum stated in the sentence that handed it down. The suspension shall be on condition that the subject does not offend during the period set, and it may be left without effect if any of the circumstances foreseen in Article 95 of this Code were evidenced again.

Article 98

1. For the purposes of the preceding Article, in the case of a security measure of deprivation of freedom, or a measure of probation that must be executed after a sentence of imprisonment is served, the Penitentiary Parole Board Judge shall be bound to submit a proposal for maintenance, substitution or suspension thereof, at least annually. In order to draw up that proposal, the Penitentiary Parole Board Judge must evaluate the reports issued

by the experts and professionals who care for the person subject to the security measure, or by the competent Public Administrations and, when appropriate, the result of the other actions ordered to such end.

2. In the case of any other measure that does not deprive of freedom, the Judge or Court of Law sentencing shall apply directly to the Administrations, experts and professionals referred to in the preceding Section, for the appropriate reports concerning the situation and progress of the convict, his degree of reinstatement and possibility of reoffending or of recidivism.

3. In all cases, the Judge or Court of Law sentencing shall issue a reasoned resolution concerning the proposal or reports respectively referred to in the preceding two Sections, having heard the person subject to the measure, as well as the Public Prosecutor and the other parties. A hearing shall also be granted to the victims of the felony who were not present when this was requested at commencement, or at any moment of the sentence execution, provided it is possible to locate them.

Article 99

In the event of both punishments and security measures depriving of freedom concurring, the Judge or Court of Law shall order fulfilment of the measure, which shall be credited in the sentence handed down. Once the security measure is raised, the Judge or Court of Law may, should execution of the sentence endanger the effects achieved thereby, suspend fulfilment of the rest of the punishment for a term not exceeding its duration, or apply any of the measures foreseen in Article 96.3.

Article 100

1. Breach of a security measure of deprivation of freedom shall lead to the Judge or Court of Law to order the subject to be returned to the same institution from which he has escaped, or another that is appropriate to his status.

2. In the case of other measures, the Judge or Court of Law may resolve substitution of that breached with that of internment, if it is foreseen in the case concerned, and if that breach were to prove the need for such.

3. In both cases, the Judge or Court of Law shall record an attestation of the breach. To these ends, refusal by the subject to submit to medical treatment or to continue medical treatment initially consented shall not be deemed a breach. However, the Judge or Court of Law may order substitution of the initial treatment or that subsequently rejected by another measure from among those applicable to the case concerned.

CHAPTER II

On application of security measures

SUBCHAPTER 1. ON MEASURES DEPRIVING OF FREEDOM

Article 101

1. Subjects declared exempt of criminal accountability pursuant to Section 1 of Article 20, may have the measure of internment for medical treatment or special education applied to them, if necessary, at an adequate institution for the type of anomaly or mental alteration appraised, or any other of the measures foreseen in Section 3 of Article 96. The internment may not exceed the time a sentence of imprisonment would have lasted, if the subject had been declared accountable, and to that end the Judge or Court of Law shall set that maximum limit in the sentence.

2. Whoever is subject to such measure may not leave the institution without authorisation from the Judge or Court of Law sentencing, pursuant to what is set forth in Article 97 of this Code.

Article 102

1. When necessary, those exempt of criminal accountability pursuant to Section 2 of Article 20 shall be subject to internment measures at a public or private detoxification centre that is duly accredited or endorsed, or any other of the measures foreseen in Section 3 of Article 96. The internment may not exceed the time a sentence of imprisonment would have lasted, had the subject been declared accountable, and the Judge or Court of Law shall set that maximum limit in the sentence on that basis.

2. The person subject to that measure may not leave the institution without authorisation from the Judge or Court of Law sentencing, pursuant to the terms foreseen in Article 97 of this Code.

Article 103

1. If necessary, those who are declared exempt from accountability, pursuant to Section 3 of Article 20, may have the measure of internment in a special education centre or ay other of the measures foreseen in Section three of Article 96 applied to them. The internment may not exceed the time a sentence of imprisonment would have lasted, had the subject been declared accountable and the Judge or Court of Law shall set that maximum limit in the sentence on that basis.

2. The person subject to that measure may not leave the institution without authorisation from the Judge or Court of Law sentencing, pursuant to the terms foreseen in Article 97 of this Code.

3. In that case, the proposal referred to in Article 98 of this Code must be made at the end of each course or educational stage.

Article 104

1. In cases of incomplete exempting circumstances in relation to Section 1, 2 and 3 of Article 20, in addition to the relevant punishment, the Judge or Court of Law may impose the measures foreseen in Articles 101, 102 and 103. However, the measure of internment shall only be applicable when the punishment imposed is imprisonment and its term may not exceed that of the punishment foreseen for that felony in the Code. The terms set forth in Article 99 shall be observed for the implementation thereof.

2. When an internment measure of those foreseen in the preceding Section or in Articles 101, 102 and 103 is applied, the Judge or Court of Law sentencing shall notify the Public Prosecutor, sufficiently in advance, when its completion is near, for the purposes foreseen under Additional Provision One of this Code.

SUBCHAPTER 2. ON MEASURES THATDO NOT DEPRIVE OF FREEDOM

Article 105

In the cases foreseen in Articles 101 to 104, when a measure depriving of freedom is imposed, or during its execution, the Judge or Court of Law may reasonably impose one or several of the measures listed below and must also impose one or several of those measures in the other cases specifically foreseen in this Code.

1. For a term not exceeding five years:

a) Probation;

b) Family custody. The person subject to this measure shall remain under the care and surveillance of a relative appointed and who agrees to the custody, who shall carry it out in liaison with the Parole Board Judge and without detracting from the schooling or work activities of the person under custody.

2. For a term of up to ten years:

   a) Probation, when specifically provided by this Code;

   b) Deprivation of right to own and carry weapons;

   c) Deprivation of right to drive motor vehicles and mopeds.

In order to decree the obligation to observe any or a number of the measures foreseen in this Article, as well as to specify that obligation when their imposition is a legal obligation, the Judge or Court of Law sentencing must evaluate the reports issued by the experts and professionals in charge of caring for the person subject to the security measure.

The Penitentiary Parole Board Judge or the services of the relevant Administration shall inform the Judge or Court of Law sentencing.

In the cases foreseen in this Article, the Judge or Court of Law sentencing shall order the competent social assistance services to provide the necessary aid or attention to which the person subject to the security measures that do not deprive of freedom is entitled to.

Article 106

1. Probation shall consist of the convict being subject to court control and having to fulfil any one or number of the following measures:

   a) The obligation to always be traceable by means of electronic devices to allow him to be traced at all times;

   b) The obligation to regularly appear at the place set by the Judge or Court of Law;

   c) That of immediately reporting, within the maximum term and by the means stated by the Judge or Court of Law for that purpose, each change of residence or place or post at work;

   d) Prohibition to leave the place of residence or a specific area without leave from the Judge or Court of Law;

   e) Prohibition to approach the victim, or his relatives or other persons determined by the Judge or Court of Law;

   f) Prohibition to communicate with the victim, or with his relatives or other persons determined by the Judge or Court of Law;

   g) Prohibition to visit specific areas, places or establishments;

   h) Prohibition to reside in specific places;

   i) Prohibition to carry out certain activities that may provide or afford him the chance to commit criminal offences of a similar kind;

   j) The obligation to participate in labour, cultural, sexual education or other similar training programmes;

   k) The obligation to follow external medical treatment, or to submit to periodic medical inspection.

2. Without prejudice to what is set forth in Article 105, the Judge or Court of Law shall impose the probation measure in the sentence for the serving thereof after the punishment of imprisonment handed down has been served, as long as this is specifically provided so in this Code.

In these cases, at least two months before completion of a sentence of imprisonment, so the probation measure may commence at that very moment, the Penitentiary Parole Board Judge, shall submit the appropriate proposal to the Judge or Court of Law sentencing using the procedure foreseen in Article 98. The latter, pursuant to such procedure, shall set the content of the measure, without prejudice to the terms established in Article 97, setting the obligations or prohibitions that must be observed by the convict, as listed in Section 1 of this Article.

Should he be subject to several custodial sentences to be served consecutively, what is set forth in the preceding Section shall be construed to refer to the moment when he has served all of these.

Likewise, convicts upon whom other specific probation measures have been imposed that may not be executed simultaneously due to the content of the obligations or prohibitions established, shall serve them consecutively, without prejudice to the Judge or Court of Law being able to exercise the powers attributed thereto in the following Section.

3. By the same procedure of Article 98, the Judge or Court of Law may:

a) Amend the obligations and prohibitions imposed thereafter;

b) Reduce the term of probation or even end it, considering, due to the positive assessment of reinstatement, that continuity of the obligations or prohibitions imposed would be unnecessary or counter-productive;

c) To leave the measure without effect when the circumstance described in the preceding Sub-Section concurs at the moment of specifying the measures regulated under Section 2 of this Article.

4. In the event of breach of one or several obligations, considering the circumstances concurring and using the same procedure indicated in the preceding Sections, the Judge or Court of Law may amend the obligations or prohibitions imposed. Should the breach be repeated or serious, evidencing refusal to submit to the obligations or prohibitions imposed, the Judge shall also issue an attestation to proceed in view of an apparent offence pursuant to Article 468 of this Code.

Article 107

The Judge or Court of Law may issue a reasoned resolution, ordering the measure of barring from a specific right, profession, trade, industry or commerce, post or employment, for a term from one to five years, when the subject has committed an offence by abuse of that office, or in relation thereto, and when an evaluation of the circumstances concurring may lead to the conclusion of the danger of him committing the same offence or other similar ones again, as long as it is not possible to impose the relevant punishment due to him being included in any of the situations foreseen in Sections 1, 2 and 3 of Article 20.

Article 108

1. Should the subject be an alien not legally resident in Spain, the Judge or Court of Law shall hand down a sentence, after hearing him, of deportation in substitution of the security measures applicable to him, except if the Judge or Court of Law, after hearing the Public Prosecutor, exceptionally and giving the reasons, were to consider the nature of the offence to justify this being served in Spain.

Deportation decreed thus shall halt all administrative proceedings to process a permit to reside or work in Spain.

In the event that, after ordering deportation to substitute the security measure, it should not be possible to implement it, the security measure originally imposed shall be carried out.

2. The alien may not return to Spain for a term of ten years from the date of his deportation.

3. Aliens who attempt to breach a court order of deportation and prohibition to enter Spain mentioned in the preceding Sections shall be returned by the governmental authority and the term of prohibition to enter the country shall then begin to be counted in full again from that moment.

TITLE V

On civil liability arising from the felonies and misdemeanours and costs

CHAPTER I

On civil liability and its scope

Article 109

1. Perpetration of an act defined as a felony or misdemeanour by Law shall entail, pursuant to the provisions contained in the laws, to repair the damages and losses caused thereby.

2. In all cases, the party damaged may opt to sue for civil liability before the Civil Jurisdiction.

Article 110

The liability established in the preceding Article includes:

1. Restitution;

2. Repairing the damage;

3. Compensation of material and moral damage.

Article 111

1. Whenever possible, the same asset shall be returned, paying for the deterioration and damage the Judge or Court of Law shall determine. Restitution shall take place, even though the asset may be in the possession of a third party who may have acquired it legally and in good faith, notwithstanding his right to take further action against the relevant party and, when appropriate, entitlement to be compensated by the party civilly accountable for the felony or misdemeanour.

2. This provision is not applicable when the third party has acquired the asset in the manner and with the requisites established by the laws to make them irretrievable.

Article 112

Reparation of the damage may consist of obligations to give, to do or to abstain from doing that the Judge or Court of Law shall establish in view of the nature thereof and the personal conditions and assets of the offender, determining whether they are to be carried out personally by him or carried out at his expense.

Article 113

Compensation of material and moral damages shall include not only those caused to the victim, but also those caused to relatives thereof or third parties.

Article 114

Should the victim have contributed to causing the damage or loss suffered with his conduct, the Judges or Courts of Law may mitigate the amount of reparation or compensation.

Article 115

When declaring the existence of civil liability, the Judges and Courts of Law shall provide a reasoned opinion in their resolutions concerning the bases on which they base the amount for damages and compensation, being able to set these in the resolution itself, or at the moment of the enforcement thereof.

CHAPTER II

On persons liable under Civil Law

Article 116

1. All persons held criminally accountable for a felony or misdemeanour shall also be held liable under Civil Law if the fact gives rise to damages or losses. If two or more persons are responsible for a felony or misdemeanour, the Judges or Courts of Law shall set the proportion for which each one must be held accountable.

2. Principals and accessories, each within their own respective category, shall be held jointly and severally liable for their proportions and, under subsidiary terms, for those of the other parties responsible. The subsidiary accountability shall first be enforced against the assets of the principals, and then those of the accessories.

In cases where the joint and several is enforced or subsidiary liability is, whoever paid the shares due from each one on behalf of the others shall be entitled to bring an action for recovery from the latter.

3. The criminal accountability of a legal person shall involve its civil liability pursuant to the provisions contained in Article 110 of this Code, jointly and severally with the natural persons who are found guilty of the same acts.

Article 117

Insurers that have underwritten the risk of monetary liabilities arising from use or exploitation of any asset, company, industry or activity when, as a consequence of a fact foreseen in this Code, an event takes place covered by the risk insured, shall have direct civil liability up to the limit of the legally established or contractually agreed compensation, without prejudice to the right bring an action for recovery against who such may be appropriate.

Article 118

1. The exemption from criminal accountability declared under Sections 1, 2, 3, 5 and 6 of Article 20, does not include exemption of civil liability, which shall be made effective pursuant to the following rules:

   1. In cases included in Sections 1 and 3, those who, *de facto* or *de jure,* are in charge of, or have custody of persons declared exempt of criminal accountability, shall be held liable for the acts they perpetrate, whenever they have acted culpably or negligently, and without prejudice to the direct civil liability of those who may be charged. The Judges or Courts of Law shall equitably assess the extent to which each of these subjects must respond with their assets.

   2. Those who are drunk and under the influence of narcotics shall also be held liable in cases included in Section 2.

   3. In cases included in Section 5, direct civil liability shall apply to the persons in whose favour the harm has been prevented, in proportion to the damage they have been prevented, if this may be calculated or, otherwise, that the Judge or Court of Law shall establish pursuant to the prudent criteria thereof.

When it is not possible for the Judge or Court of Law to assign equitable proportions for which the party concerned shall be held liable, or when the liability affects the Public Administrations, or the majority of a village or town and, in all cases, as long as the damage has been caused with the assent of the authority or its agents, compensation shall be ordered, as appropriate, in the manner established by the special laws and regulations.

4. In cases included in Section 6, mainly those who have caused the fear shall be liable, and failing these, those who have committed the act.

2. In cases included in Article 14, those held civilly liable shall be the principals of the act.

Article 119

In all the cases of the preceding Article, the Judge or Court of Law on handing down a sentence of not guilty due to any of the causes of exemption mentioned concurring shall proceed to setting the civil liabilities, except for specific reservation of the actions to claim them in the relevant channel.

Article 120

The following persons shall be held civilly liable, failing those held criminally accountable:

1. The parents or guardians, for the damages and losses caused by the felonies or misdemeanours committed by those over eighteen years of age subject to their parental rights or guardianship and who cohabit with them, provided their is culpability or negligence on their part;

2. Natural or legal persons owning publishing houses, newspapers, magazines, radio stations or television channels, or any other means of written, spoken or visual diffusion, for felonies or misdemeanours committed using the media they own, notwithstanding what is set forth in Article 212 of this Code;

3. Natural or legal persons, in cases of felonies or misdemeanours committed in the establishments they own, when those that manage or administer them, or their assistants or employees have breached the police by-laws or provisions by the authority related to the punishable offence committed, so that would not have happened had that infringement not taken place;

4. Natural or legal persons dedicated to any kind of industry or commerce, for felonies or misdemeanours their employees or assistants, representatives or managers may have committed in the carrying out of their obligations or services;

5. Natural or legal persons owning vehicles liable to create risks to third parties, for the felonies or misdemeanours committed in use of these by their assistants, representatives or authorised persons.

Article 121

The State, Autonomous Communities, provinces, islands, municipalities and other public entities, as appropriate, shall be subject to subsidiary liability for damage caused by those criminally accountable for malicious or negligent felonies, when these are authorities, agents and employees of those bodies, or civil servants carrying out their duties or functions of office, as long as the damage is caused directly by operation of the public services they are entrusted with, without prejudice to patrimonial liability arising from normal or abnormal operation of those services, which may be demanded pursuant to the rules of administrative procedure and without double compensation arising in any case.

If civil liability is claimed in criminal proceedings against the authority, agents and employees thereof, or civil servants, the claim must be filed simultaneously against the public administration or entity presumably subject to subsidiary civil liability.

Article 122

Whoever may have participated for gain in the effects of a felony or misdemeanour shall be bound to restore the item or to compensate the damage up to the amount of his share therein.

CHAPTER III

On the costs

Article 123

Costs are deemed to be imposed by Law upon those criminally accountable for all felonies or misdemeanours.

Article 124

Costs shall include the fees and compensations arising from the judicial actions and they shall always include the fees of the private prosecution for offences that may only be prosecuted by the party concerned.

CHAPTER IV

On fulfilment of civil liability and other monetary liabilities

Article 125

When the assets of the party held liable under Civil Law are not sufficient to pay all the monetary liabilities at once, the Judge or Court of Law, after hearing the party damaged, may split up the payment thereof, setting the amounts and terms of the instalments, according his prudent criterion, the needs of the victim and the financial capacity of the party responsible,

Article 126

1. Payments made by the convict or party with subsidiary civil liability shall be applied in the following order:

    1. To repairing the damage caused and to compensating the losses;

    2. To compensating the State for the amounts expended on the case;

    3. To the costs of the specific or private prosecutor when payment thereof is imposed in the sentence;

    4. To the other costs, even those of defence of the accused, without preference among the interested parties;

    5. To the fine.

2. When the offence was one of those that may only be prosecuted at the instance of the party concerned, the costs of the private prosecutor shall be paid, with preference to compensation to the State.

TITLE VI

On ancillary consequences

Article 127

1. All penalties imposed for a malicious felony or misdemeanour shall lead to loss of the assets obtained therefrom and of the goods, means or instruments with which they were prepared or executed, as well as the gains obtained from the felony or misdemeanour, whatever the transformations these may have undergone. All shall be seized, unless they belong to a third party in good faith who is not responsible for the felony, who has acquired them legally.

The Judge or Court of Law shall extend the seizure of assets, goods, instruments and gains for criminal activities committed within the setting of a criminal or terrorist organisation or group, or for an offence of terrorism. For these purposes, the property of each and every one of the persons found guilty of felonies committed within the criminal or terrorist organisation or group or for an offence of terrorism that is disproportionate in relation to the revenue lawfully obtained by each one of those persons shall be deemed to have been obtained by the criminal activity.

2. In cases in which the Law foresees imposing a sentence of imprisonment exceeding one year for committing an imprudent felony, the Judge or Court of Law may order the loss of the assets obtained thereby and of the assets, means or instruments with which this has been prepared or executed, as well as the gains from the offence, whatever transformations they may have undergone.

3. If, for any circumstance, it were not possible to seize the assets stated in the preceding Sections of this Article, seizure of other assets for an equivalent value pertaining to those criminally accountable for the act shall be seized.

4. The Judge or Court of Law may order the seizure foreseen in the preceding Sections of this Article even when no punishment is imposed on any person due exemption from criminal accountability or due to the statute of limitations, in the latter case, as long as the unlawful status of the assets is proven.

5. The assets seized shall be sold, if of lawful trade, applying the sums obtained to covering the civil liabilities of the convict if the Law does not foresee otherwise and, if not of lawful trade, they shall be applied to the use provided by the laws and, failing that, shall be destroyed.

Article 128

When those assets and instruments are of lawful trade and their value is not proportional to the nature or severity of the crime, or when the civil liabilities have been fully settled, the Judge or Court of Law may decide not to order the seizure, or may order only a partial one.

Article 129

1. In the case of felonies or misdemeanours committed within, in collaboration with, or through or by means of firms, organisations, groups or any other kind of entities or groups of persons that, due to not having legal personality, are not included in Article 31 bis of this Code, the Judge or Court of Law may hand down a reasoned resolution ordering on those companies, organisations, groups, entities or groups one or several ancillary consequences of the relevant punishment imposed on the principal, with the content foreseen in Sections c) to g) of Article 33.7. The Judge or Court may also order definitive prohibition to carry out any activity, even if lawful.

2. The ancillary consequences referred to in the preceding Section may only be applied to firms, organisations, groups, entities or assemblies mentioned therein when this Code specifically foresees this, or in the case of any of the felonies or misdemeanours for which it allows criminal accountability of legal persons to be demanded.

3. Temporary closure of premises or establishments, suspension of the corporate activities and judicial intervention might also be ordered by the Investigating Judge as a provisional measure during the investigation proceedings for the purposes established in this Article and within the limits stated in Article 33.7.

TITLE VII

On expiration of criminal accountability and its effects

CHAPTER I

On the causes that extinguish criminal accountability

Article 130

1. Criminal accountability is extinguished:

    1. On death of the convict.

    2. When the sentence is fully served.

    3. By definitive remission of the sentence, as set forth in Article 85.2 of this Code.

    4. By the granting of the royal pardon.

    5. When forgiven by the victim, when the Law foresees this. Such forgiveness must be granted specifically before the sentence is handed down, to which end the Judge or Court of Law sentencing must hear the victim of the offence before handing it down.

        In felonies or misdemeanours against minors or the incapacitated, Judges or Courts of Law, having heard the Public Prosecutor, may reject the effectiveness of the forgiveness granted by their representatives, ordering proceedings to continue, with intervention by the Public Prosecutor, or the serving of the sentence.

        In order to reject the forgiveness to which the preceding Section refers, the Judge or Court of Law must hear the representative of the minor or incapacitated person again.

    6. By prescription of the offence.

    7. By prescription of the sentence or the security measure.

2. Transformation, merger, absorption or split of a legal person does not extinguish its criminal accountability, which shall be transferred to the firm or firms into which it is transformed, is merged or absorbed, and it shall extend to the firm or firms arising from the split. The Judge or Court of Law may order the punishment to be transferred to the legal person in view of the proportion that the legal person originally accountable for the offence has therein.

Criminal accountability is not extinguished by concealed or merely apparent dissolution of the legal person. It shall be deemed, in all cases, that there is concealed or merely apparent dissolution of the legal person when its economic activity continues and it maintains a substantial identity of clients, providers and employees, or the most important part thereof.

Article 131

1. Felonies prescribe:

After twenty years, when the maximum punishment set for the offence is imprisonment of fifteen or more years.

After fifteen, when the maximum punishment set by Law is barring for more than ten years, or imprisonment for more than ten and less than fifteen years.

After ten, when the maximum punishment set by Law is imprisonment or barring for more than five years and does not exceed ten.

After five, all other felonies, except those of slander and defamation, which shall prescribe in one year.

2. Misdemeanours prescribe in six months.

3. When the punishment stated in the Law is a compound one, that requiring the longest time to prescription shall be considered to apply the rules considered in this Article.

4. Crimes against humanity and of genocide and offences against persons and assets protected in the case of armed conflict, except those punished under Article 614, shall not have a statute of limitations.

Nor shall offences of terrorism have a statute of limitations, if they have caused the death of a person.

5. In cases of concurrent or related felonies, the term for prescription shall be that of the most serious offence.

Article 132

1. The terms foreseen in the preceding Article these shall be calculated from the day on which the punishable crime was committed. In cases of continued offence, permanent offence, as well as offences requiring assiduity, those terms shall be calculated, respectively, from the day on which the last infraction took place, from when the unlawful situation or the conduct ceased.

In attempted homicide and offences of non-consensual abortion, injury, against liberty, of tortures and against moral integrity, sexual freedom and indemnity, privacy, the right to personal dignity and the inviolability of the dwelling, when the victim is a minor, the terms shall be calculated from the day on which he has come of age, and if he were to die before coming of age, as of the date of his death.

2. Prescription shall be interrupted, leaving the time elapsed without effect, when proceedings are brought against the person deemed to be responsible for the felony or misdemeanour, and shall begin to elapse again from the proceedings halting or ending without sentencing, pursuant to the following rules:

1. Proceedings shall be deemed as being conducted against a specific person from the moment when, at the suit's inception, or thereafter, a reasoned judicial resolution is handed down attributing him the presumed participation in an event that might constitute a felony or misdemeanour.

2. Notwithstanding the foregoing, filing a suit or the accusation brought before a judicial body, in which a specific person is charged with presumed participation in an act that might constitute a felony or misdemeanour, shall suspend calculation of the prescription for a maximum term of six months in the case of an felony and for two months in the case of a misdemeanour, to be counted from the very date the suit is filed or the accusation brought.

   If any of the court resolutions mentioned in the preceding Section is issued against the accused or defendant within that term, or against any other person involved in the events, the interruption of prescription shall be deemed to have taken place retroactively, for all purposes, on the date of the suit or accusation being filed.

   On the contrary, calculation of the term of prescription shall continue from the date of the suit or accusation being filed if, within the term of six or two months, in the respective cases of felony or misdemeanour, a final court order of non-admission of the suit or accusation is handed down or the Court decides not to proceed against the person sued or accused. Continuation of the calculation shall also take place if the Investigating Judge does not adopt any of the resolutions foreseen in this Article within those terms.

3. For the purposes of this Article, the person against whom the proceedings are filed must be sufficiently determined in the court order, either by direct identification or by data that allow subsequent specification of that identification within the organisation or group of persons charged with the act.

Article 133

1. Penalties imposed by final judgement prescribe:

In thirty years, those of imprisonment for more than twenty years.

In twenty- five years, those of imprisonment of fifteen years or more, without exceeding twenty.

In twenty, those of barring for more than ten years and those of imprisonment for more than ten and less than fifteen.

In fifteen, those of barring for more than six years and that do not exceed ten, and those of imprisonment for more than five years and that do not exceed ten.

After ten, the remaining serious penalties.

After five, less serious penalties.

After one year, minor penalties.

2. Penalties imposed for crimes against humanity and of genocide and for offences against protected persons and assets in the event of armed conflict, except those punished under Article 614, shall not have a the statute of limitations.

Nor shall penalties for offences of terrorism have a statute of limitations, if the latter have caused the death of a person.

Article 134

The time until prescription of the punishment shall be calculated from the date of the final judgement, or from breach of the sentence, if it had begun to be served.

Article 135

1. Security measures shall prescribe in ten years, if depriving of freedom for a term exceeding three years, and in five years if depriving of freedom for a term equal to or less than three years, or if they have another content.

2. The time for prescription shall be calculated from the day on which the resolution imposing the measure became final or, when consecutively served, from when it should have begun to be served.

3. Should fulfilment of a security measure be later than that of a punishment, the term shall be calculated from extinction of the latter.

CHAPTER II

On cancellation of criminal records

Article 136

1. Convicts whose criminal accountability has been extinguished shall be entitled to obtain cancellation of their criminal record by the Ministry of Justice, on its own motion or at the request of the party, following report by the Judge or Court of Law sentencing.

2. The following shall be indispensable requisites for this right to be recognised:

1. Having settled the civil liabilities arising from the offence, except in cases of insolvency declared by the Judge or Court of Law sentencing, except if the financial circumstances of the convict have improved.

   Notwithstanding what is set forth in the preceding Section, in the case foreseen in Article 125, it shall suffice for the convict to be up to date with the instalment payments he was set by the Judge or Court of Law and for him to provide what is considered a sufficient guarantee of the sum left to be paid by instalments.

2. When the following terms have elapsed without the convict reoffending: six months for minor penalties; two years for penalties that do not exceed twelve months and those imposed for negligent offences; three years for the remaining less serious penalties; and five for serious penalties.

3. These terms shall be counted from the day following that on which the punishment was extinguished, although if this were to happen without conditional remission, the term, after having obtained final remission, shall be calculated with backdating to the day following that on which the punishment should have been completed, should such benefit not have been made use of. In such case, the initial date taken for calculation of the term of the sentence shall be the day following the suspension being granted.

4. Entries of criminal records at the different Sections of the Central Criminal Records Bureau shall not be public. While they are in force, certifications shall only be issued with the limitations and guarantees foreseen in the specific rules thereof and in the cases established by Law. In all cases, those requested by Judges or Courts of Law shall be issued, whether or not they refer to cancelled entries, specifically stating the latter circumstance when it concurs.

5. In cases in which, in spite of fulfilling the requisites established in this Article for cancellation, either at the request of the person concerned, or by the Ministry of Justice on its own motion, this has not been carried out, the Judge or Court of Law, having verified these circumstances, shall order the cancellation and shall not take those records into account.

Article 137

Annotations of the security measures imposed pursuant to the terms provided in this Code or in other criminal laws shall be cancelled once the respective measure has been fulfilled or has expired; meanwhile, they shall only be recorded in the certifications the Bureau issues for use by the Judges or Courts of Law, or the administrative authorities, and in the cases established by Law.

BOOK II

Felonies and their penalties

TITLE I

On unlawful killing and its forms

Article 138

Whoever kills another shall convicted of manslaughter, punishable with a sentence of imprisonment from ten to fifteen years.

Article 139

Whoever kills another when any of the following circumstances concur shall be convicted of murder and punished with a sentence of imprisonment from fifteen to twenty years:

5.1. With premeditation;

5.2. For a price, reward or promise;

5.3. With wanton cruelty, deliberately and inhumanely increasing the victim's suffering.

Article 140

When more than one of the circumstances foreseen in the preceding Article concur in a murder, a sentence of imprisonment shall be from twenty to twenty- five years.

Article 141

Provocation, conspiracy and solicitation to commit the offences foreseen in the preceding three Articles shall be punished with the penalty lower by one or two degrees to that stated as appropriate in the preceding Articles.

Article 142

1. Whoever causes the death of another by serious negligence shall be convicted of manslaughter and punished with a sentence of imprisonment of one to four years.

2. When the manslaughter is committed using a motor vehicle, a moped or a firearm, the punishment shall also, and respectively, include deprivation of the right to drive motor vehicles and mopeds or deprivation of the right to own and carry weapons from one to six years.

3. When the manslaughter is committed due to professional negligence, the punishment of special barring from exercise of the profession, trade or cargo shall also be imposed, for a period of three to six years.

Article 143

1. Whoever induces another to suicide shall be punished with a sentence of imprisonment from four to eight years.

2. A sentence of imprisonment of two to five years shall be imposed on whoever co-operates in the necessary acts for a person to commit suicide.

3. Punishment shall involve a sentence of imprisonment from six to ten years if such co-operation were to reach the point of death ensuing.

4. Whoever causes or actively co-operates in the necessary, direct acts causing the death of another, at the specific, serious, unequivocal request of that person, in the event of the victim suffering a serious disease that would unavoidably lead to death, or that causes permanent suffering that is hard to bear, shall be punished with a punishment lower by one or two degrees to those described in Sections 2 and 3 of this Article.

TITLE II

On abortion

Article 144

Whoever perpetrates an abortion on a woman without her consent shall be punished with a sentence of imprisonment from four to eight years and special barring from practising any health profession or from providing services of any kind at public or private gynaecological clinics, institutions or surgeries, for a term of three to ten years.

The same penalties shall be applied to whoever perpetrates an abortion having obtained the consent by the woman through violence, intimidation or deceit.

Article 145

1. Whoever perpetrates an abortion on a woman, with her consent, outside the cases allowed by Law shall be punished with a sentence of imprisonment from one to three years and special barring from practising any health profession and from providing services of any kind at public or private gynaecological clinics, institutions or surgeries, for a term of one to six years. The Judge may hand down the sentence in its higher half when the acts described in this Section are perpetrated outside an authorised public or private centre or institution.

2. The woman who causes herself an abortion or allows another person to cause it, outside the cases allowed by Law, shall be punished with a fine from six to twenty- four months.

3. In all cases, the Judge or Court of Law shall impose the penalties respectively foreseen in this Article in the upper half when perpetrated after the twenty- second week of gestation.

Article 145 bis

1. Punishment with a fine from six to twelve months and special barring from providing services of any kind at public or private gynaecological clinics, institutions or surgeries shall be applied, for a term of six months to two years, to whoever, within the cases admitted by the Law, perpetrates an abortion:

a) Without having verified that the woman has received prior information on the rights, public subsidies and aid to support maternity;

b) Without the waiting period established in the legislation having elapsed;

c) Without having obtained the required prior reports;

d) Outside an authorised public or private centre or institution. In this case, the judge may impose the punishment in its upper half.

2. In all cases, the Judge or Court of Law shall impose the penalties foreseen in this Article in the upper half, when the abortion is perpetrated as of the twenty- second week of gestation.

3. The pregnant woman shall not be penalised under this provision.

Article 146

Whoever causes an abortion due to serious negligence shall be punished with a sentence of imprisonment of three to five months, or a fine from six to ten months.

When an abortion is perpetrated due to professional negligence, the punishment of special barring from practising the profession trade or holding office shall also be imposed for a term from one to three years.
The pregnant woman shall not be penalised under this provision.

TITLE III

On bodily harm

Article 147

1. Whoever, by any means or procedure, causes another an injury that detracts from his bodily integrity or his physical or mental health, shall be convicted of the offence of grievous bodily harm, with a sentence of imprisonment of six months to three years, whenever the injury objectively requires medical or surgical treatment for health purposes, in addition to qualified first aid. Simple qualified surveillance or monitoring of the course of the injury shall not be deemed medical treatment.

Punishment by the same penalty shall be applied to whoever, within the term of one year, has perpetrated the action described in Article 617 of this Code four times.

2. However, the act described in the preceding Section shall be punished with a sentence of imprisonment of three to six months or a fine from six to twelve months, when less serious, in view of the means used or the result caused.

Article 148

The injuries foreseen in Section 1 of the preceding Article may be punished with a sentence of imprisonment of two to five years, in view of the result caused or the risk produced:

1. If weapons, instruments, objects, means, methods or ways that are specifically dangerous to life or health, both physical and mental, of the injured party, were used;

2. If perpetrated with wanton cruelty and premeditation;

3. If the victim is under twelve years old or is incapacitated;

4. If the victim is or has been the wife, or woman bound to the offender by a similar emotional relation, even when not cohabitating;

5. If the victim is an especially vulnerable person who lives with the offender.

Article 149

1. Whoever causes to another person, by any means or procedure, to forfeit or lose the use of a major organ or limb, or a sense, or sexual impotence, sterility, serious deformity or to suffer a serious physical or mental illness, shall be punished with a sentence of imprisonment from six to twelve years.

2. Whoever causes to another person a genital mutilation in any form shall be punished with a sentence of imprisonment from six to twelve years. Should the victim be a minor or incapacitated, the punishment of special barring from exercise of parental rights, guardianship, care, safekeeping or fostership shall be applicable for a term from four to ten years, should the Judge deem it appropriate in the interest of the minor or incapacitated person.

Article 150

Whoever causes another person to forfeit or lose the use of a non-major or limb, or a deformity, shall be punished with a sentence of imprisonment from three to six years.

Article 151

Provocation, conspiracy and the solicitation to commit the offences foreseen in the preceding Articles of this Title shall be punished with a penalty one or two degrees below that set for the relevant offence.

Article 152

1. Whoever causes any of the injuries foreseen in the preceding Articles due to serious negligence shall be punished:

   1. With a sentence of imprisonment from three to six months, in the case of the injuries described in Article 147.1;

   2. With a sentence of imprisonment of one to three years, in the case of the injuries described in Article 149;

   3. With a sentence of imprisonment of six months to two years, in the case of the injuries in Article 150.

2. When the acts referred to in this Article have been committed using a motor vehicle, moped or firearm, the punishment of deprivation of the right to drive motor vehicles and mopeds or the right to own and carry weapons for a term of one to four years, respectively, shall also be imposed.

3. When the injuries are committed due to professional negligence, the punishment of special barring from practice of the profession, trade or office shall also be applied, for a term from one to four years.

Article 153

1. Whoever, by any means or procedure, causes another mental damage or an injury not defined as a felony in this Code, or who hits or abuses another by action, without causing such person an injury, when the victim is or has been his wife, or a woman with whom he has been bound by a similar emotional relation, even when not cohabitating, or an especially vulnerable person who lives with the offender, the offender shall be punished with a sentence of imprisonment of six months to one year, or community service from thirty one to eighty days and, in all cases, deprivation of the right to own and carry weapons from a year and a day to three years, as well as, when the Judge or Court of Law deems it appropriate in the interest of the minor or incapacitated person, barring from the exercise parental rights, guardianship, care, safekeeping or fostership for up to five years.

2. If the victim of the offence foreseen in the preceding Section were any of the persons referred to in Article 173.2, except the persons considered in the preceding Section of this Article, the offender shall be punished with a sentence of imprisonment from three months to a year or community service of thirty- one to eighty days and, in all cases, deprivation of the right to own and carry weapons from a year and a day to three years, as well as, when the Judge or Court of Law deems it adequate in the interest of the minor or incapacitated person, barring from the exercise of parental rights, guardianship, care, safekeeping or fostership from six months to three years.

3. The penalties foreseen in Sections 1 and 2 shall be imposed in the upper half when the offence is perpetrated in the presence of minors, or using weapons, or when it takes place in the common dwelling or in the dwelling of the victim, or when perpetrated in breach of a penalty of those set forth in Article 48 of this Code, or an precautionary or security measure of the same nature.

4. Notwithstanding the terms foreseen in the preceding Sections, the Judge or Court of Law, giving the reasons in the judgement, in view of the offender's personal circumstances and those arising in perpetrating the event, may impose the lower degree punishment.

Article 154

Those who brawl, attacking each other in a disorderly manner and using means or instruments that endanger the life or integrity of persons, shall be punished for their participation in the brawl with a sentence of imprisonment from three months to a year or fine from six to twenty- four months.

Article 155

In felonies involving bodily harm, if valid, free, spontaneous consent is involved expressed by the victim, a punishment lower by one or two degrees shall be imposed.

Consent granted by a minor or incapacitated person shall not be valid.

Article 156

Notwithstanding what is set forth in the preceding Article, valid free, conscious and specifically expressed consent shall exempt from criminal accountability in cases of organ transplant carried out pursuant to the terms of the Law, sterilisations and transsexual surgery carried out by a surgeon, except if the consent obtained is flawed, or obtained by price or reward, or when the person consenting is a minor or incapacitated person, in which case that provided by these or their legal representatives shall not be valid.

However, sterilisation of an incapacitated person suffering from serious mental deficiency shall not be punishable when this is carried out pursuant to the overriding criterion of the best interest of the incapacitated person and it has been authorised by a Judge, either in the actual procedure of incapacitation, or through voluntary jurisdiction proceedings, processed thereafter at the request of the legal representative of the incapacitated person, having heard the opinion of two specialists, the Public Prosecutor and having examined the incapacitated person.

Article 156 bis

1. Those who promote, favour, facilitate or publicise the unlawful obtaining or trafficking in human organs or their transplantation shall be punished with a sentence of imprisonment from six to twelve years in the case of a main organ, and of prison from three to six years if not a main organ.

2. Should the receiver of the organ consent to the carrying out of the transplant while being aware of its unlawful origin, he shall punished with the same penalties as in the preceding Section, that may be lowered by one or two degrees in view of the circumstances of case and of the offender.

3. When, pursuant to the terms established in Article 31 bis, a legal person is responsible for the offences defined in this Article, it shall be sentenced to pay a fine of three to five times the profit obtained.

Pursuant to the rules established in Article 66 bis, the Judges and Courts of Law may also impose the penalties described in Sub-Sections b) to g) of Section 7 of Article 33.

TITLE IV

On injuries to the foetus

Article 157

Whoever, by any means or procedure, were to cause a foetus an injury or disease that seriously damages the normal development thereof or causes such foetus a serious physical or mental handicap, shall be punished with a prison sentence of one to four years and special barring from practising any health profession, or providing services of all kinds at public or private gynaecological clinics, institutions or surgeries, for a term of two to eight years.

Article 158

Whoever, due to serious negligence, were to commit the acts described in the preceding Article, shall be punished with a sentence of imprisonment of three to five months or a fine from six to ten months.

When the acts described in the preceding Article are committed by professional negligence, the punishment of special barring from practice of the profession, trade or office for a term of six months to two years shall also be imposed.

The pregnant woman shall not be penalised under this provision.

TITLE V

Felonies related to genetic engineering

Article 159

1. Those who manipulate the human genes so as to alter the genome for purposes other than eliminating or decreasing serious flaws or diseases, shall be punished with a sentence of imprisonment from two to six years and special barring from public employment and office, profession or trade for seven to ten years.

2 Should alteration of the genome be perpetrated due to serious negligence, the punishment shall be a fine from six to fifteen months and special barring from public employment and office, profession or trade from one to three years.

Article 160

1. The use of genetic engineering to produce biological weapons or those intended to exterminate human beings shall be punished with a sentence of imprisonment of three to seven years and special barring from public employment and office, profession or trade for a term of seven to ten years.

2. Those who fertilise human ovules for any purpose other than human procreation shall be punished with a sentence of imprisonment from one to five years and special barring from public employment and office, profession or trade from six to ten years.

3. The same penalty shall apply to punish creation of identical human beings by cloning or other procedures aimed at racial selection.

Article 161

1. Whoever carries out assisted reproduction techniques on a woman without her consent shall be punished with a sentence of imprisonment from two to six years and special barring from public employment and office, profession or trade for a term of one to four years.

2. Prosecution of this offence shall require it to be denounced by the victim or her legal representative. Should she be a minor, incapacitated, or a handicapped person, the Public Prosecutor may also denounce the offence.

Article 162

In the felonies defined in this Title, the judicial authority may impose any one or number of the consequences foreseen in Article 129 of this Code when the offender belongs to a company, organisation or assembly which engages in these activities, even though only transitionally.

TITLE VI

Felonies against freedom

CHAPTER I

On illegal detention and kidnapping

Article 163

1. A private individual who locks up or detains another person, depriving him of his liberty, shall be punished with a sentence of imprisonment from four to six years.

2. Should the offender release the person locked up or detained within the first three days of detention, without having achieved his intended objective, he shall have the lower degree punishment imposed.

3. A sentence of imprisonment from five to eight years shall be handed down if the victim is locked up or detained for more than fifteen days.

4. A private individual who, outside the cases allowed by the laws, arrests a person to immediately hand him over to the authorities, shall be punished with the penalty of a fine from three to six months.

Article 164

Kidnapping a person when setting a condition for release shall be punished with a sentence of imprisonment from six to ten years. If the circumstance of Article 163.3 has concurred with the kidnap, the higher degree punishment shall be imposed, and the lower degree one if the conditions of Article 163.2 are fulfilled.

Article 165

The penalties of the preceding Articles shall be imposed in the upper half, in the respective cases, if an unlawful detention or kidnapping has been carried out simulating being an authority or public officer, or if the victim is a minor, an incapacitated person, or a civil servant exercising his duties.

Article 166

A convict for illegal detention or kidnapping who does not declare the whereabouts of the person detained shall be punished, as appropriate, with higher degree penalties than those stated in the preceding Articles of this Chapter, except if he has released the victim.

Article 167

The authority or civil servant who, outside the cases allowed by Law, and without there being a reason due to a felony, were to commit any of the acts described in the preceding Articles, shall be punished with the penalties respectively foreseen therein, in the upper half, and also with absolute barring for a term of eight to twelve years.

Article 168

Provocation, conspiracy and solicitation to commit the offences foreseen in this Chapter shall be punished with the penalty lower by one or two degrees to that set for the offence concerned.

CHAPTER II

On intimidation

Article 169

Whoever threatens another with causing him, his family or other persons with whom he is intimately related harm consisting of felonies of unlawful killing, bodily harm, abortion, against liberty, torture and against moral integrity, sexual freedom, privacy, honour, property and the social-economic order, shall be punished:

1. With a sentence of imprisonment from one to five years, if he has made the threat demanding a sum or imposing any other condition, even though not unlawful, and the offender has achieved what he intended. If not achieved, a sentence of imprisonment of six months to three years shall be handed down.

   The penalties stated in the preceding Section shall be imposed in the upper half if the intimidation is made in writing, by telephone or by any means of communication or reproduction, or on behalf of real or supposed entities or groups.

2. With a sentence of imprisonment of six months to two years, when the intimidation has not been conditional.

Article 170

1. Should the intimidation be of a harm which constitutes a felony is intended to cause fear among the inhabitants of a location, ethnic, cultural or religious group, or a social or professional group, or any other group of persons, and if serious enough for such harm to be inflicted, the respective higher degree of penalties than those foreseen in the preceding Article shall be imposed.

2. A sentence of imprisonment from six months to two years shall be applied to those who, for the same purpose and severity, publicly call for violent actions to be committed by armed gangs, organisations or terrorist groups.

Article 171

1. Threats of harm that does not constitute a felony shall be punished with a prison sentence from three months to a year or fine from six to twenty- four months, in view of the severity and circumstances of the facts, when the intimidation is conditional and the condition does not consist in a conduct that is due. Should the offender have achieved his purpose, the upper half of the punishment shall be applied.

2. Should any person demand any other sum or compensation under the threat of disclosing or broadcasting facts concerning his private life or family relations that are not publicly known and that may affect his reputation, credit or interest, he shall be punished with a sentence of imprisonment from two to four years, if he has obtained delivery of all or part of what has been demanded, and from four months to two years, should this not be achieved.

3. Should the act described in the preceding Section consist of a threat to reveal or report that a felony has been committed, the Public Prosecutor may, in order to facilitate punishment of the intimidation, abstain from accusing the person threatened with disclosure of the latter offence, except if punishable with a prison sentence exceeding two years. In the latter case, the Judge or Court of Law may lower the punishment by one or two degrees.

4. Whoever lightly intimidates his wife or former wife, or woman with whom he has been bound by a similar emotional relation even without cohabitation, shall be punished with a sentence of imprisonment of six months to one year or community service from thirty- one to eighty days and, in all cases, deprivation of the right to own and carry weapons from a year and a day to three years, as well as, when the Judge or Court of Law sees it fit in the interest of the minor or incapacitated person, special barring from exercise of parental rights, guardianship, care, safekeeping or fostership for up to five years.

The same punishment shall be imposed on whoever lightly intimidates an especially vulnerable person who lives with the offender.

5. Whoever lightly intimidates any of the persons referred to in Article 173.2 with weapons or other dangerous instruments, except those stated in the preceding Section of this Article, shall be punished with a sentence of imprisonment from three months to a year or community service of thirty- one to eighty days and, in all cases, deprivation of the right to own and carry weapons from one to three years, as well as, when the Judge or Court of Law sees it fit in the interest of the minor or incapacitated person, special barring from exercise of parental rights, guardianship, care, safekeeping or fostership for a term of six months to three years.

The penalties foreseen in Sections 4 and 5, in the upper half, shall be applied when the offence is committed in the presence of minors, or when it takes place in the common dwelling or in the dwelling of the victim, or is perpetrated in breach of a punishment of those set forth in Article 48 of this Code or an precautionary or security measure of the same kind.

6. Notwithstanding what is set forth in Sections 4 and 5, the Judge or Court of Law, may, giving the reasons in the judgement, in view of the offender's personal circumstances and those arising in the perpetration of the act, handing down a punishment one degree lower.

CHAPTER III

On coercion

Article 172

1. Whoever, without being lawfully authorised, were to use violence to prevent another from doing something the law does not prohibit, or who forces him to do something he does not want to do, whether just or unjust, shall be punished with a sentence of imprisonment of six months to three years or with a fine of twelve to twenty- four months, in view of the severity of the coercion or the means used.

When the object of the coercion exercised is to prevent someone from exercising a fundamental right, the penalties shall be imposed in the upper half, except if a higher punishment is set for the offence under another provision of this Code.

The penalties shall also be imposed in the upper half when the coercion perpetrated is intended to prevent someone from lawfully enjoying his dwelling.

2. Whoever lightly coerces his wife or former wife or woman to whom he is or has been bound by a similar emotional relation, even without cohabitation, shall be punished with a sentence of imprisonment of six months to one year or of community service of thirty- one to eighty days and, in all cases, deprivation of the right to own and carry weapons from a year and a day to three years, as well as, when the Judge or Court of Law sees it fit in the interest of the minor or incapacitated person, special barring from exercise of parental rights, guardianship, care, safekeeping or fostership up to five years.

The same punishment shall be imposed on whoever slightly coerces an especially vulnerable person who lives with the offender.

The punishment shall be imposed in the upper half when the offence is committed in the presence of minors, or when it takes place in the common dwelling or in the dwelling of the victim, or is perpetrated in breach of a punishment of those set forth in Article 48 of this Code or an precautionary or security measure of the same kind.

Notwithstanding what is set forth in the preceding Sections, the Judge or Court of Law may, giving the reasons in the judgement, in view of the offender's personal circumstances and those arising in perpetrating the act, hand down a punishment one degree lower.

TITLE VII

On torture and other felonies against moral integrity

Article 173

1. Whoever inflicts a degrading treatment on another person, seriously damaging his moral integrity, shall be punished with a sentence of imprisonment of six months to two years.

The same punishment shall be imposed on those who, within the setting of any labour relation or the civil service, availing themselves of their superior status, repeatedly perpetrate hostile or humiliating acts against another that, while not reaching the status of degrading treatment, amount to serious harassment of the victim.

The same punishment shall also be imposed on those who repeatedly perpetrate hostile or humiliating acts that, while not reaching the statement of degrading treatment, are aimed at preventing lawful enjoyment of a dwelling.

2. Whoever habitually uses physical or mental violence against the person who is or has been his spouse or the person who is or has been bound to him by a similar emotional relation, even without cohabitation, or against descendents, ascendants or biological, adopted or fostered siblings, against that person or the spouse or cohabitating partner, or against minors or the incapacitated who live with him or who are subject to the parental rights, guardianship, care, fostership or safekeeping of the spouse or cohabitating partner, or against a person protected by any other relation by which that person is a member of the core family unit, as well as against persons who, due to their special vulnerability are subject to custody or safekeeping in public or private centres, shall be punished with a sentence of imprisonment of six months to three years, deprivation of the right to own and carry weapons from two to five years and, when appropriate, when the Judge or Court of Law sees it fit in the interest of the minor or incapacitated person, special barring from exercise of parental rights, guardianship, care, safekeeping or fostership for a term from one to five years, without prejudice to the penalties that may be relevant for the felonies or misdemeanours in which the acts of physical or mental violence have been materialised.

The penalties shall be imposed in the upper half when any one or number of the acts of violence are committed in the presence of minors, or using weapons, or take place in the common dwelling or in the dwelling of the victim, or are perpetrated in breach of any of the penalties foreseen in Article 48 of this Code, or of an precautionary or security measure or prohibition of the same kind.

3. In order to appraise the habitual nature referred to in the preceding Section, the number of proven acts of violence shall be considered, as well as the nearness of these in time, regardless of whether that violence has been perpetrated against the same or different victims described in this Article, and whether the violent acts have or have not been judged in previous proceedings.

Article 174

1. Torture is committed by the public authority or officer who, abusing his office, and in order to obtain a confession or information from any person, or to punish him for any act he may have committed, or is suspected to have

committed, or for any reason based on any kind of discrimination, subjects that person to conditions or procedures that, due to their nature, duration or other circumstances, cause him physical or mental suffering, suppression or decrease in his powers of cognizance, discernment or decision, or that in any other way attack his moral integrity. Those found guilty of torture shall be punished with a sentence of imprisonment from two to six years if the offence is serious, and of imprisonment from one to three years if it is not. In addition to the penalties stated, in all cases, the punishment of absolute barring shall be imposed, from eight to twelve years.

2. The same penalties shall be incurred, respectively, by the authority or officer of penitentiary institutions or correctional or protection centres for minors who may commit the acts referred to in the preceding Section in relation to the detainees, interns or prisoners.

Article 175

The authority or public officer who, abusing his office and outside the cases considered in the preceding Article, attacks the moral integrity of a person, shall be punished with a sentence of imprisonment of two to four years if the attack is serious and of six months to two years imprisonment if it is not. In all cases, in addition to the penalties stated, the offender shall be subject to that of special barring from public employment and office for two to four years.

Article 176

The penalties, as respectively established in the preceding Articles, shall be imposed on the authority or officer who, in breach of the duties of his office, were to allow other persons to perpetrate the acts foreseen therein.

Article 177

If the offences described in the preceding Sections, in addition to attacking moral integrity, were to cause injury or damage to life, physical integrity, health, sexual freedom or the assets of the victim or a third party, such acts shall be punished separately with the relevant punishment for the felonies or misdemeanours committed, except when they are already specifically punished with the Law.

TITLE VII BIS

On trafficking in human beings

Article 177 bis

1. Whoever, using violence, intimidation or deceit, or abusing a situation of superiority or need, or the vulnerability of a national or alien victim, were to induce, transport, transfer, receive or house such a victim for any of the purposes described below, within Spain, from Spain, in transit or with destination therein, shall be convicted of human trafficking and punished with the penalty of five to eight years imprisonment,:

a) Imposing on the victim forced work or services, slavery or practices similar to slavery or servitude or begging;

b) Sexual exploitation, including pornography;

c) Extraction of their bodily organs.

2. Even when not resorting to any of the means listed in the preceding Section, the actions stated in the preceding Section shall be deemed human trafficking when perpetrated with minors for the purposes of exploitation.

3. The consent of a victim of human trafficking shall be irrelevant when any of the means stated in Section one of this Article has been resorted to.

4. A higher degree punishment than that foreseen in Section 1 of this Article shall be applied when:

   a) The trafficking puts the victim in serious danger;

   b) The victim is a minor;

   c) The victim is especially vulnerable due to illness, disability or his situation.

Should more than one circumstance concur, the punishment shall be imposed in its upper half.

5. A punishment higher in one degree than that foreseen in Section 1 of this Article shall be imposed, and absolute barring from six to twelve years for those who perpetrate such acts availing themselves of their status as an authority due to being agent or public officer thereof . If any of the circumstances also foreseen in Section 4 of this Article should also concur, the penalties shall be imposed in the upper half.

6. A punishment higher in one degree than foreseen in Section 1 of this Article shall be imposed and special barring from profession, trade, industry or commerce for the time of the sentence, when the offender belongs to an organisation or assembly of more than two persons, even if transitory in nature, which perpetrates such activities. Should any of the circumstances foreseen in Section 4 of this Article concur, the penalties imposed shall be in the upper half. If the circumstance foreseen in Section 5 of this Article concurs, the penalties imposed shall be those stated the upper half thereof.

In the case of the managers, directors or persons in charge of such organisations or assemblies, the upper half of the punishment shall be applied, which may raised to the one immediately above it in degree.

In all cases, the punishment shall be raised to the one immediately above in degree if any of the circumstances foreseen in Section 4 or the circumstance foreseen in Section 5 of this Article concurs.

7. When, pursuant to the terms established in Article 31 bis, a legal person is responsible for the offences described in the Article, the punishment imposed thereon shall be a fine from three to five times the profit obtained. Pursuant to the rules established in Article 66 bis, the Judges and Courts of Law may also impose the penalties established in Sub-Sections b) to g) of Section 7 of Article 33.

8. Provocation, conspiracy and solicitation to commit the offence of trafficking in human beings shall be punished with the penalty lower by one or two degrees to that of the relevant offence.

9. In all cases, the penalties foreseen in this Article shall be imposed without prejudice to the relevant one, as appropriate, for the offence of Article 318 bis of this Code and other offences effectively committed, including those related to the relevant exploitation.

10. Sentences by foreign Judges or Courts of Law for offences of the same kind as those foreseen in this Article shall have the effect of recidivism, except if the criminal record has been cancelled or may be, pursuant to Spanish Law.

11. Without prejudice to application of the general rules of this Code, the victims of trafficking in human beings shall be exempt of punishment for the criminal offences that might have been committed while suffering exploitation, as long as participation therein has been a direct consequence of the situation of violence, intimidation, deceit or abuse to which they may have been subjected to and provided there is an adequate proportionality between that situation and the criminal act perpetrated.

TITLE VIII

Felonies against sexual freedom and indemnity

CHAPTER I

On sexual assault

Article 178

Whoever offends against the sexual freedom of another person, using violence or intimidation, shall be punished for sexual assault with a sentence of imprisonment from one to five years.

Article 179

When the sexual assault consists of vaginal, anal or oral penetration, or inserting body parts or objects into either of the former two orifices, the offender shall be convicted of rape with a sentence of imprisonment from six to twelve years.

Article 180

1. The preceding conduct shall be punished with prison sentences of five to ten years for assaults pursuant to Article 178, and from twelve to fifteen years for those of Article 179, when any of the following circumstances concur:

   1. When the violence or intimidation made are of a particularly degrading or humiliating nature;

   2. When the acts are committed by joint action of two or more persons;

   3. When the victim is especially vulnerable due to age, illness, handicap or circumstances, except for what is set forth in Article 183;

   4. When, in order to execute the offence, the offender has availed himself of a superiority or relationship, due to being the ascendant, descendent or brother or sister, biological or adopted or in-law of the victim;

   5. When the doer uses weapons or other equally dangerous means which may cause death or any of the injuries foreseen in Articles 149 and 150 of this Code, without prejudice to the relevant punishment for the death or injuries caused.

2. Should two or more of the above circumstances concur, the penalties foreseen in this Article shall be imposed in the upper half.

CHAPTER II

On sexual abuse

Article 181

1. Whoever, without violence or intimidation and without there being consent, perpetrates acts against the sexual freedom or indemnity of another person, shall be convicted of sexual abuse, with a sentence of imprisonment from one to three years or a fine of eighteen to twenty- four months.

2. For the purposes of the preceding Section, non-consensual sexual abuse is deemed to be that perpetrated on persons who are unconscious, or whose mental disorder is taken advantage of, as well as those committed by

overcoming the will of the victim using narcotics, drugs or any other natural or chemical substance that is appropriate for such purpose.

3. The same punishment shall be imposed when consent is obtained by the offender availing himself of a situation of manifest superiority that deprives the victim of liberty.

4. In all the preceding cases, when the sexual abuse consists of vaginal, anal or oral penetration, or inserting body parts or objects into either of the former two orifices, the offender shall be punished with a sentence of imprisonment from four to ten years.

5. The penalties stated in this Article shall be imposed in the upper half if the circumstance of 3a. or that of 4a. of those foreseen in Section 1 of Article 180 of this Code concur.

Article 182

1. Whoever, by deceit, engages in acts of a sexual nature with a person over the age of thirteen and under the age of sixteen shall be punished with a sentence of imprisonment from one to two years, or a fine of twelve to twenty- four months.

2. When the acts consist of vaginal, anal or oral penetration, or inserting body parts or objects into either of the former two orifices, the punishment shall be prison from two to six years. The punishment shall be imposed in its the upper half if circumstances 3 or 4 of those foreseen in Article 180.1 of this Code concur.

CHAPTER II BIS

On sexual abuse and assault on children under the age of thirteen years

Article 183

1. Whoever perpetrates acts against the sexual indemnity of a child under the age of thirteen years shall be convicted of sexual abuse of the child, with a sentence of imprisonment from two to six years.

2. When the assault takes place by means of violence or intimidation, the offender shall convicted of the offence of sexual assault of the child, with the punishment of five to ten years imprisonment.

3. When the assault consists of vaginal, anal or oral penetration, or inserting body parts or objects into either of the former two orifices, the offender shall be punished with a sentence of imprisonment from eight to twelve years, in the case of Section 1 and with the punishment of twelve to fifteen years, in the case of Section 2.

4. The conducts foreseen in the preceding three numbers shall be punished with the relevant sentence of imprisonment in its upper half when any of the following circumstances concur:

a) When the scarce intellectual or physical development of the victim has caused a situation of total defencelessness and, in all cases, when under four years old;

b) When the acts are committed by the joint action of two or more persons;

c) When the violence or intimidation made are of a particularly degrading or humiliating nature;

d) When, in order to execute the offence, the offender has availed himself of a superiority or relationship, due to being the ascendant, descendent or brother, biological, adopted or in-law of the victim;

e) When the offender has endangered the life of the minor;

f) When the offence has been committed within a criminal organisation or group with the purpose of perpetrating those activities.

5. In all the cases foreseen in this Article, when the offender has availed itself of his condition as an authority, agent or public officer thereof, the punishment of absolute barring from six to twelve years shall also be applied.

Article 183 bis

Whoever uses the Internet, telephone or any other information and communication technology to contact a person under the age of thirteen years and proposes to meet that person in order to commit any of the offences described in Articles 178 to 183 and 189, as long as such a solicitation is accompanied by material acts aimed at such an approach, shall be punished with the penalty of one to three years imprisonment or a fine of twelve to twenty- four months, without prejudice to the relevant penalties for the offences actually committed. The penalties shall be imposed in the upper half when the approach is obtained by coercion, intimidation or deceit.

CHAPTER III

On sexual harassment

Article 184

1. Whoever solicits favours of a sexual nature, for himself or for a third party, within the setting of a continuous or usual work relation, teaching or service provision relation, and by such conduct causes the victim a situation that is objective and seriously intimidating, hostile or humiliating, shall convicted of sexual harassment and punished with a sentence of imprisonment of three to five months or a fine from six to ten months.

2. Should the party guilty of sexual harassment have committed the act availing himself of a situation of labour, teaching or hierarchical superiority, or specifically or tacitly warning of harm to the victim in relation to the lawful expectations that person may have within the setting of that relation, the punishment shall be five to seven months imprisonment or a fine of ten to fourteen months.

3. When the victim is especially vulnerable, due to age, illness or the circumstances, the punishment shall five to seven months imprisonment or a fine of ten to fourteen months in the cases foreseen in Section 1, and of imprisonment for six months to one year in the cases foreseen in Section 2 of this Article.

CHAPTER IV

On felonies of exhibitionism and sexual provocation

Article 185

Whoever perpetrates or has another perpetrate acts of obscene exhibitionism before minors or the incapacitated, shall be punished with a sentence of imprisonment of six months to one year or fine from twelve to twenty- four months.

Article 186

Whoever, by any direct means, were to sell, distribute or exhibit pornographic material among minors or the incapacitated, shall be punished with a sentence of imprisonment of six months to one year or a fine from twelve to twenty- four months.

CHAPTER V

On felonies related to prostitution and corruption of minors

Article 187

1. Whoever induces, promotes, favours or facilitates the prostitution of a person who is underage or incapacitated shall be punished with the penalties from one to five years and a fine of twelve to twenty- four months. The same punishment shall be imposed on whoever solicits, accepts or obtains a sexual relation with a person who is a minor or incapacitated in exchange for a remuneration or promise.

2. Whoever perpetrates the conducts described in Section 1 of this Article when the victim is under thirteen years old shall be punished with a sentence of imprisonment from four to six years.

3. Those who perpetrate the acts availing themselves of their status as an authority, agent or public officer thereof shall be subject, in a sentence of imprisonment stated, in the upper half, and also that of absolute barring from six to twelve years.

4. The penalties shall be imposed in a higher degree to those foreseen in the preceding Sections, in the respective cases, when the offender belongs to an organisation or assembly, even if transitory in nature, with the purpose of perpetrating those activities.

5. The penalties stated shall be imposed, in the respective cases, without prejudice to the relevant ones for offences against sexual freedom or indemnity committed against minors or the incapacitated.

Article 188

1. Whoever uses violence, intimidation or deceit, or abuse of a situation of superiority or need or vulnerability of the victim, to force a person who is of legal age to practice prostitution, or to continue to do so, shall be punished with the prison sentences of two to four years and a fine from twelve to twenty- four months. The same punishment shall be incurred by whoever makes a profit from exploiting prostitution by another person, even when that person consents.

2. Should the conduct mentioned by perpetrated against a minor or incapacitated person, to initiate or maintain that person in prostitution, the offender shall be handed down a sentence of imprisonment from four to six years.

3. Whoever behaves as foreseen in the preceding Section, when the victim is under thirteen years old, shall be punished with a sentence of imprisonment from five to ten years.

4. The penalties shall be imposed as foreseen in the preceding Sections, in the upper half, in the respective cases, when any of the following circumstances concur:

   a) When the offender has availed himself of his status as an authority, agent or public officer thereof. In that case, the punishment of absolute barring from six to twelve years shall also be applied;

   b) When the offender belongs to a criminal organisation or group with the purpose of perpetrating those activities;

   c) When the offender has endangered the life or health of the victim, maliciously or due to serious negligence.

5. The penalties stated shall be imposed in the respective cases, without prejudice to the relevant one for the sexual assaults or abuses committed against the person prostituted.

Article 189

1. A sentence of imprisonment from one to five years shall be handed down to:

a) Whoever recruits or uses minors or the incapacitated for exhibitionistic or pornographic purposes or shows, both public or private, or to prepare any kind of pornographic material, whatever the media, or who finances or profits from any of these activities.

b) Whoever produces, sells, distributes, displays, offers or facilitates the production, sale, diffusion or display by any means of pornographic material, in the preparation of which minors or incapacitated persons have been used, or possesses such material for such purposes, even though the material is of foreign or unknown origin.

2. Whoever possesses pornographic material for his own use, in the preparation of which minors or the incapacitated have been used, shall be punished with the penalty from three months to a year of imprisonment or with a fine of six months to two years.

3. Whoever perpetrates the acts foreseen in Section 1 of this Article shall be punish with a sentence of imprisonment from five to nine years when any of the following circumstances concur:

a) When using children under the age of thirteen years;

b) When the acts are particularly degrading or humiliating in nature;

c) When the acts are especially serious in view of the financial value of the pornographic material;

d) When the pornographic material displays children or the incapacitated who are victims of physical or sexual violence;

e) When the offender belongs to an organisation or assembly, even if transitory in nature, with the purpose of perpetrating those activities;

f) When the offender is an ascendant, tutor, carer, minder, teacher or any other person in charge, *de facto* or *de jure*, of the minor or incapacitated person.

4. Whoever makes a minor or incapacitated person participate in a conduct of a sexual nature that damages the personal evolution or development of that person shall be punished with a sentence of imprisonment of six months to one year.

5. Whoever has a minor or incapacitated person under his care, guardianship, protection or fostership and who, being aware of his state of prostitution or corruption, does not do everything possible to prevent such situation continuing, or does not resort to the competent authority for such purpose, if lacking the resources for custody of the minor or incapacitated person, shall be punished with a sentence of imprisonment from three to six months or a fine from six to twelve months.

6. The Public Prosecutor shall promote the pertinent actions in order to deprive whoever commits any conduct described in the preceding Section of his parental rights, guardianship, safekeeping or family fostership, as appropriate.

7. Whoever produces, sells, distributes, displays or facilitates pornographic material by any means in which, while minors or incapacitated persons have not been used directly, makes use of their altered or modified voice or image, shall be punished with a sentence of imprisonment from three months to a year or a fine of six months to two years.

8. (Suppressed)

Article 189 bis

When, pursuant to the terms established in Article 31 bis, a legal person is responsible for the offences included in this Chapter, it shall have the following penalties imposed thereon:

a) Fine from three to five times the profit obtained, if the offence committed by a natural person has a punishment of imprisonment foreseen exceeding five years;

b) Fine of two to four times the profit obtained, if the offence committed by a natural person has a punishment of imprisonment foreseen exceeding two years not included in the preceding Section;

c) Fine of two to three times the profit obtained, in the rest of the cases.

Pursuant to the rules established in Article 66 bis, the Judges and Courts of Law may also impose the penalties established in Sub-Sections b) to g) of Section 7 of Article 33.

Article 190

Sentencing by a foreign Judge or Court of Law, for offences included in this Chapter, shall be equivalent to sentences by Spanish Judges or Courts of Law for the purposes of applying the aggravating circumstance of recidivism.

CHAPTER VI

Provisions common to the preceding Chapters

Article 191

1. Prosecution of felonies of sexual assault, harassment or abuse, shall require this to be reported by the victim, his legal representative or a suit to be filed by the Public Prosecutor, who shall act in line with the lawful interests concerned. When the victim is a minor, incapacitated or handicapped person, the report by the Public Prosecutor shall suffice.

2. In these felonies, forgiveness by the victim or legal representative does not extinguish the criminal action or the criminal liability.

Article 192

1. Those sentenced to imprisonment for one or more felonies included in this Title shall also be subject to a probation measure to be carried out after the sentence of imprisonment is served. The duration of such measure shall be five to ten years, if any of the offences is serious, and from one to five years, if one or more less serious offences are involved. In the latter case, in the case of a single offence committed by a first time offender, the Court of Law may order the probation measure based on the lower danger of the convict.

2. The ascendants, tutors, carers, minders, teachers or any other person in charge *de facto* or *de jure* of the minor or incapacitated person, who acted as principals or accomplices of commit the felonies included in this Title, shall be punished with the relevant punishment, in its upper half.

This rule shall not be applied when the circumstance it contains is specifically included in the definition of the crime concerned.

3. The Judge or Court of Law may also hand down a reasoned punishment of special barring from the exercise of parental rights, guardianship, care, safekeeping, public employment and office or practice of the profession or trade, for the term of six months to six years, or permanent deprivation of parental rights.

Article 193

Judgements convicting of offences against sexual freedom, in addition to the relevant pronouncements on civil liability, shall duly make the appropriate pronouncements concerning filiation and establishment of maintenance allowances.

Article 194

In the cases defined in Chapters IV and V of this Title, when establishments or premises are used, whether or not they are open to the public, to perpetrate the acts, a sentence of conviction may order their temporary or definitive closure. Temporary closure, which may not exceed five years, may also be adopted precautionary.

TITLE IX

On failure in the duty to assist

Article 195

1. Whoever does not assist a person who is unprotected or in serious, manifest danger, when able to do so without risk to himself or third parties, shall be punished with the penalty of a fine of three to twelve months.

2. The same penalties shall be incurred by whoever, being unable to provide assistance, does not urgently call for outside help.

3. If the party concerned is the victim of a fortuitous accident caused by whom omits the assistance, the punishment shall be six months to eighteen months imprisonment, and if the accident was due to negligence, six months to four years imprisonment.

Article 196

A medical practitioner who, while under obligation to do so, were to refuse health assistance or abandon the provision of health services, when refusal or abandonment were to cause serious risk to personal health, shall be punished with the penalties of the preceding Article, in the upper half and with that of special barring from public employment and office, profession or trade, for a term of six months to three years.

TITLE X

Felonies against privacy, the right to personal dignityand the inviolability of the dwelling

CHAPTER I

On discovery and revelation of secrets

Article 197

1. Whoever, in order to discover the secrets or to breach the privacy of another, without his consent, seizes his papers, letters, electronic mail messages or any other documents or personal belongings, or intercepts his telecommunications or uses technical devices for listening, transmitting, recording or to play sound or image, or any other communication signal, shall be punished with imprisonment of one to four years and a fine of twelve to twenty- four months.

2. The same penalties shall be imposed upon whoever, without being authorised, seizes, uses or amends, to the detriment of a third party, reserved data of a personal or family nature of another that are recorded in computer, electronic or telematic files or media, or in any other kind of file or public or private record. The same penalties shall be imposed on whoever, without being authorised, accesses these by any means, and whoever alters or uses them to the detriment of the data subject or a third party.

3. Whoever, by any means or procedure and in breach of the security measures established to prevent it, obtains unauthorised access to computer data or programs within a computer system or part thereof, or who remains within it against the will of whoever has the lawful right to exclude him, shall be punished with a prison sentence of six months to two years.

When, pursuant to the terms established in Article 31 bis, a legal person is responsible for the offences included in this Article, the punishment of a fine from six months to two years shall be imposed thereon. Pursuant to the rules established in Article 66 bis, the Judges and Courts of Law may also impose the penalties established in Sub- Sections b) to g) of Section 7 of Article 33.

4. A sentence of imprisonment shall be imposed from two to five years if the data or facts discovered, or the images captured to which the preceding numbers refer, are broadcast, disclosed or ceded to third parties. Whoever, being aware of their unlawful origin and without having taken part in their discovery, perpetrates the conduct described in the preceding Section shall be punished with imprisonment from one to three years and a fine of twelve to twenty- four months.

5. Should the acts described in Sections 1 and 2 of this Article be perpetrated by persons in charge of or responsible for the files, computer, electronic or telematic media, archives or records, a sentence of imprisonment of three to five years shall be imposed on them, and if they disclose, communicate or reveal reserved data, the upper half shall be imposed.

6. Likewise, when the acts described in the preceding Sections concern personal data that reveal the ideology, religion, belief, health, racial origin or sexual preference, or when the victim is a minor or incapacitated, the penalties imposed shall be those foreseen in the upper half.

7. If the acts are perpetrated for profit- making purposes, the penalties shall be imposed as foreseen in Sections 1 to 4 respectively of this Article in the upper half. If they also affect the data mentioned in the preceding Section, the punishment to be imposed shall be that of imprisonment from four to seven years.

8. Should the acts described in the preceding Sections be committed within a criminal organisation or group, the higher degree penalties shall be applied respectively.

Article 198

The authority or public officer who, outside the cases permitted by Law, without there being a legal cause due to an offence having being committed, and availing himself of his office, acts in any of the manners described in the preceding Article, shall be punished with the penalties respectively foreseen therein, in the upper half and also with that of absolute barring for a term from six to twelve years.

Article 199

1. Whoever discloses secrets of others that he obtains knowledge whereof through his trade or labour relations, shall be punished with a sentence of imprisonment from one to three years and a fine from six to twelve months.

2. Professionals who, in breach of their obligation of secrecy or reserve, reveal secrets of another person, shall be punished with a sentence of imprisonment of one to four years, a fine of twelve to twenty- four months and special barring from that profession for a term from two to six years.

Article 200

The terms set forth this Chapter shall be applicable to whoever, discloses, reveals or communicates reserved data of legal persons without the consent of their representatives, except for what is set forth in other provisions of this Code.

Article 201

1. Prosecution of offences foreseen in this Chapter requires a report by the victim or his legal representative. When the former is a minor, incapacitated or handicapped person, it may also be reported by the Public Prosecutor.

2. The report required in the preceding Section shall not be necessary to prosecute the acts described in Article 198 of this Code nor when the offence committed affects general interests or persons at large.

3. Forgiveness by the victim or his legal representative, as appropriate, extinguishes the penal action without prejudice to what is set forth in Paragraph Two of Sub-Section 5 of Section 1 of Article 130.

CHAPTER II

On trespassing a dwelling, the registered address of legal persons andestablishments open to the public

Article 202

1. The individual who, without being resident therein, enters the dwelling of another, or were to remain therein against the will of its dweller, shall be punished with a sentence of imprisonment of six months to two years.

2. Should the act be perpetrated with violence or intimidation, the punishment shall be imprisonment from one to four years and a fine from six to twelve months.

Article 203

1. Whoever enters the domicile of a public or private legal person, professional firm or office, a trading establishment or premises open the public after opening hours against the will of its owner shall be punished with imprisonment of six months to one year and a fine from six to ten months.

2. Whoever, by means of violence or intimidation, enters or remains in the domicile of a public or private legal person, professional firm or office, in a trading establishment or premises open to the public against the will of its owner, shall punished with a sentence of imprisonment of six months to three years.

Article 204

The authority or public officer who, outside the cases permitted by Law and without there being a legal cause due to an offence being committed, were to commit any of the acts described in the preceding two Articles, shall be punished with the penalty foreseen respectively therein, in the upper half, and to absolute barring from six to twelve years.

TITLE XI

Felonies against honour

CHAPTER I

On slander

Article 205

Slander involves accusing another person of a felony while knowing it is false or recklessly disregarding the truth.

Article 206

Slander shall be punished with imprisonment of six months to two years or a fine of twelve to twenty- four months, if propagated with publicity and, in other cases, by a fine from six to twelve months.

Article 207

Whoever is accused of the offence of slander shall be exempt from all punishment by proving the criminal act of which he has accused the other person.

CHAPTER II

On defamation

Article 208

Defamation is the action or expression that harms the dignity of another person, detracting from his reputation or attacking his self-esteem.

Only defamation that, due to its nature, effects and circumstances, is considered serious by the public at large, shall be deemed to constitute a felony.

Defamation consisting of attributing acts to another shall not be deemed serious, except when this has been carried out knowingly of the falsehood thereof or with recklessly disregards of the truth.

Article 209

Severe defamation perpetrated with publicity shall be punished with the penalty of a fine from six to fourteen months and, otherwise, with that of three to seven months.

Article 210

Whoever is accused of defamation shall be exempt of all accountability by proving the truth of the statements when these are against civil servants concerning events in exercise of their duties of office or referring to the commission of criminal or administrative offences.

CHAPTER III

General provisions

Article 211

Slander and defamation shall be deemed to have been perpetrated with publicity when propagated by means of the printing press, by radio broadcasting or any other similarly effective means.

Article 212

In the cases referred to in the preceding Article, the natural or legal person owning the media through which the slander or defamation was propagated shall be subject to joint and several civil liability as a consequence thereof.

Article 213

Should slander or defamation be committed for a price, reward or promise, in addition to the penalties stated for the offences concerned, the Courts of Law shall impose that of special barring foreseen in Articles 42 or 45 of this Code, for a term of six months to two years.

Article 214

Should whoever is accused of slander or defamation recognise the falsity or lack of truth of the accusations and withdraw them, the Judge or Court of Law shall impose the punishment immediately lower by degree and may abstain from imposing the punishment of barring established in the preceding Article.

The Judge or Court of Law before whom the registration takes place shall order an attestation of retraction to be delivered to the victim and, should the latter so request it, order its publication in the same media us used to commit the slander or defamation, with an identical or similar space to that in which its diffusion took place, and within the term set by the Judge or Court of Law sentencing.

Article 215

1. Nobody shall be convicted of slander or defamation other than by means of a suit filed by the person offended by the felony or his legal representative. Prosecution shall be effected on the Court's own motion when the offence is against a civil servant, authority or agent thereof, over events related to exercise of his duties of office.

2. Nobody may bring action for slander or defamation arising during a trial, without prior leave from the Judge or Court of Law in which the proceedings are heard or have been heard.

3. Forgiveness of the victim or his legal representative, as appropriate, extinguishes the penal action without prejudice to what is set forth in Paragraph Two of Sub-Section 5 of Section 1 of Article 130 of this Code.

Article 216

In offences of slander or defamation, it is deemed that repairing the damage also includes publication or diffusion of the conviction, at the expense of the party convicted of those offences, within the time and in the manner the Judge or Court of Law deems most appropriate for the purpose, having heard both parties.

TITLE XII

Felonies against relatives

CHAPTER I

On unlawful wedlocks

Article 217

Whoever contracts a second or subsequent marriage while knowing that the previous matrimony legally subsists, shall be punished with a sentence of imprisonment of six months to one year.

Article 218

1. Whoever, in order to harm the other spouse, solemnises an invalid matrimony, shall be punished with a sentence of imprisonment of six months to two years.

2. The person responsible shall be exempt of the punishment if the marriage is subsequently convalidated.

Article 219

1. Whoever authorises a marriage in which any known cause of nullity or one which is on record in the file, shall be punished with a sentence of imprisonment of six months to two years and special barring from public employment and office from two to six years.

2. Should the cause of nullity be dispensable, the punishment shall be suspension from public employment and office of six months to two years.

CHAPTER II

On pretended birth of a child and on alteration of the paternity, status or condition of the child

Article 220

1. A pretended birth shall be punished with imprisonment of six months to two years.

2. That same punishment shall be imposed on whoever conceals or delivers a child to third parties to alter or change the parentage thereof.

3. Swapping one child for another shall be punished with imprisonment from one to five years.

4. Ascendants, by nature or adoption, who commit the acts described in the preceding three Sections may be punished, in addition to the punishment of special barring from exercise of parental rights they may have in relation to the child or descendent supposed, concealed, delivered or substituted, and, when appropriate, to the rest of their offspring or descendents, for a term from four to ten years.

5. Swapping one child for another arising at hospitals or social health centres due to serious negligence by those responsible for their identification and custody shall be punished with a sentence of imprisonment of six months to one year.

Article 221

1. Those who, for a financial consideration, deliver a child, descendent or any minor to another person, even though there is no bond of affiliation or consanguinity, eluding the legal procedures for safekeeping, fostership or adoption, in order to establish a similar relation to that of filiation, shall be punished with imprisonment from one to five years and to special barring from exercise of parental rights, guardianship, care or safekeeping for a term from four to ten years.

2. The same punishment shall apply to punish the person receiving that child and the intermediary, even though the delivery may have taken place in a foreign country.

3. Should the acts be committed using crèches, schools or other premises or establishments where children are cared for, those found guilty shall have the punishment of special barring from practice of those activities imposed for a term from two to six years, and temporary or definitive closure of the establishments may be ordered. The term of temporary closure may not exceed five years.

Article 222

An educational or medical practitioner, authority or public officer who, while carrying out the duties of his profession or office, acts as described the preceding two Articles, shall incur the punishment stated therein and also that of special barring from public employment and office, profession or trade, from two to six years.

For the purposes of this Article, the term medical practitioner includes doctors, midwives, nursing staff and any other person who carries out health or social-health activities.

CHAPTER III

On felonies against family rights and duties

SUBCHAPTER 1. ON BREACH OF THE DUTIES OF CUSTODY AND OF INDUCING MINORS TO ABANDON THEIR HOME

Article 223

Whoever, being entrusted with the custody of a minor or an incapacitated person, who does not return him to his parents or carers without due reason, when called to do so by them, shall be punished with a sentence of imprisonment of six months to two years, without prejudice to the facts constituting another more serious offence.

Article 224

Whoever leads a minor or an incapacitated person to abandon the family dwelling, or place where he resides with the approval of his parents, tutors or minders shall be punished with a sentence of imprisonment of six months to two years.

The same punishment shall be incurred by a parent who induces his minor child to breach the custody regime established by a judicial or administrative authority.

Article 225

When the person responsible for the offences foreseen in the preceding two Articles returns the minor or incapacitated person to his domicile or residence, or leaves him in a known safe place, without him having been subjected to humiliation, cruelty or any criminal act whatsoever, nor having endangered his life, health, physical integrity or sexual freedom, the act shall be punished with a sentence of imprisonment from three months to a year, or fine from six to twenty- four months, as long as the parents, tutors or minders have been notified of the place where the minor or incapacitated person is staying, or the absence has not exceeded 24 hours.

SUBCHAPTER 2. ON ABDUCTION OF CHILDREN

Article 225 bis

1. A parent who, without a justified cause, abducts his child who is a minor, shall be punished with a sentence of imprisonment of two to four years and special barring from exercise of parental rights for a term from four to ten years.

2. For the purposes of this Article, abduction is deemed to be:

   1. Transporting a child from his place of residence without consent by the custodial parent or the persons or institutions to whom his safekeeping or custody is entrusted;

   2. Detention of the minor in serious breach of the duty established by a judicial or administrative order.

3. When the minor is transported out of Spain or any condition is demanded for his return, the punishment stated in Section 1 shall be imposed in its upper half.

4. When the abductor has notified the other parent, or person legally charged with his care, of the place where he is staying, within twenty- four hours of the abduction, with the commitment to immediately return the child that is effectively carried out, or when the absence does not exceed the term of twenty- four hours, he shall be exempt of punishment.

Should the child be returned, without the notification stated in the preceding Section, within fifteen days following the abduction, a sentence of imprisonment of six months to two years shall be imposed.

These terms shall be calculated from the date of the abduction being reported.

5. The penalties stated in this Article shall also be imposed on the ascendants of the minor and the relatives of the parent up to the second degree of consanguinity or affinity who act as described above.

SUBCHAPTER 3. ON ABANDONING THE FAMILY, MINORS OR INCAPACITATED

Article 226

1. Whoever fails to fulfil the legal duties of assistance inherent to parental rights, guardianship, safekeeping or fostership, or to provide the legally established necessary assistance for sustenance of his descendents, ascendants or spouse, who are in need, shall be punished with a sentence of imprisonment from three to six months, or a fine from six to twelve months.

2. The Judge or Court of Law may punish the convict giving the reasons with special barring from exercising parental rights, guardianship, safekeeping or fostership for a term from four to ten years.

Article 227

1. Whoever ceases to pay any kind of financial aid to his spouse or children, established by a judicially approved composition or court order in cases of legal separation, divorce, declaration of nullity of marriage, filiation proceedings,

or maintenance allowance proceedings in favour of his children, shall be punished with a sentence of imprisonment from three months to a year or fine from six to twenty- four months.

2. The same punishment shall be applied to punish whoever ceases to pay any other financial aid established jointly or by itself in the cases foreseen in the preceding Section.

3. Reparation of the damage arising from the offence shall always include payment of the sums owed.

Article 228

The offences foreseen in the preceding two Articles, shall only be pursued when reported by the person offended or his legal representative. When the former is a minor, incapacitated or handicapped person, it may also be reported by the Public Prosecutor.

Article 229

1. Abandoning a minor or an incapacitated person by the person entrusted with his safekeeping shall be punished with a sentence of imprisonment from one to two years.

2. Should the abandonment be perpetrated by his parents, tutors or legal minders, a sentence of imprisonment from eighteen months to three years shall be imposed.

3. A sentence of imprisonment shall be imposed of two to four years when, due to the circumstances of the abandonment the life, health, physical integrity or sexual freedom of the minor or incapacitated person has been specifically endangered, without prejudice to punishment of the act as appropriate, if it were to constitute a more serious offence.

Article 230

Temporary abandonment of a minor or incapacitated person shall be punished, in the respective cases, with the penalties a degree lower than those foreseen in the preceding Article.

Article 231

1. Whoever, while in charge of the upbringing or education of a minor or incapacitated person, delivers him to a third party or a public establishment without the approval of the person who has entrusted him such person, or an authority, in absence thereof, shall be punished with the penalty of a fine from six to twelve months.

2. If, by virtue of such delivery, the life, health, physical integrity or sexual freedom of the minor or incapacitated person has been endangered, a sentence of imprisonment of six months to two years shall be imposed.

Article 232

1. Those who use or lend minors or incapacitated persons to beg, even if this is concealed, shall be punished with a sentence of imprisonment of six months to one year.

2. If trafficking of minors or incapacitated persons takes place for the purposes of the preceding Section, using violence or intimidation against them, or providing them substances that are harmful to their health, a sentence of imprisonment of one to four years shall be imposed.

Article 233

1. Should this be deemed appropriate in view of the circumstances of the minor, the Judge or Court of Law may sentence those responsible the offences foreseen in Articles 229 to 232 to the punishment of special barring from exercise of parental rights or rights of safekeeping, guardianship, care or fostership for a term from four to ten years.

2. Should the offender have been entrusted with safekeeping of the minor due to his condition as a civil servant, he shall also be subject to the punishment of special barring from public employment and office for a term from two to six years.

3. In all cases, the Public Prosecutor shall call on the competent authority to take the appropriate measures for due custody and protection of the minor.

TITLE XIII

Felonies against property and against social-economic order

CHAPTER I

On larceny

Article 234

Whoever, for profit, were to take moveable property pertaining to others without the permission of their owner, shall be convicted of larceny, with a sentence of imprisonment from six to eighteen months if the amount of what was stolen exceeds four hundred euros.

Whoever perpetrates the action described in Section 1 of Article 623 of this Code three times within the term of one year, as long as the accumulated amount of the offences exceeds the minimum figure set for the felony, shall be punished with the same penalty.

Article 235

Larceny shall be punished with a sentence of imprisonment from one to three years:

1. When items of artistic, historic, cultural or society value are stolen;

2. When the items concerned are a primary necessity or those assigned to a public service, whenever their theft causes serious disturbance thereof or shortage of supply;

3. When especially serious, in view of the value of the items stolen, or when particularly major damage is caused;

4. When the larceny causes the victim or his family serious financial distress, or when perpetrated taking advantage of the personal circumstances of the victim;

5. When using children under fourteen years of age to commit the offence.

Article 236

Whoever, being the owner of an item of moveable property or acting with the owner's consent, takes it from whoever lawfully has it in his possession, to his detriment or that of a third party, when the value thereof exceeds four hundred euros, shall be punished with a fine of three to twelve months.

CHAPTER II

On robbery and burglary

Article 237

Those who seize moveable assets pertaining to others for profit, using forcible means to access the place where these are located, or violence or intimidation of persons, shall be convicted of burglary or robbery, respectively.

Article 238

Those perpetrating these acts shall be convicted of burglary when any of the following circumstances concur:

1. Climbing;

2. Breaking walls, ceilings or floors, forcing doors or windows;

3. Breaking open cabinets, trunks or other kinds of furniture or closed or sealed objects, or forcing their locks, or discovering their codes to steal the content, whether at the place of the burglary or outside it;

4. Use of forged keys;

5. Deactivating alarm or security systems.

Article 239

The following shall be deemed forged keys:

1. Lock picks or other similar instruments;

2. The lawful keys lost by the owner or obtained by a method that amounts to a felony or misdemeanour;

3. Any others that are not those used by the owner to open the lock the convict has forced.

For the purposes of this Article, magnetic or punched cards, remote controls or instruments to open remotely, and any other technological instrument with a similar effectiveness shall be deemed keys.

Article 240

Whoever is found guilty of burglary shall be punished with a sentence of imprisonment from one to three years.

Article 241

1. A sentence of imprisonment shall be imposed from two to five years when any of the circumstances foreseen in Article 235 concurs, or when the robbery is committed in an inhabited house, a building or premises open to the public or in any of the annexes thereof.

2. An inhabited house is deemed to be any accommodation that is the dwelling place of one or more persons, even though they may circumstantially be absent from it when the robbery takes place.

3. The annexes of an inhabited house or a building or premise open to the public are deemed to be its courtyards, garages and other spaces or locations that are fenced in and adjoining the building and internally linked to form a physical unit therewith.

Article 242

1. Whoever is found guilty of robbery with violence or intimidation against persons shall be punished with a sentence of imprisonment from two to five years, without prejudice to the relevant punishment for the acts of physical violence he may have perpetrated.

2. When the robbery is committed in an inhabited house or in any of its annexes, a sentence of imprisonment of three years and six months to five years shall be imposed.

3. The penalties stated in the preceding Sections shall be imposed in the upper half when the criminal uses weapons or equally dangerous means, either to commit the offence or to protect flight therefrom, and when he attacks those who come to aid the victim or those who pursue him.

4. A lower degree punishment than that foreseen in the preceding Sections may be handed down in cases of lesser violence or intimidation, and also appraising the remaining circumstances of the event.

CHAPTER III

On extortion

Article 243

Whoever, for profit, forces another, by means of violence or intimidation, to carry out or omit an act or legal transaction to the detriment of his own wealth or that of a third party, shall be punished with a sentence of imprisonment from one to five years, without prejudice to the penalties that might be imposed for the acts of physical violence perpetrated.

CHAPTER IV

On robbery and theft to use vehicles

Article 244

1. Whoever steals a motor vehicle or moped pertaining to another without due authorisation by its owner, when its value exceeds four hundred euros, without intending to keep it, shall be punished with the penalty of community service from thirty one to ninety days, or a fine from six to twelve months if he returns it, directly or indirectly, within a term not exceeding forty- eight hours, without, in any case, the punishment imposed being equal to or exceeding that which would be applied if he had definitely appropriated the vehicle.

The same punishment shall apply to whoever perpetrates the same action as described in Article 623.3 of this Code four times in a year, as long as the accumulated amount of the offences exceeds the minimum of that figure for the offence.

2. Should the act be perpetrated by forced entry, the punishment shall be applied in its upper half.

3. Should the vehicle not be returned within the term stated, it shall be punished as larceny or robbery as appropriate.

4. If the act is committed by means of violence or intimidation of persons, in all cases, the penalties of Article 242 shall be imposed.

CHAPTER V

On usurpation

Article 245

1. Whoever, by means of violence or intimidation of persons, occupies real property or usurps a right *in rem* over real property pertaining to another, in addition to the penalties incurred for the violence committed, shall have a sentence of imprisonment from one to two years imposed; that shall be set taking into account the utility obtained and the damage caused.

2. Whoever occupies a property, dwelling or building pertaining to another that are not a dwelling, without due authorisation, or who remains there against the will of their owner, shall be punished with the penalty of a fine from three to six months.

Article 246

Whoever alters the boundaries or borders of towns or estates or any kind of signals or markers intended to set the limits of properties or the borders with adjoining estates, both public as well as privately owned, shall be punished with the penalty of a fine of three to eighteen months, if the utility reported or intended exceeds four hundred euros.

Article 247

Whoever, without being authorised, diverts water for public or private use from their course, or from their natural or artificial reservoir, shall be punished with the penalty of a fine from three to six months if the utility reported exceeds four hundred euros.

CHAPTER VI

On fraud

SUBCHAPTER 1. ON SWINDLING

Article 248

1. Those who use sufficient deceit, for profit, to cause lead another into error so as to have him carry out an act of disposal in his own detriment or that of another, commit swindling.

2. The following shall also be deemed guilty of swindling:

a) Those who, for profit and making use of any computer manipulation or similar scheme, manage to perpetrate an unauthorised transfer of any patrimonial assets to the detriment of another;

b) Those who manufacture, upload, possess or provide computer programs specifically intended to commit the swindles foreseen in this Article;

c) Those who, using credit or debit cards, or travellers' cheques, or the data any of these bear, perpetrate operations of any kind to the detriment of their owner or a third party.

Article 249

Those convicted of swindling shall be punished with a sentence of imprisonment of six months to three years, if the amount swindled exceeds four hundred euros. The amount swindled, the financial damage caused to the victim, the relations between him and the swindler, the means used by the latter and any other circumstances pertinent to evaluate the seriousness of the offence shall be taken into account when setting the punishment.

Article 250

1. The offence of swindling shall be punished with imprisonment from one year to six years and a fine from six to twelve months, when:

   1. It affects belongings of prime necessity, dwellings or other assets of recognised social utility;

   2. When perpetrated by forging the signature of another, or by stealing, concealing or fully or partially destroying any process, file, archive or public or official document of any kind;

   3. When it affects assets forming artistic, heritage, cultural or scientific property;

   4. It is especially serious, in view of the magnitude of the damage and the financial situation in which it leaves the victim or his family:

   5. When the amount of what is swindled exceeds 50,000 euros;

   6. When perpetrated abusing the personal relations that exist between the victim and swindler, or when the latter takes advantage of the latter's corporate or professional credibility;

   7. When procedural fraud is committed. This is incurred by those who manipulate the evidence on which they intend to found base allegations or use any other similar procedural fraud in judicial proceedings of any kind, causing the Judge or Court of Law to mistakenly be led to hand down a resolution that damages the financial interests of the other party or a third party.

2. Should circumstances 4, 5 or 6 concur with 1 of the preceding Section, a prison sentence from four to eight years and a fine of twelve to twenty- four months shall be imposed.

Article 251

A sentence of imprisonment of one to four years shall be handed down to punish:

1. Whoever, falsely attributing powers of disposal he does not have over a real or personal property, either due to never having had such powers or due to already having exercised them, proceeds to dispose of, encumber or let such property to another, to the detriment of the latter or a third party;

2. Whoever disposes of a real or personal property, concealing the existence of any charge thereon, or who, having disposed of it as a property free of encumbrances, were to encumber or dispose of it again, prior to definitively conveying it to the acquirer, to the detriment thereof, or of a third party;

3. Whoever were to execute a simulated contract to the detriment of another.

Article 251 bis

When, pursuant to the terms established in Article 31 bis, a legal person is responsible for the offences included in this Subchapter, it shall have the following penalties imposed thereon:

   a) Fine of three to five times the sum swindled, if the offence committed by a natural person has a punishment of imprisonment foreseen exceeding five years;

b) Fine of two to four times the sum swindled, in the rest of the cases. Pursuant to the rules established in Article 66 bis, the Judges and Courts of Law may also impose the penalties mentioned in Sub-Sections b) to g) of Section 7 of Article 33.

SUBCHAPTER 2. ON MISAPPROPRIATION

Article 252

Those who, to the detriment of another, appropriate or steal moneys, belongings, valuables or any other moveable or personal property they have received in deposit, in trust or for administration, or by any other title that produces the obligation to deliver or return them, or who deny having received them, when the amount of what has been appropriated exceeds four hundred euros, shall be punished with the penalties of Article 249 or 250, as appropriate. Such punishment shall be imposed in its upper half in the case of necessary deposit or deposit in distress.

Article 253

Those who appropriate an item that is lost or has an unknown owner for profit, as long as, in both cases, the value of what is appropriated exceeds four hundred euros. If they are items of artistic, historic, cultural or scientific value, the punishment shall be imprisonment from six months to two years.

Article 254

Whoever, having unduly received moneys or any other moveable or personal property, due to an error by the conveyor, denies having received it or, having noticed the error, does not proceed to return it, when the sum of what is received exceeds four hundred euros, shall be punished with the penalty of a fine from three to six months.

SUBCHAPTER 3. ON ELECTRICITY THEFT AND THE LIKE

Article 255

Whoever steals electricity, gas, water, telecommunications signals or any other element, energy or fluid pertaining to another, by any of the means described below, in an amount exceeding four hundred euros, shall be punished with the penalty of a fine from three to twelve months:

1. Using mechanisms installed to perpetrate the fraud;

2. Maliciously altering the signs or meter appliances;

3. Using any other clandestine means.

Article 256

Whoever makes use of any telecommunications terminal equipment, without the consent of its owner, causing him a damage exceeding four hundred euros shall be punished with the penalty of a fine from three to twelve months.

CHAPTER VII

On punishable insolvency

Article 257

1. Punishment by imprisonment of one to four years and a fine of twelve to twenty- four months is imposed on:

   1. Whoever absconds with his assets to the detriment of his creditors;

   2. Whoever, to the same end, carries out any act of disposal of assets or generation of obligations that draws out, hinders or prevents the effectiveness of an embargo or enforcement or collection proceedings, either in or out of court, or administrative ones, commenced, or that may predictably be commenced.

2. The terms set forth in this Article shall be applicable whatever the nature or origin of the obligation or debt, the settlement or payment of which he intends to avoid, including the financial rights of the workers, and regardless of whether the creditor is a natural person or any legal person, public or private.

3. In the event of the debt or obligation the felon attempts to elude being one under public law and when the creditor is a public corporation, the punishment to be imposed shall be one to six years and a fine of twelve to twenty- four months.

4. The penalties foreseen in this Article shall be imposed in the upper half in the cases foreseen in Sub-Section 1, 4 and 5 of Section 1 of Article 250.

5. This offence shall be pursued even when bankruptcy proceedings are commenced after it is committed.

Article 258

Whoever is responsible for any criminal act who, after having committed it and in order to avoid honouring the civil liabilities arising therefrom, carries out acts of disposal or contracts obligations that decrease his assets, making himself fully or partially insolvent, shall be punished with a sentence of imprisonment of one to four years and a fine of twelve to twenty- four months.

Article 259

The debtor who, once the application for insolvency has been admitted to proceedings, without being authorised to do so either by the court or the receivers, and outside the cases allowed by the law, carries out any act of disposal of assets or of generation of obligations, aimed at paying one or several creditors, either privileged or otherwise, to the detriment of the rest, shall be punished with the penalty of one to four years imprisonment and a fine from twelve to twenty- four months.

Article 260

1. Whoever is declared insolvent shall be punished with a sentence of imprisonment from two to six years and a fine from eight to twenty- four months, when the situation of economic crisis or insolvency is caused or aggravated maliciously by the debtor or person acting on his behalf.

2. The amount of damage the creditors are caused, their number and financial status, shall be taken into account to appraise the punishment.

3. This offence and the individual offences related thereto, committed by the debtor or person who has acted on his behalf, may be pursued without awaiting conclusion of the civil proceedings and without prejudice to continuation thereof. The sum of civil liability arising from such offences shall be included in the insolvent's estate as appropriate.

4. Under no circumstance whatsoever shall the insolvency classification in the civil proceedings be binding in the criminal proceedings.

Article 261

Whoever were to knowingly present false data concerning his accounting status during insolvency proceedings, in order to unduly obtain a declaration thereof, shall be punished with a sentence of imprisonment from one to two years and a fine from six to twelve months.

Article 261 bis

When, pursuant to the terms established in Article 31 bis, a legal person is responsible for the offences included in this Chapter, it shall have the following penalties imposed thereon:

a) Fine from two to five years, if the offence committed by a natural person has a punishment of imprisonment foreseen exceeding five years;

b) Fine from one to three years, if the offence committed by a natural person has a punishment of imprisonment foreseen exceeding two years not included in the preceding Section;

c) Fine of six months to two years, in the rest of the cases.

Pursuant to the rules established in Article 66 bis, the Judges and Courts of Law may also impose the penalties established in Sub-Sections b) to g) of Section 7 of Article 33.

CHAPTER VIII

On alteration of prices in public tenders and auctions

Article 262

1. Those who request handouts or promises in order not to take part in a public tender or auction; those who attempt to drive bidders away from it by means of intimidation, handouts, promises or any other contrivance; those who make arrangements among themselves in order to alter the final bid, or those who fraudulently default or abandon the auction after obtaining the award, shall be punished with a sentence of imprisonment from one to three years and a fine from twelve to twenty- four months, as well as special barring from bidding in judicial auctions from three to five years. In the case of a tender or auction called by the public administrations or entities, the agent and the person or company represented by him shall also have the punishment imposed of special barring that shall, in all cases, involve barring from the right to contract with the Public Administrations for a term of three to five years.

2. The Judge or Court of Law may hand down any or several of the penalties foreseen in Article 129 if the offender were to belong to any company, organisation or assembly, even if transitory in nature, with the purpose of perpetrating those activities.

CHAPTER IX

On damages

Article 263

1. Whoever were to cause damage to the property of another not included in other Titles of this Code, shall be punished with the penalty of a fine from six to twenty- four months, in view of the financial status of the victim and the amount of the damage, if this exceeds four hundred euros.

2. Whoever causes the damage stated in the preceding Section shall be punished with a sentence of imprisonment from one to three years and a fine of twelve to twenty- four months, if any of the following cases were to concur:

1. When perpetrated to prevent free exercise of authority or as a consequence of actions committed while carrying out the duties of office, or if the offence were to be committed against civil servants, or against individuals who, as witnesses, or in any other capacity, have contributed or may contribute to the implementation or application of the laws or general provisions;

2. When caused by any means, infection or contagion against cattle;

3. When using poisonous or corrosive substances;

4. When affecting assets that are publicly or commonly owned or used;

5. When these ruin the party damaged or seriously affect his financial status.

Article 264

1. Whoever, by any means, without authorisation and in a serious way, were to erase, damage, deteriorate, alter, suppress, or make data, computer programs or electronic documents pertaining to others inaccessible, when the result produced is serious, shall be punished with a sentence of imprisonment of six months to two years.

2. Whoever, by any means, without being authorised and in a serious way, were to hinder or interrupt operation of a computer system pertaining to another, introducing, transmitting, damaging, erasing, deteriorating, altering, suppressing or making computer data inaccessible, when the result produced is serious, shall be punished, with a sentence of imprisonment of six months to three years.

3. The penalties imposed shall be higher by one degree to those respectively stated in the previous two Sections and, in all cases, the punishment of a fine ranging from one to ten times the amount of damage caused, when any of the following circumstances concur in the conduct described:

1. When committed within the setting of a criminal organisation;

2. When special damage has been caused or general interest has been affected;

4. When, pursuant to the terms established in Article 31 bis, a legal person is responsible for the offences included in this Article, it shall have the following penalties imposed thereon:

a) Fine of two to four times the damage caused, if the offence committed by a natural person has a punishment of imprisonment foreseen exceeding two years;

b) Fine of two to three times the damage caused, in the rest of the cases.

Pursuant to the rules established in Article 66 bis, the Judges and Courts of Law may also impose the penalties established in Sub-Sections b) to g) of Section 7 of Article 33.

Article 265

Whoever destroys, seriously damages, or puts out of service, even if temporarily, military works, establishments or installations, warships, military aircraft, means of military transport or transmission, war materiel, provisions or other means or resources assigned to the service of the Armed Forces or the Police and Security Forces, shall be punished with a sentence of imprisonment of two to four years if the damage caused exceeds fifty thousand pesetas.

Article 266

1. Whoever commits the damage described in Article 263 by means of fire, or causing explosions or using any other means of a similar destructive power, or endangering the life or integrity of persons, shall be punished with a sentence of imprisonment from one to three years.

2. Whoever commits the damage described in Article 264, in any of the circumstances mentioned in the preceding Section, shall be punished with a sentence of imprisonment of three to five years and a fine of twelve to twenty-four months.

3. Whoever commits the damage described in Articles 265, 323 and 560, in any of the circumstances mentioned in Section 1 of this Article, shall be punished with a sentence of imprisonment from four to eight years.

4. In any of the cases foreseen in the preceding Sections, when the damage is committed with the provocation of explosions or the use of other means of a similar explosive power and also endanger the life or integrity of persons, the punishment shall be imposed in its upper half.

What is set forth in Article 351 shall apply to the case of fire.

Article 267

Damage caused due to serious negligence, in an amount exceeding 80,000 euros, shall be punished with the penalty of a fine from three to nine months, in view of the extent thereof.

The offences to which this Article refers shall only be pursuable when reported by the person offended or his legal representative. The Public Prosecutor may also report them when the victim is a minor, incapacitated or handicapped person.

In these cases, forgiveness by the victim or his legal representative, as appropriate, extinguishes the penal action without prejudice to what is set forth in Paragraph Two of Sub-Section 5 of Section 1 of Article 130 of this Code.

CHAPTER X

Provisions common to the preceding Chapters

Article 268

1. Spouses who are not separated legally or *de facto*, or who are subject to judicial proceedings for separation, divorce or nullity of their marriage, and the ascendants, descendents and biological or adoptive siblings, as well as those of first degree affinity, if cohabiting, shall be exempt of criminal accountability and only subject to civil liability for offences against property they were to cause each other, as long as neither violence nor intimidation is involved.

2. This provision is not applicable to third parties who participate in the offence.

Article 269

Provocation, conspiracy and solicitation to commit the offences of robbery, burglary, extortion, swindling or misappropriation, shall be punished with the penalty lower by one or two degrees to that of the relevant offence.

CHAPTER XI

On felonies against intellectual and industrial property, the market and consumers

SUBCHAPTER 1. ON FELONIES RELATED TO INTELLECTUAL PROPERTY

Article 270

1. Whoever, for profit and to the detriment of a third party, reproduces, plagiarises, distributes or publicly discloses all or part of a literary, artistic or scientific work, or transforms, interprets or performs it in any kind of medium, or broadcast by any medium, without authorisation by the holders of the relevant intellectual property rights or their assignees, shall be punished with a sentence of imprisonment of six months to two years and a fine from twelve to twenty- four months.

However, in cases of retail distribution, in view of the circumstances of the offender and the small amount of financial profit, as long as none of the circumstances of the following Article concur, the Judge may hand down the punishment of a fine from three to six months, or community service of thirty- one to sixty days. In the same cases, when the profit does not exceed four hundred euros, the act shall be punished as a misdemeanour under Article 623.5.

2. Whoever intentionally exports or stores copies of the works, productions or performances to which the preceding Section refers without due authorisation shall be punished with a sentence of imprisonment of six months to two years and a fine from twelve to twenty- four months. Likewise, the same punishment shall be incurred by those who intentionally import these products without such authorisation, regardless of whether these have a lawful or unlawful origin in their country of origin. However, importing those products from a State pertaining to the European Union shall not be punishable when these have been acquired directly from the holder of the rights in that State, or with his consent.

3. Whoever manufactures, imports, puts into circulation or possesses any means specifically intended to facilitate unauthorised suppression or neutralisation of any technical device that has been used to protect computer programs or any of the other works, interpretations or performances under the terms foreseen in Section 1 of this Article shall also be punished with the same penalty.

Article 271

A sentence of imprisonment of one to four years, a fine from twelve to twenty- four months and special barring from practice of the profession related with the offence committed, for a term from two to five years, shall be imposed when any of the following circumstances concur:

a) When the profit obtained is of special economic importance;

b) When the events are especially serious, in view of the value of the objects produced unlawfully or the special importance of the damage caused;

c) When the offender belongs to an organisation or assembly, even if transitory in nature, whose purpose is to perpetrate activities that infringe intellectual property rights.

d) When persons under eighteen years of age are used to commit those offences.

Article 272

1. The extent of civil liability arising from the felonies defined in the preceding two Articles shall be governed by the provisions of the Intellectual Property Act on cessation of the unlawful activity and reparation of damages and losses.

2. In the event of conviction, the Judge or Court of Law may decree publication thereof in an official newspaper, at the expense of the offender.

SUBCHAPTER 2. ON FELONIES AGAINST INDUSTRIAL PROPERTY

Article 273

1. Whoever, for industrial or commercial purposes, without the consent of the holder of a patent or utility model and being aware of registration thereof, manufactures, imports, possesses, uses, offers or markets objects protected by those rights, shall be punished with a sentence of imprisonment of six months to two years and a fine from twelve to twenty- four months.

2. The same penalties shall be imposed upon whoever, likewise and for the purposes stated, uses or offers the use of a patented procedure, or possesses, offers, markets or uses a product directly obtained by the patented procedure.

3. Whoever perpetrates any of the acts described in Section 1 of this Article when equal circumstances concur with regard to objects protected in favour of a third party by an industrial, artistic or topographic model or design of a semiconductor product, shall be punished with the same penalties.

Article 274

1. Whoever, for industrial or commercial purposes, without the consent by the holder of a registered industrial property right pursuant to the trademarks legislation and being aware of registration thereof, reproduces, imitates, amends or in any other way usurps a distinctive sign that is identical or may be mistaken for the former, to distinguish the same or similar products, services, activities or establishments for which the industrial property right is registered, shall be punished with the penalties of six months to two years imprisonment and a fine of twelve to twenty- four months. The same punishment shall be incurred by those who import such products.

2. The same penalties shall be imposed upon whoever, knowingly possesses products or services with distinctive signs that, pursuant to Section 1 of this Article, amount to infringement of the exclusive rights of the holder thereof, even in the case of imported products, in order to commercialise or market these.

However, in cases of retail distribution, in view of the characteristics of the offender and the low amount of the financial profit, as long as none of the circumstances of Article 276 concurs, the Judge may hand down the punishment of a fine from three to six months or community service of thirty one to sixty days. In the same cases, when the profit does not exceed four hundred euros, the act shall be punished as a misdemeanour under Article 623.5.

3. Whoever, for agricultural or commercial purposes, without the consent of the owner of a new plant variety title and being aware of its registration, produces or reproduces, conditions with a view to production or reproduction, offers on sale, sells or otherwise commercialises, exports, imports or possesses, for any of the purposes mentioned, plant material for reproduction or propagation of a protected plant variety pursuant to the laws on protection of new plant varieties shall be punished with the same penalty.

4. Whoever perpetrates any of the acts described in the preceding Section using, plant material for reproduction or propagation that does not belong to the variety stated, under the denomination of a protected plant variety, shall be punished with the same penalty.

Article 275

The same penalties foreseen in the preceding Article shall be imposed on whoever intentionally and without being authorised to do so, uses a denomination of origin or a geographic indication representing a legally protected specific quality used to distinguish the products obtained thereby, being aware of such protection, to trade therewith.

Article 276

A sentence of imprisonment of one to four years, a fine from twelve to twenty- four months and special barring from practice of the profession related with the offence committed, for a term from two to five years, shall be imposed when any of the following circumstances concur:

a) When the profit obtained is of special economic importance;

b) When the events are especially serious, in view of the value of the objects unlawfully produced or the special importance of the damage caused;

c) When the offender belongs to an organisation or assembly, even if transitory in nature, whose purpose is to perpetrate activities that infringe industrial property rights;

d) When persons under eighteen years of age are used to commit those offences.

Article 277

Punishment by imprisonment of six months to two years and a fine from six to twenty- four months shall be imposed on whoever intentionally discloses the invention subject to a secret patent application, in breach of what is set forth in the patent legislation, whenever this is to the detriment of national defence.

SUBCHAPTER 3. ON FELONIES RELATED TO THE MARKET AND CONSUMERS

Article 278

1. Whoever obtains data, written or electronic documents, computer media or other objects related thereto in order to discover a company secret, or who uses any of the means or instruments described in Section 1 of Article 197, shall be punished with a sentence of imprisonment of two to four years and a fine of twelve to twenty- four months.

2. A sentence of imprisonment of three to five years and a fine of twelve to twenty- four months shall be imposed if the secrets discovered are disclosed, revealed or communicated to third parties.

3. The terms set forth in this Article shall be construed to be without prejudice to the penalties that might be relevant for appropriating or destroying the computer media.

Article 279

Diffusion, disclosure or communication of a company secret perpetrated by whoever has the legal or contractual obligation of confidentiality, shall be punished with a sentence of imprisonment of two to four years and a fine of twelve to twenty- four months.

Should the secret be used to his own advantage, the penalties shall be imposed in their lower half.

Article 280

Whoever, with knowledge of their unlawful origin, and without having taken part in their discovery, perpetrates any of the actions described in the preceding two Articles shall be punished with a sentence of imprisonment from one to three years and a fine of twelve to twenty- four months.

Article 281

1. Whoever removes raw materials or products of basic need from the market in order to interrupt supplies to a sector thereof, to force an alteration in prices, or to seriously affect consumers, shall be punished with a sentence of imprisonment from one to five years and a fine of twelve to twenty- four months.

2. A punishment higher in one degree shall be imposed if the act is carried out in situations of serious or catastrophic need.

Article 282

Manufacturers or traders who make false claims or declare untrue features in their offers or publicly of products or services, so as to cause serious, manifest harm to consumers, without prejudice to the relevant punishment for having committed other felonies, shall be punished with a sentence of imprisonment of six months to one year or fine from twelve to twenty- four months

Article 282 bis

Those who, as *de facto* or *de jure* managers of a company that issues securities listed on the stock markets, falsify the economic-financial information contained in the prospectuses used to issue any financial instruments or information that the company must publish and make known pursuant to the stock market legislation, concerning its resources, activities and present and future business, in order to attract investors or depositors, to place any kind of financial asset, or to obtain financing by any means, shall be punished with a sentence of imprisonment of one to four years, without prejudice to what is set forth in Article 308 of this Code.

Should the investment, deposit, placement of the asset or financing be eventually obtained, causing damage to the investor, depositor, acquirer of the financial assets or creditor, the punishment shall be imposed in its upper half. Should the damage caused be notoriously serious, the punishment to be imposed shall be one to six years imprisonment and a fine from six to twelve months.

Article 283

Prison sentences of six months to one year and fines from six to eighteen months shall be imposed on those who, to the detriment of the consumer, bill higher amounts for products or services whose cost or price is measured by automatic appliances, by altering or manipulating these.

Article 284

A sentence of imprisonment shall be imposed of six months to two years or a fine of twelve to twenty- four months upon those who:

1. Using violence, intimidation or deceit, were to attempt to alter the prices that would arise from free competition of products, merchandise, securities or financial instruments, services or any other moveable assets or real estate that is subject to contract, without prejudice to the punishment that may be imposed on them for other felonies committed;

2. Disseminate news or rumours, themselves or through the media, on persons or companies, in which they knowingly provide fully or partially false economic data in order to alter or preserve the listed price of a financial security or instrument, obtaining financial profit for themselves or others exceeding 300,000 euros, or causing an identical amount of damage.

3. Using privileged information for insider dealing, carry out transactions or give operating orders liable to provide deceitful signs concerning the offer, demand or price of financial securities or instruments, or using that same information, themselves or in collusion with others, assure themselves a dominant position on the market for such securities or instruments, in order to set their prices at abnormal or artificial levels.

In all cases, the punishment shall be imposed of barring from one to two years to trade on the financial market as a principal, agent or broker or analyst.

Article 285

1. Whoever, directly or through an intermediary, uses any relevant information for the price of any kind of securities or instruments traded on any organised, official or recognised market, to which he has had reserved access due to exercising his professional or corporate activity, or who supplies this obtaining financial profit for himself or a third party exceeding 600,000 euros, or causing damage of an equal amount, shall be punished with a sentence of imprisonment of one to four years, a fine of one to three times the profit obtained or favoured, and special barring from practice of the profession or activity from two to five years.

2. A sentence of imprisonment from four to six years, a fine of one to three times the profit obtained or favoured and special barring from practice of the profession or activity from two to five years shall be handed down when, in the conduct described in the preceding Section, any of the following circumstances concur:

1. That the subjects habitually perpetrate such abusive practices;

2. That the profit obtained be notoriously large;

3. That serious damage to general interests was caused.

Article 286

1. Punishment by imprisonment of six months to two years and a fine from six to twenty- four months shall be handed down to whoever, without the consent of the service provider and for commercial purposes, provides intelligible access to a radio or television broadcasting sound or image service, to interactive services provided remotely by electronic means, or who provides conditional access to these, considered as an independent service, by means of:

1. Manufacturing, importation, distribution, making available by electronic means, sale, rental, or possession of any computer equipment or program that is unauthorised in another member State of the European Union, designed or adapted to make such access possible;

2. Installation, maintenance or replacement of the equipment or computer programs mentioned in Section 1.

2. An identical punishment shall be applied to whoever, for profit, were to alter or duplicate the identifying number of telecommunications equipment or sell equipment that has undergone fraudulent manipulation.

3. Whoever, for non-profit purposes, provides third parties the access described in Section 1, or through public communication, whether for commercial purposes or not, provides information to multiple persons on the way to obtain unauthorised access to a service or use of a device or program, of those stated in that same Section 1, inciting them to attain this, shall have the punishment of the fine foreseen therein imposed.

4. Whoever uses equipment or programs that allow unauthorised access to conditional access services or telecommunications equipment shall have the punishment foreseen in Article 255 of this Code imposed, regardless of the amount obtained by such fraud.

SUBCHAPTER 4. ON CORRUPTION BETWEEN PRIVATE INDIVIDUALS

Article 286 bis

1. Whoever, personally or through an intermediary, promises, offers or grants executives, directors, employees or collaborators of a trading company or any other firm, partnership, foundation or organisation an unfair benefit or advantage of any nature, in order for the to favour him or a third party against others, breaching their obligations in acquisition or sale of goods or in hiring of professional services, shall be punished with a sentence of imprisonment of six months to four years, special barring from practice of industry or commerce for a term from one to six years and a fine of up to three times the value of the value of the profit or advantage obtained.

2. The same penalties shall be imposed on executives, directors, employees or collaborators of trading companies, or firms, associations, foundations or organisation who, personally or through an intermediary, receive, request or accept a benefit or advantage of any unjustified nature, in order to favour whoever grants, or whoever expects the profit or advantage over third parties, breaching their obligations in the acquisition or the sale of goods or in the hiring professional services.

3. The Judges and Courts of Law may impose a lower degree of punishment and reduce the fine, at their prudent criteria, in view of the amount of profit obtained or value of the advantage and the importance of the duties of the offender.

4. The terms set forth this Article shall be applicable, in the respective cases, to executives, directors, employees or collaborators of a sporting company, whatever its legal status, as well as sportsmen, referees or judges, regarding conduct aimed at deliberately and fraudulently predetermining or altering the result of a professional sport match, game or competition.

SUBCHAPTER 5. PROVISIONS COMMON TO ALL THE PRECEDING SUBCHAPTERS

Article 287

1. Prosecution of the offences foreseen in Section 3 of this Chapter, except those foreseen in Articles 284 and 285, must necessarily be reported by the victim or by his legal representatives. When the victim is a minor, incapacitated or handicapped person, they may also be reported by the Public Prosecutor.

2. The report required in the preceding Section shall not be necessary when commission of the offence affects general interests or multiple persons.

Article 288

In the cases foreseen in the preceding Articles, publication of the sentence in the official journals shall be provided and, if requested by the offended, the Judge or Court of Law may order full or partial reproduction in any other medium, at the expense of the convict.

When, pursuant to the terms established in Article 31 bis, a legal person is responsible for the offences defined in this Chapter, it shall have the following penalties imposed thereon:

1. In the case of the offences foreseen in Articles 270, 271, 273, 274, 275, 276, 283, 285 and 286:

  a) Fine of two to four times the profit obtained or favoured, if the offence committed by a natural person has a punishment of imprisonment foreseen exceeding two years;

  b) Fine of two to three times the profit obtained or favoured, in the rest of the cases.

In the case of the offences foreseen in Articles 277, 278, 279, 280, 281, 282, 282 bis, 284 and 286 bis:

  a) Fine from one to three years, if the offence committed by a natural person has a punishment foreseen of more than two years custodial sentence;

  b) Fine of six months to two years, in the rest of the cases.

2. According to the rules established in Article 66 bis, the Judges and Courts of Law may also impose the penalties established in Sub-Sections b) to g) of Section 7 of Article 33.

CHAPTER XII

On making an asset unavailable for its social or cultural use

Article 289

Whoever, by any means, destroys, puts out of service or damages an asset belong to himself assigned to social or cultural use, or in any way makes it unavailable for fulfilment of the legal duties imposed thereon in the interest of the community, shall be punished with a sentence of imprisonment of three to five months or a fine from six to ten months.

CHAPTER XIII

On corporate offences

Article 290

The *de facto* or *de jure* directors of a company incorporated or under formation, who falsify the annual accounts or other documents that should record the legal or financial status of the company, in such a way to cause financial damage thereto or to any of its shareholders or partners, or to a third party, shall be punished with a sentence of imprisonment from one to three years and a fine from six to twelve months.

If financial damage were actually caused, the penalties shall be imposed in the upper half.

Article 291

Those who, availing themselves of their majority at the General Meeting of Shareholders or on the governing body of any company incorporated or under formation, impose abusive resolutions, for own profit or that of others, to the detriment of the other shareholders or partners, and without this providing profit thereto, shall be punished with a sentence of imprisonment of six months to three years or a fine of one to three times the profit obtained.

Article 292

The same punishment as in the preceding Article shall be imposed on those who impose or take advantage of, for themselves or for a third party, to the detriment of the company or some of its shareholders or partners, a damaging resolution passed by a fictitious majority, obtained by use of blank signed orders, by undue attribution of the voting rights of whoever legally lacks them, by unlawfully refusing voting rights to whoever are legally recognised as having them, or by any other similar means or procedure, and without prejudice to punishment of the act as appropriate should it constitute another felony.

Article 293

De facto or *de jure* directors of any company incorporated or under formation who, without a legal reason, refuse or prevent a shareholder or partner from exercising his rights of information, participation in the management or control of the corporate activity, or pre-emptive subscription of shares recognised by the laws, shall be punished with the penalty of a fine from six to twelve months.

Article 294

Those who, as *de facto* or *de jure* directors of any company incorporated or under formation, subject to or that acts on markets subject to administrative supervision, deny or prevent action by the inspection or supervisory persons or bodies, shall be punished with a sentence of imprisonment of six months to three years or a fine of twelve to twenty- four months.

In addition to the penalties foreseen in the preceding Section, the judicial authority may decree some of the measures foreseen in Article 129 of this Code.

Article 295

De facto or *de jure* directors or the shareholders or partners of any company incorporated or under formation who fraudulently dispose of the assets of the company or contract obligations at its expense, directly causing financial damage that may be evaluated to its shareholders or partners, depositors, account holders or to the owners of the assets, stock or capital they administer, for their own profit or that of a third party, abusing the duties inherent to their office, shall be punished with a sentence of imprisonment of six months to four years, or a fine of one to three times the profit obtained.

Article 296

1. The acts described in this Chapter may only be prosecuted when reported by the person offended or his legal representative. When the former is a minor, incapacitated or handicapped person, it may also be reported by the Public Prosecutor.

2. The report required in the preceding Section shall not be necessary when commission of the offence affects general interests or multiple persons.

Article 297

For the purposes of this Chapter, all co-operatives, savings banks, mutual societies, financial or lending institutions, foundations, trading companies or any other corporation of a similar nature, with a permanent participation in the market to fulfil its ends, shall be construed to be a company.

CHAPTER XIV

On receiving stolen goods and money laundering

Article 298

1. Whoever, for profit and being aware that a felony against property or the social-economic order is being committed, in which he has not intervened either as a principal or accomplice, aids those responsible to take advantage of the proceeds thereof, or receives, acquires or conceals those proceeds, shall be punished with a sentence of imprisonment of six months to two years.

2. That punishment shall be imposed in its upper half on whoever receives, acquires or conceals the proceeds of the felony to traffic therewith. Should the trade be carried out using a commercial or industrial establishment or premises, the punishment of a fine from twelve to twenty-four months shall also be imposed. In these cases, the Judges or Courts of Law, in view of the severity of the act and the personal circumstances of the criminal, may also sentence him to the punishment of special barring from exercise of his profession or industry, for a term from two to five years, and order the measure of temporary or definitive closing of the establishment or premises. If the closing is temporary, its duration may not exceed five years.

3. Under no circumstances whatsoever may a sentence of imprisonment be handed down that exceeds that set for the felony concealed. Should this be punished with a punishment of another nature, the sentence of imprisonment shall be substituted by that of a fine from twelve to twenty-four months, except if the felony concealed is assigned a punishment is assigned a punishment equal to or lower than this. In such an event, the offender shall have the punishment for the felony in its lower half imposed.

Article 299

1. Whoever for profit and being aware of the acts constituting a misdemeanour against property being committed, habitually takes advantage of or aids and abets the offenders to take advantage of the effects thereof, shall be punished with a sentence of imprisonment of six months to one year.

2. Should he receive or acquire the products to trade with them, the punishment shall be imposed in its upper half and, if perpetrated on premises open to the public, a fine from twelve to twenty-four months shall also be imposed.

In these cases, the Judges or Courts of Law, in view of the severity of the act and the personal circumstances of the criminal, may also sentence him to the punishment of special barring from the exercise of his profession or industry for a term from one to three years, and order the measure of temporary or definitive closing of the establishment or premises. If the closing is temporary, its duration may not exceed five years.

Article 300

The provisions of this Chapter shall be applied even when the principal or the accomplice of the act from which the proceeds originate is not responsible or is personally exempt from punishment.

Article 301

1. Whoever acquires, possesses, uses, converts, or conveys assets, knowing they originate from a criminal activity, committed by himself or by any third party, or who perpetrates any other act to hide or conceal their unlawful origin, or to aid the person who participated in the felony or felonies to avoid the legal consequences of his acts, shall be punished with a sentence of imprisonment of six months to six years and a fine from one to three times the value of the goods. In these cases, the Judges or Courts of Law, in view of the severity of the act and the personal circumstances of the criminal, may also sentence him to the punishment of special barring from exercise of his profession or industry for a term from one to three years, and order the measure of temporary or definitive closing of the establishment or premises. If the closing is temporary, its duration may not exceed five years.

The punishment shall be imposed in its upper half when the assets have their origin in any of the felonies related to trafficking toxic drugs, narcotics or psychotropic substances described in Articles 368 to 372 of this Code. In these cases, the provisions set forth in Article 374 of this Code shall be applied.

The punishment shall also be imposed in its upper half when the assets originate from any of the felonies included in Chapters V, VI, VII, VIII, IX and X of Title XIX or in any of the felonies of Chapter I of Title XVI.

2. The same penalties shall be used to punish, as appropriate, hiding or concealment of the true nature, origin, location, destination, movement or rights to the assets, or their ownership, knowing that they originate from any of the felonies described in the preceding Section or an act of participation therein.

3. Should the acts be perpetrated due to serious negligence, the punishment shall be imprisonment from six months to two years and a fine of one to three times thereof.

4. The offender shall be also be punished even though the felony from which the assets, or the acts punishable pursuant to the preceding Sections may have been committed, full or partially, abroad.

5. Should the offender have obtained gains, these shall be seized pursuant to the rules of Article 127 of this Code.

Article 302

1. In the cases foreseen in the preceding Article the custodial sentences shall be imposed in the upper half on those pertaining to an organisation dedicated to the purposes stated therein, and the higher degree punishment on the bosses, managers or persons in charge of those organisations.

2. In such cases, when pursuant to the terms established in Article 31 bis, a legal person is responsible, it shall have the following penalties imposed thereon:

   a) Fine from two to five years, if the offence committed by a natural person has a punishment of imprisonment foreseen exceeding five years;

   b) Fine of six months to two years, in the rest of the cases.

Pursuant to the rules established in Article 66 bis, the Judges and Courts of Law may also impose the penalties established in Sub-Sections b) to g) of Section 7 of Article 33.

Article 303

Should the acts foreseen in the preceding Articles be perpetrated by an entrepreneur, intermediary in the financial sector, a medical practitioner, civil servant, social worker, teacher or educator, when carrying out the duties of his office, profession or trade, in addition to the relevant punishment, he shall also be sentenced to special barring from public employment and office, profession or trade, industry or commerce, for three to ten years. The punishment of absolute barring shall be imposed from ten to twenty years when such acts are carried out by an authority or agent thereof.

To that end, medical practitioners are construed to be doctors, psychologists, persons who hold higher education health and veterinary qualifications, pharmacists and their employees.

Article 304

Provocation, conspiracy and solicitation to commit the offences foreseen in Articles 301 to 303 shall be punished, respectively, with the punishment lower by one or two degrees.

TITLE XIV

On felonies against the Exchequer and the Social Security

Article 305[2]

1. Any person who, whether by action or omission, defrauds the state, regional or local treasury, avoiding the payment of taxes or deductions, or amounts that should have been deducted, or payments on account, wrongfully obtaining rebates or likewise enjoying fiscal benefits, provided that the amount of the defrauded payment, the unpaid amount of deductions or payments on account or the amount of the rebates or fiscal benefits wrongfully obtained or enjoyed exceeds one hundred and twenty thousand euros, shall be punished with a prison sentence of between one and five years and a fine of up to six times the aforesaid amount, unless his tax situation has been brought into compliance with the terms of section 4 of this article.

The mere filing of returns or making of voluntary payments does not preclude fraud, where other facts provide evidence of that.

In addition to the sentences stated, the person accountable shall lose the possibility of receiving state grants and aid and the right to enjoy fiscal or social security benefits or incentives for a period of between three and six years.

2. For the purposes of determining the amount referred to in the preceding section:

a) Where periodic or periodically declared taxes, deductions, payments on account or rebates are concerned, the amount defrauded in each tax or declaration period shall apply, and if those periods are less than twelve months, the amount defrauded shall refer to the calendar year. The foregoing notwithstanding, in those cases where the fraud is committed within an organisation or criminal group, or by persons or entities acting under the appearance of a genuine economic activity without in fact carrying it out, the offence may be prosecuted from the very moment at which the sum established in section 1 is reached.

b) In the remaining cases, the amount shall be deemed to refer to each of the different items for which a tax may have to be paid.

3. The same sentences shall be imposed where the acts described in section 1 of this article are committed against the treasury of the European Union, provided that the amount defrauded exceeds fifty thousand euros in a period of one calendar year. The foregoing notwithstanding, in those cases where the fraud is committed within an organisation or criminal group, or by persons or entities acting under the appearance of a genuine economic activity

---

[2] Amended by single art. 2 of Organic Law 7/2012 of 27 December.

without in fact carrying it out, the offence may be prosecuted from the very moment at which the sum established in this section is reached.

If the amount defrauded does not exceed fifty thousand euros, but does exceed four thousand, a prison sentence of between three months and one year or a fine of up to three times the aforesaid amount shall be imposed, as well as the loss of the possibility of receiving state grants and aid and the right to enjoy fiscal or social security benefits or incentives for a period of between six months and two years.

4. The tax situation of the taxpayer shall be deemed to have been brought into compliance where he has wholly acknowledged the tax liability and paid it in full, before being notified by the tax authorities of the commencement of investigative proceedings aimed at determining the tax liabilities to be met, or, if such proceedings do not take place, before the public prosecutor's office, the legal representative of the state or the procedural representative of the regional or local government, brings a charge or files a complaint against him, or before the public prosecutor's office or the investigating judge take steps that allow him to be formally aware of the commencement of proceedings.

The effects of bringing the tax situation into compliance provided for in the preceding paragraph shall also apply where tax liabilities are settled once the right of the authorities to determine them under the rules of administrative law has expired.

Where the taxpayer brings his tax situation into compliance, it shall prevent him being prosecuted for possible accounting irregularities or other documentary misrepresentations which, exclusively in relation to the tax liability in question, he may have committed prior to bringing his tax situation into compliance.

5. Where the tax authorities find indications of an offence having been committed against the treasury, they may collect separately, on the one hand, the items and amounts that are not linked to the possible offence against the treasury and, on the other hand, those that are linked to the possible offence against the treasury.

The collection referred to first in the preceding paragraph shall be processed in the ordinary way and subject to the arrangement for collection of own resources accruing from all tax settlements. And collection, where appropriate, arising from those items and amounts that are linked to the possible offence against the treasury shall follow the process established by the tax regulations for that purpose, without prejudice to it ultimately being adapted to what is decided in criminal proceedings.

The existence of criminal proceedings for an offence against the treasury shall not freeze the collection of the tax liability. The tax authorities may commence steps aimed at collection, unless the judge, on his own initiative or at the request of one of the parties, has ordered the suspension of enforcement action, subject to the provision of guarantees. If it has not been possible to provide guarantees, in full or in part, the judge may exceptionally order the suspension, fully or partially dispensing with guarantees, if he finds that enforcement could cause irreparable damage or damage only repaired with great difficulty.

6. The judges and courts may impose on the taxpayer or the offender a lesser sentence by one or two degrees, provided that, within two months of receiving the judicial notice of the charge, he settles the tax liability and acknowledges the facts in court. The above shall likewise apply to participants in the offence other than the taxpayer or the offender, where they actively collaborate to obtain decisive evidence to identify or capture others responsible, to fully clarify the facts of the offence or to establish the assets of the taxpayer or others responsible for the offence.

7. In the proceedings for the offence provided for in this article, to enforce the fine and civil liability, which includes the amount of the tax liability that the tax authorities have not collected on grounds of prescription or other legal grounds in accordance with Law 58/2003, the General Taxation Act, of 17 December, including interest on arrears, the judges and courts shall request the help of the tax authorities' services, which shall enforce them with administrative proceedings for debt collection in accordance with the provisions of the aforesaid Law.

Article 305 bis[3].

1. Offences against the treasury shall be punished with a prison sentence of between two and six years and a fine of between twice and six times the amount defrauded, where the fraud takes is committed in any of the following circumstances:

[3] Added by single art. 3 of Organic Law 7/2012 of 27 December

a) The amount defrauded exceeds six hundred thousand euros.

b) The fraud was committed within an organisation or criminal group.

c) Where the use of natural or legal persons or entities without legal personality as proxies, businesses or trust instruments or tax havens or territories with no taxation obscures or makes it difficult to determine the identity of the taxpayer or the person responsible for the office, the amount defrauded or the assets of the taxpayer or the person responsible for the offence.

2. In the cases described in this article, all the remaining provisions contained in article 305 shall apply.
In these cases, in addition to the sentences stated, the person accountable shall lose the possibility of receiving state grants and aid and the right to enjoy fiscal or social security benefits or incentives for a period of between four and eight years.

Article 306[4]

Any person who, whether by action or omission, defrauds the general budget of the European Union, or any other budget managed by that entity, of an amount greater than fifty thousand euros, avoiding, other than in the cases provided for in section 3 of article 305, the payment of amounts that should be paid, using the funds obtained for a purpose different from that for which they were intended or wrongfully obtaining funds by falsifying the conditions required for being granted them or hiding those that would have prevented them being granted, shall be punished with a prison sentence of between one and five years and a fine of up to six times the aforesaid amount.

If the amount defrauded or wrongfully used does not exceed fifty thousand euros, but does exceed four thousand, a prison sentence of between three months and one year or a fine of up to three times the aforesaid amount shall be imposed, as well as the loss of the possibility of receiving state grants and aid and the right to enjoy fiscal or social security benefits or incentives for a period of between six months and two years.

Article 307[5]

1. Any person who, whether by action or omission, defrauds the social security system by avoiding social security contributions and jointly collected items, wrongfully obtaining rebates or enjoying deductions in relation to any item, provided that the amounts defrauded or the wrongful rebates or deductions exceed fifty thousand euros, shall be punished with a prison sentence of between one and five years and a fine of up to six times the aforesaid amount, unless he has brought his situation with regard to social security into compliance in accordance with the terms of section 3 of this article.

The mere filing of social security contribution documents does not preclude fraud, where other facts provide evidence of that.

In addition to the sentences stated, the person accountable shall lose the possibility of receiving state grants and aid and the right to enjoy fiscal or social security benefits or incentives for a period of between three and six years.

2. For the purposes of determining the amount referred to in the preceding section, the total amount defrauded in four calendar years shall apply.

3. The situation with regard to social security of the person liable shall be deemed to have been brought into compliance where he has wholly acknowledged and paid the debt before being notified of the commencement of inspection proceedings aimed at determining the debt, or, if such proceedings do not take place, before the public prosecutor's office or the lawyer for the social security system brings a charge or files a complaint against him, or before the public prosecutor's office or the investigating judge takes steps that allow him to be formally aware of the commencement of proceedings.

---

[4] Amended by single art. 4 of Organic Law 7/2012 of 27 December
[5] Amended by single art. 5 of Organic Law 7/2012 of 27 December.

The effects of bringing the situation with regard to social security into compliance provided for in the preceding paragraph shall also apply where debts are settled once the right of the authorities to determine them under the rules of administrative law has expired.

If the individual brings his situation with regard to social security into compliance, it shall prevent him being prosecuted for possible accounting irregularities or other documentary misrepresentations which, exclusively in relation to the debt in question, he may have committed prior to bringing his situation into compliance.

4. The existence of criminal proceedings for an offence against the social security system shall not freeze administrative proceedings for settlement and collection of the social security debt incurred, unless the judge orders it subject to the provision of a guarantee. If it has not been possible to provide a guarantee, in full or in part, the judge may exceptionally order the suspension, wholly or partially dispensing with guarantees, should he find that enforcement could cause irreparable damage or damage only repaired with great difficulty. The administrative settlement proceedings shall ultimately be adapted to what is decided in the criminal proceedings.

5. The judges and courts may impose on the person liable to the social security system or the offender a lesser sentence by one or two degrees, provided that, within two months of receiving the judicial notice of the charge, he settles the social security debt and acknowledges the facts in court. The above shall likewise apply to participants in the offence other than the social security debtor or the offender, where they actively collaborate to obtain decisive evidence to identify or capture others responsible, to fully clarify the facts of the offence or to establish the assets of the person liable to the social security system or others responsible for the offence.

6. In the proceedings for the offence provided for in this article, to enforce the fine and civil liability, which includes the amount of the debt to the social security system that the authorities have not collected on grounds of prescription or other legal grounds, including interest on arrears, the judges and courts shall request the help of the social security authorities' services, which shall enforce them with administrative proceedings for debt collection.

Article 307 bis[6]

1. The offence against the social security system shall be punished with a prison sentence of between two and six years and a fine of between twice and six times the amount, where any of the following circumstances apply to the commission of the offence:

a) The amount of the defrauded contributions or wrongful rebates or deductions exceeds one hundred and twenty thousand euros.

b) The fraud was committed within an organisation or criminal group.

c) Where the use of natural or legal persons or entities without legal personality as proxies, businesses or fiduciary instruments or tax havens or territories with no taxation obscures or makes it difficult to determine the identity of the person liable to the social security system or the person responsible for the office, the amount defrauded or the assets of the person liable to the social security system or the person responsible for the offence.

2. In the cases described in this article, all the remaining provisions contained in article 307 shall apply.

3. In these cases, in addition to the sentences stated, the person accountable shall lose the possibility of receiving state grants and aid and the right to enjoy fiscal or social security benefits or incentives for a period of between four and eight years.

Article 307 ter[7]

1. Any person who, for himself or for another person, obtains social security benefits, their wrongful prolongation, or helps others to obtain them, by means of error induced by simulating or distorting facts, or knowingly concealing

---

[6] Added by single art. 6 of Organic Law 7/2012 of 27 December
[7] Added by single art. 7 of Organic Law 7/2012 of 27 December

facts that he has a duty to report, thereby causing harm to the public authorities, shall be punished with a prison sentence of between six months and three years.

Where, in view of the amount defrauded, the means used and the personal circumstances of the offender, the facts of the offence are not especially serious, he will be punished with a fine of up to six times the amount.

In addition to the sentences stated, the person accountable shall lose the possibility of receiving grants and the right to enjoy fiscal or social security benefits or incentives for a period of between three and six years.

2. Where the value of the benefits exceeds fifty thousand euros or any of the circumstances referred to in letters b) or c) of section 1 article 307 bis apply, a prison sentence of between two and six years and a fine of up to six times the amount shall be imposed.

In these cases, in addition to the sentences stated, the person accountable shall lose the possibility of receiving grants and aid and the right to enjoy fiscal or social security benefits or incentives for a period of between four and eight years.

3. The person accountable shall be exempt from criminal liability if he repays an amount equivalent to the value of the benefits received in addition to annual interest equivalent to the statutory interest rate plus two per cent, from the time that he received the benefits, before being notified of the commencement of inspection and control proceedings in relation to those benefits or, if such proceedings do not take place, before the public prosecutor's office, or the legal representative of the state, the lawyer for the social security system or the representative of the regional or local government in question, brings a charge or files a complaint against him, or before the public prosecutor's office or the investigating judge take steps that allow him to be formally aware of the commencement of proceedings.

The exemption from criminal liability provided for in the preceding paragraph shall also extend to that individual for any possible documentary misrepresentations which, exclusively in relation to the defrauded benefits to be repaid, he may have committed prior to bringing his situation into compliance.

4. The existence of criminal proceedings for any of the offences in sections 1 and 2 of this article shall not prevent the relevant authorities demanding repayment of the wrongfully obtained benefits in the administrative courts. The amount that must be repaid shall provisionally be set by the authorities and shall later be adapted to what is ultimately decided in the criminal proceedings.

Nor shall the criminal proceedings freeze the collection action of the relevant authorities, which may commence proceedings aimed at collection, unless the judge, on his own initiative or at the request of one of the parties, orders the suspension of enforcement action, subject to the provision of a guarantee. If it has not been possible to provide a guarantee, in full or in part, the judge may exceptionally order the suspension, fully or partially dispensing with guarantees, if he finds that enforcement could cause irreparable damage or damage only repaired with great difficulty.

5. In proceedings for the offence provided for in this article, to enforce the fine and civil liability, the judges and courts shall request the help of the social security authorities' services, which shall enforce them with administrative proceedings for debt collection.

6. In the cases governed by this article, the provisions of section 5 of article 307 of the Criminal Code shall apply.

Article 308[8]

1. Any person who obtains grants or aid from the public authorities for an amount or with a value greater than one hundred and twenty thousand euros by falsifying the conditions required for being awarded them or hiding those that would have prevented them being granted, shall be punished with a prison sentence of between one and five years and a fine of up to six times the amount, unless he makes repayment as referred to in section 5 of this article.

---

[8] Amended by single art. 8 of Organic Law 7/2012 of 27 December

2. The same sentences shall be imposed on any person who, carrying out an activity that is fully or partially defrayed with funds from the public authorities, uses them for purposes other than those for which the subsidy or aid was granted, where the amount in question is greater than one hundred and twenty thousand euros, unless he makes repayment as referred to section 5 of this article.

3. In addition to the sentences stated, the person accountable shall lose the possibility of receiving state grants and aid and the right to enjoy fiscal or social security benefits or incentives for a period of between three and six years.

4. To determine the amount defrauded, the calendar year shall apply and the subsidies or aid in question must be obtained for the same private activity eligible for subsidy, even if they come from different public authorities or entities.

5. The repayment referred to sections 1 and 2 shall be deemed to have been made, where the person receiving the subsidy or aid returns the wrongfully received or used subsidy or aid, in addition to the late payment interest applicable in relation to subsidies, from the moment that he received it, and does so before being notified of the commencement of inspection or control proceedings in relation to that subsidy or aid, or, if such proceedings do not take place, before the public prosecutor's office, the legal representative of the state or the representative of the regional or local government in question, brings a charge or files a complaint against him, of before the public prosecutor's office or the investigating judge take steps that allow him to be formally aware of the commencement of proceedings. Such repayment shall prevent the individual being prosecuted for any possible documentary misrepresentations which, exclusively in relation to the debt in question, he may have committed prior to bringing his situation into compliance.

6. The existence of criminal proceedings for any of the offences in sections 1 and 2 of this article shall not prevent the relevant authorities demanding repayment of the wrongfully used subsidy or aid in the administrative courts. The amount that must be repaid shall provisionally be set by the authorities and shall later be adapted to what is ultimately decided in the criminal proceedings.

Nor shall the criminal proceedings freeze the collection action of the authorities, which may commence proceedings aimed at collection, unless the judge, on his own initiative or at the request of one of the parties, orders the suspension of enforcement action, subject to the provision of a guarantee. If it has not been possible to provide a guarantee, in full or in part, the judge may exceptionally order the suspension, fully or partially dispensing with guarantees, if he finds that enforcement could cause irreparable damage or damage only repaired with great difficulty.

7. The judges and courts may impose on the person accountable for this offence a lesser sentence by one or two degrees, provided that, within two months of receiving the judicial notice of the charge, he makes repayment as referred to in section 5 and acknowledges the facts in court. The above shall likewise apply to participants in the offence other than the person obliged to make repayment or the offender, where they actively collaborate to obtain decisive evidence to identify or capture others responsible, to fully clarify the facts of the offence or to establish the assets of the person obliged to make repayment or the person responsible for the offence.

Article 309[9]

(Repealed)

Article 310

He who is obliged by law to keep corporate accounting, books or tax records shall be punished with a sentence of imprisonment from five to seven months when:

a) He absolutely fails to fulfil that obligation under the direct assessment of the tax bases regime;

b) He keeps different accounts that, related to the same activity and business year, conceal or simulate the true situation of the business;

---

[9] Repealed by single repealing provision 1 of Organic Law 7/2012 of 27 December

c) He has not recorded businesses, acts, operations or economic transactions in general, in the obligatory books, or has recorded them with figures different to the true ones;

d) He has recorded fictitious accounting entries in the obligatory books.

The consideration as a felony of the cases of fact referred to in Sections c) and d) above, shall require the tax returns to have been omitted, or for those submitted to provide a record of the false accounting and that the amount, by more or less, of the charges or payments omitted or forged exceeds, without arithmetic compensation between them, 240,000 euros for each business year.

Article 310 bis[10]

Where, in accordance with the provisions of article 31 bis, a legal person is responsible for the offences contained in this heading, the following sentences shall be imposed on it:

a) A fine of up to twice the amount defrauded or wrongfully obtained, if the offence when committed by a natural person is punishable with a prison sentence of more than two years.

b) A fine of between twice and four times the amount defrauded or wrongfully obtained, if the offence when committed by a natural person is punishable with a prison sentence of more than five years.

c) A fine of between six months and one year, in the circumstances contained in article 310.

In addition to the sentences stated, the legal person accountable shall lose the possibility of receiving state grants and aid and the right to enjoy fiscal or social security benefits or incentives for a period of between three and six years. A ban on contracting with the public authorities may also be imposed on the entity.

Taking into account the rules laid down in article 66 bis, the judges and courts may also impose the sentences contained in article 33, section 7, letters b), c), d), e).

TITLE XV

On felonies against the rights of workers

Article 311[11]

Prison sentences of between six months and six years and a fine of between six and twelve months shall be imposed on:

1. Those who, by means of deception or abuse of a situation of need, impose on the workers in their service working or social security conditions that are detrimental to, suppress or restrict the rights granted to them by law, by collective bargaining agreements or by individual contracts.

2. Those who simultaneously employ a number of workers without appropriately registering them with the social security system or, where appropriate, without having obtained the relevant work permit, provided that the number of workers affected is less than:

    a) twenty-five per cent, in companies or workplaces where there are more than one hundred workers,

    b) fifty per cent, in companies or workplaces where there are more than ten workers and not more than one hundred, or

    c) all of them, in companies or workplaces where there are more than five and not more than ten workers.

---

[10] Amended by single art. 9 of Organic Law 7/2012 of 27 December
[11] Amended by single art. 10 of Organic Law 7/2012 of 27 December

3. Those who, in the event of business transfers, being aware of the procedures described in the preceding sections, maintain the aforesaid conditions imposed by some other person.

4. If the conduct described in the preceding sections is accompanied by violence or intimidation, sentences of a higher degree shall be imposed.

Article 312

1. Punishment by imprisonment from two to five years and a fine from six to twelve months shall apply to those who unlawfully traffic with labour.

2. The same punishment shall be incurred by whoever recruits persons or leads them to leave their place of work by offering deceitful or false employment or working conditions and whoever employs foreign citizens without work permits under conditions that negatively affect, suppress or restrict the rights they are recognised by the legal provisions, collective bargaining agreements or individual contracts.

Article 313

Whoever were to bring about or favour emigration of any person to another country simulating a contract or placement, or using another similar deceit, shall be punished with the penalty foreseen in the preceding Article.

Article 314

Those who commit a serious discrimination in public or private employment, against any person due to his ideology, religion or belief, belonging to an ethic group, race or nation, gender, sexual preference, family situation, illness or handicap, due to appointment as the legal or Trade Union representative of the workers, due to relationship to other workers at the company, or due to use of any of the official languages of the Spanish State, and who do not reinstate him to the situation of equality before the law after an administrative demand or punishment, compensating the financial damage arising therefrom, shall be punished with a sentence of imprisonment of six months to two years or a fine from twelve to twenty- four months.

Article 315

1. Punishment by imprisonment of six months to three years and a fine from six to twelve months shall be handed down to those who, by deceit or abuse of a situation of need, were to prevent or limit the exercise of Trade Union freedom or the right to strike.

2. Should the conduct described in the preceding Section be carried out by force, violence or intimidation, the higher degree penalties shall be imposed.

3. The same penalties as in Section 2 shall be imposed on those who, acting in a group or individually, although in collusion with another, coerce other persons to begin or continue a strike.

Article 316

Those who, breaching the rules on labour risk prevention, being legally obliged, do not provide the necessary resources for the workers to carry out their activity with the appropriate health and safety measures, so that they seriously endanger their life, health or physical integrity, shall be punished with imprisonment of six months to three years and a fine from six to twelve months.

Article 317

When the felony to which the preceding Article refers is committed due to serious negligence, it shall be punished with the lower degree punishment.

Article 318

When the acts foreseen in the Articles of this Title are attributed to legal persons, the punishment set shall be imposed on the directors or service managers who were responsible for these and on whoever, being aware of and able to put these right, did not adopt measures to do so. In these cases, the judicial authority may also decree any one or number of measures foreseen in Article 129 of this Code.

TITLE XV BIS

Offences against the rights of aliens

Article 318 bis

1. Whoever, directly or indirectly, promotes, favours or facilitates illegal trafficking or clandestine immigration of persons from, in transit and with their destination in Spain, or with their destination in another country in the European Union, shall be punished with the penalty from four to eight years imprisonment.

2. Those who perpetrate the conduct described the preceding Section for profit or using violence, intimidation, deceit, or abusing a situation of superiority or of special vulnerability of the victim, or endangering life, personal health or integrity, shall be punished with the penalties in the upper half. Should the victim be a minor or incapacitated, this shall be punished with the penalties higher by one degree to those foreseen in the preceding Section.

3. The same penalties as in the preceding Section, and also that of absolute barring from six to twelve years, shall be incurred by those who perpetrate the acts availing themselves of their status as an authority, agent thereof or public officer.

4. The penalties higher by one degree to those foreseen in Sections 1 to 3 of this Article shall be imposed, in the respective cases, and special barring from profession, trade, industry or commerce for the term of the conviction, when the offender belongs to an organisation or assembly, even if transitory in nature, which perpetrates such operations.

In the case of managers, directors or those in charge of those organisations or assemblies, the upper half of the punishment shall be applied, that may be raised to the one immediately above it in degree.

When, pursuant to the terms established in Article 31 bis, a legal person is responsible for the offences defined in this Title, the punishment of a fine from two to five years shall be imposed, or that from three to five times the profit obtained if the resulting amount were to be higher.

Pursuant to the rules established in Article 66 bis, the Judges and Courts of Law may also impose the penalties established in Sub-Sections b) to g) of Section 7 of Article 33.

5. The Courts of Law, taking into account the seriousness of the act and its circumstances, the conditions of the offender and the purpose he had intended, may impose the punishment lower by one degree to the relevant one stated.

TITLE XVI

On felonies concerning organisation of the territory and town planning, protection of the historic heritage and the environment

CHAPTER I

On felonies concerning organisation of the territory and town planning

Article 319

1. Prison sentences of one year and six months to four years, a fine of twelve to twenty- four months shall be imposed, except if the profit obtained from the offence exceeds the resulting amount, in which case the fine shall be from one to three times the amount of that profit, and special barring from profession or trade for a term of one to four years, for promoters, builders or technical directors who carry out unauthorised town planning, construction or building works on land assigned to roadways, park zones, public property, or places that the legal or administrative regulations recognise landscape, ecological, artistic, historic or cultural value, or that have been deemed worthy for special protection for the same reasons.

2. A sentence of imprisonment shall be imposed from one to three years, a fine of twelve to twenty- four months, except if the profit obtained by the offence were to exceed the resulting sum, in which case the fine shall be from one to three times the amount of that profit, and special barring from profession or trade for a term of one to four years, for promoters, builders or technical directors who carry out unauthorised town planning, construction or building works on land not zoned for urbanisation.

3. In any event, the Judges or Courts of Law, may issue a reasoned order to demolish the works and restore the physical reality altered at the expense of the principal thereof, without prejudice to the compensations due to third parties in good faith. In all cases, seizure of the gains obtained by the offence shall be ordered, whatever the transformations they may have undergone.

4. In the cases foreseen in this Article, when a legal person is responsible pursuant to the terms established in Article 31 bis of this Code, the punishment of a fine from one to three years shall be imposed, except if the profit obtained by the offence exceeds the sum resulting, in which case the fine shall be two to four times the amount of that profit.

Pursuant to the rules established in Article 66 bis, the Judges and Courts of Law may also impose the penalties established in Sub-Sections b) to g) of Section 7 of Article 33.

Article 320

1. The authority or public officer who, being aware of the injustice thereof, has advised favourably on planning instruments, projects for town planning, allotment division and subdivision, construction or building, or the granting of permits that violate the regulations of territorial organisation or town planning in force, or who, during inspections, has silenced the breach of those regulations or has omitted carrying out the mandatory inspections, shall be punished with the penalty established in Article 404 of this Code and, moreover, with that of imprisonment for one year and six months to four years and that of a fine from twelve to twenty- four months.

2. The same penalties shall be imposed on the authority or public officer who, himself, or as a member of a collegiate body, has resolved or voted in favour of approval of the planning instruments, the town planning projects, allotment, sub-allotment, construction or building or the granting the permits referred to in the preceding Section, being aware of the injustice thereof.

CHAPTER II

On felonies against historical heritage assets

Article 321

Those who demolish or seriously alter buildings uniquely protected due to their historic, artistic, cultural or monumental interest shall be punished with imprisonment of six months to three years, a fine of twelve to twenty-four months and, in all cases, special barring from profession or trade for a term from one to five years.

In any event, the Judges or Courts of Law, on reasoned grounds, may order reconstruction or restoration of the works at the expense of the doer, without prejudice to the compensations due to third parties in good faith.

Article 322

1. The authority or public officer who, being aware of the injustice thereof, has favourably reported on projects to demolish or alter uniquely protected buildings, shall be punished, in addition to the punishment established in Article 404 of this Code, with that of imprisonment for six months to two years or a fine of twelve to twenty- four months.

2. The same penalties shall be applied to the authority or public officer who, himself or as a member of a collegiate body has resolved or voted in favour of the granting thereof despite being aware of the injustice thereof.

Article 323

A sentence of imprisonment from one to three years and a fine of twelve to twenty- four months shall be imposed on whoever causes damage to an archive, registry, museum, library, teaching centre, scientific laboratory, similar institution or to assets of historical artistic, scientific, cultural or monumental value, as well as to archaeological sites.

In these cases, the Judges or Courts of Law may order, at the expense of the doer of the damage, adoption of measures aimed at restoration of the damaged asset to the extent possible.

Article 324

Whoever, due to serious negligence, causes damage, in an amount exceeding four hundred euros, to an archive, registry, museum, library, teaching centre, scientific laboratory, similar institution or to assets of historical, artistic, scientific, cultural or monumental value, as well as to archaeological sites, shall be punished with a penalty of a fine from three to eighteen months, in view of the extent thereof.

CHAPTER III

On felonies against natural resources and the environment

Article 325

Whoever, breaking the laws or other provisions of a general nature that protect the environment, directly or indirectly causes or makes emissions, spillages, radiation, extractions or excavations, filling with earth, noises, vibrations, injections or deposits, in the atmosphere, the ground, the subsoil or the surface water, ground water or sea water, including the high seas, even those affecting cross border spaces, as well as the water catchment basins, that may seriously damage the balance of the natural systems shall be punished with a sentence of imprisonment from two to five years, a fine from eight to twenty-four months and with special barring from his profession or trade for a period from one to three years. Should there be risk of serious damage to the health of persons, the sentence of imprisonment shall be imposed in its upper half.

Article 326

A punishment higher in one degree shall be imposed, without prejudice to those that may be appropriate pursuant to other provisions of this Code, when commission of any of the acts described in the preceding Article takes place with any of the following circumstances concurring:

a) When the industry or activity is operating unlawfully, without having obtained the requisite authorisation or administrative approval of its facilities;

b) When the specific orders by the administrative authority on correction or suspension of the activities defined in the preceding Section have been disobeyed;

c) When information on the environmental aspects thereof has been forged or concealed;

d) When the inspection activity of the Administration has been hindered;

e) When a risk of irreversible or catastrophic deterioration has ensued;

f) When there has been unlawful extraction of water during a period of restrictions.

Article 327

When, pursuant to the terms established in Article 31 bis a legal person is responsible for the offences established in the preceding two Articles, it shall have the following penalties imposed thereon:

a) Fine from two to five years, if the offence committed by a natural person has a punishment foreseen of imprisonment exceeding five years;

b) Fine from one to three years, in the rest of the cases.

Pursuant to the rules established in Article 66 bis, the Judges and Courts of Law may also impose the penalties established in Sub-Sections b) to g) of Section 7 of Article 33.

Article 328

1. A sentence of imprisonment of six months to two years, a fine from ten to fourteen months and special barring from profession or trade for a term from one to two years shall be imposed on whoever establishes deposits or landfills of solid or liquid waste or residues that are toxic or hazardous and may seriously damage the balance of natural systems or the health of individuals.

2. The same punishment foreseen in the preceding Section shall apply to whoever, breaching the laws or other general provisions, carries out exploitation of installations where a hazardous activity is perpetrated, or where hazardous substances or preparations are stored or used, that cause or might cause death or serious injury to persons, or substantial damage to the quality of the air, soil quality, water quality, or to animals or plants.

3. A sentence of imprisonment from one to two years shall be imposed on those who, when assembling, transporting, recycling, eliminating or recycling waste, including omission of the duty of surveillance of such procedures, seriously endanger the life, integrity or health of persons, or the quality of the air, ground or water, or animals or plants.

4. Whoever, breaching the laws or other general provisions, transports a major quantity of waste, both in the case of one as well as several related transfers, shall be punished with a sentence of imprisonment from one to two years.

5. When, due to the conduct foreseen in the preceding Sections, in addition to the risk considered, a result an injury that constitutes a felony ensues, whatever its seriousness, the Judges or Courts of Law shall only consider the most seriously penalised offence, applying the upper half of the punishment.

6. When, pursuant to the terms established in Article 31 bis, a legal person is responsible for the offences defined in this Article, it shall have the following penalties imposed thereon:

a) Fine from one to three years, or of two to four times the damage caused when the resulting amount is higher, if the offence committed by a natural person has a punishment foreseen of more than two years custodial sentence;

b) Fine of six months to two years or of two to three times the damage caused if the resulting amount is higher, in the rest of the cases.

Pursuant to the rules established in Article 66 bis, the Judges and Courts of Law may also impose the penalties established in Sub-Sections b) to g) of Section 7 of Article 33.

7. When, in committing any of the acts foreseen in the preceding Sections of this Article, any of the circumstances established in Sections a), b), c) or d) of Article 326 concur, the penalties shall be imposed higher by one degree to those respectively foreseen, without prejudice to those that might be appropriate pursuant to other provisions of this Code.

Article 329

1. The authority or public officer who, knowingly, has reported favourably on granting manifestly unlawful permits that authorise operation of the polluting industries or activities referred to in the preceding Articles, or who has silenced breach of laws or provisions of regulations of a general nature thereon during his inspections, or who has omitted the carrying out of the mandatory inspections, shall be punished with the penalty established in Article 404 of this Code and, moreover, with that of imprisonment from six months to three years and a fine from eight to twenty-four months.

2. The same penalties shall be applied to the authority or public officer who, himself or as a member of a collegiate body, may have resolved or voted in favour of such granting, being aware of the injustice thereof.

Article 330

Whoever seriously damages any of the elements of a protected natural space that were used to classify it as such, shall incur a sentence of imprisonment from one to four years and a fine of twelve to twenty-four months.

Article 331

The acts foreseen in this Chapter shall be penalised, as appropriate, by the lower degree punishment, in their respective cases, when committed by serious negligence.

CHAPTER IV

On felonies related to the flora, fauna and pets

Article 332

Whoever, with serious damage to environment, cuts, fells, burns, tears up, harvests or conducts unlawful trafficking in any species or sub-species of threatened flora or its shoots, or destroys or seriously alters its habitat, shall be punished with a sentence of imprisonment from four months to two years or fine from eight to twenty-four months.

Article 333

Whoever introduces non autochthonous species of flora or fauna so as to damage the biological balance, against the laws or provisions of a general nature that protect species of flora or fauna, shall be punished with a sentence of imprisonment from four months to two years or fine from eight to twenty- four months and, in all cases, special barring from profession or trade for a term from one to three years.

Article 334

1. Whoever hunts or fishes endangered species, perpetrates activities that prevent or hinder their reproduction or migration, or who destroys or seriously alters their habitat, against the laws or provisions of a general nature that protect species of wild fauna, or who trades or traffics with them or their remains, shall be punished with a sentence of imprisonment from four months to two years or a fine from eight to twenty- four months and, in all cases, that of special barring from profession or trade and special barring from exercise of the right to hunt or fish for a term of two to four years.

2. The punishment shall be imposed in its upper half if they are species or subspecies classified as endangered by extinction.

Article 335

1. Whoever hunts or fishes species other than those stated in the previous Article, when this is specifically prohibited by the specific rules on their hunting or fishing, shall be punished with the penalty of a fine from eight to twelve months and special barring from exercise of the right to hunt or fish for a term from two to five years.

2. Whoever hunts or fishes species referred to in the preceding Section on public or private land pertaining to others, subject to special hunting regime, without due permission by their owner, shall be punished with the penalty of a fine from four to eight months and special barring from exercise of the right to hunt or fish for a term from one to three years, in addition to the penalties that may befall him, as appropriate, for committing the offence foreseen in Section 1 of this Article.

3. Should the preceding conduct cause serious damage to hunting property on an estate subject to a special hunting regime, a sentence of imprisonment of six months to two years and special barring from exercising the right to hunt and fish for a term from two to five years shall be imposed.

4. The punishment shall be imposed in its upper half when the conduct classified in this Article is perpetrated by groups of three or more persons using tackle or means that are prohibited by law or by-laws.

Article 336

Whoever, without being legally authorised, uses poison, explosive devices or other instruments or tackle of a similar destructive, non- selective effect on the fauna to hunt or fish, shall be punished with a sentence of imprisonment from four months to two years or fine from eight to twenty- four months and, in all cases, that of special barring from profession or trade and special barring from exercise of the right to hunt or fish for a term from one to three years. Should the damage caused be notoriously important, the upper half of the aforesaid sentence of imprisonment shall be imposed.

Article 337

Whoever, by any means or procedure, unfairly mistreats a pet or tame animal, causing it death or injuries that seriously damage its health, shall be punished with the penalty from three months to a year of imprisonment and special barring from one to three years to carry out a profession, trade or commerce related to animals.

CHAPTER V

Common provisions

Article 338

When the conduct defined in this Title affects any protected natural space, the penalties shall be imposed higher by one degree to those respectively foreseen.

Article 339

The Judges or Courts of Law shall order adoption, at the expense of the doer, of the necessary measures aimed at restoring the ecological balance disturbed, as well as any other precautionary measure required to protect the assets safeguarded under this Title.

Article 340

Should the principal of any of the acts defined in this Title have voluntarily proceeded to repair the damage caused, the Judges and Courts of Law shall impose the lower degree punishment of those respectively foreseen.

TITLE XVII

On felonies against collective safety

CHAPTER I

On felonies of catastrophic risk

SUBCHAPTER 1. ON FELONIES RELATED TO NUCLEAR ENERGY AND IONISING RADIATIONS

Article 341

Whoever releases nuclear energy or radioactive elements that endanger the life or health of persons or their property, even though an explosion does not take place, shall be punished with a sentence of imprisonment from fifteen to twenty years, and special barring from public employment and office, profession or trade for a term of ten to twenty years.

Article 342

Whoever, without being included in the preceding Article, disturbs operation of a nuclear or radioactive facility, or alters the carrying out of activities in which materials or equipment producing ionizing radiation are used, creating a situation of serious hazard to life or health of persons, shall be punished with a sentence of imprisonment from four to ten years, and special barring from public employment and office, profession or trade for a term from six to ten years.

Article 343

1. Whoever, by tipping, emission or release into the air, the ground or water, of a quantity of materials or ionising radiation, or exposure to such radiation by any other means that endangers the life, integrity, health or assets of one

or several persons, shall be punished with a sentence of imprisonment from six to twelve years and special barring from public employment and office, profession or trade for a term from six to ten years. The same punishment shall be imposed when, by means of such conduct, the quality of the air, the soil or water or animals or plants is endangered.

2. When, due to the conduct described in the preceding Section, in addition to the risk foreseen, a result of injury constituting a felony is produced, whatever its seriousness, the Judges or Courts of Law shall only consider the most seriously penalised offence, applying the upper half of the punishment.

3. When, pursuant to the terms established in Article 31 bis, a legal person is responsible for the offences defined in this Article, the punishment of a fine from two to five years shall be imposed thereon.

Pursuant to the rules established in Article 66 bis, the Judges and Courts of Law may also impose the penalties established in Sub-Sections b) to g) of Section 7 of Article 33.

Article 344

The acts foreseen in the preceding Articles shall be punished with the lower degree punishment, in their respective cases, when committed by serious negligence.

Article 345

1. Whoever seizes nuclear materials or radioactive elements, even for non-profit purposes, shall be punished with a sentence of imprisonment from one to five years. That same punishment shall be imposed on whoever, without due authorisation, possesses, traffics, facilitates, processes, transforms, uses, stores, transports or eliminates nuclear materials or other hazardous radioactive substances that cause or may cause persons death or serious injury, or substantial damage to the quality of the air, soil quality or the quality of the water, or to animals or plants.

2. Should the act be carried out by forcible means, the punishment shall be imposed in its upper half.

3. Should the act be committed by means of violence or intimidation of persons, the offender shall be punished with the higher degree punishment.

4. Whoever, without due authorisation, were to produce such materials or substances, shall be punished with the higher degree punishment.

SUBCHAPTER 2. ON HAVOC

Article 346

1. Those who, by causing explosions or using any other means with a similar destructive power, were to cause the destruction of airports, ports, stations, buildings, public premises, deposits containing flammable or explosive materials, means of communication, mass transport resources, or sinking or running a ship aground, flooding, explosion of a mine or industrial facility, tearing up the rails of a railway, maliciously changing the signals used in such service for the safety of transportation resources, blowing up a bridge, destroying public highways, serious disturbance of any kind or means of communication, disturbance or interruption of the water or electricity supply, or of any other fundamental natural resource, shall be punished with a sentence of imprisonment from ten to twenty years, when the havoc caused necessarily endangered the life or integrity of persons.

2. When such a danger does not arise, the action shall be punished as damages ad defined in Article 266 of this Code.

3. If, in addition to that hazard, loss of life, damage to physical integrity or the health of persons has ensued, the acts shall be punished separately with the relevant punishment for each felony committed.

Article 347

Whoever, due to serious negligence, were to cause havoc, shall be punished with a sentence of imprisonment of one to four years.

SUBCHAPTER 3. ON OTHER OFFENCES OF RISK CAUSED BY EXPLOSIVES AND OTHER SUCH AGENTS

Article 348

1. Those who, in manufacturing, handling, transporting, holding or marketing explosives, flammable or corrosive, toxic or asphyxiating substances, or any other materials, appliances or devices that may cause havoc, breach the established safety regulations, specifically endangering life, the physical integrity or health of persons, or the environment, shall be punished with a sentence of imprisonment of six months to three years, a fine of twelve to twenty- four months and special barring from public employment and office, profession or trade for a term from six to twelve years. The same penalties shall be imposed on whoever unlawfully produces, imports, exports, commercialises or uses substances that destroy ozone.

2. Those responsible for surveillance, control and use of explosives that might cause havoc who, breaching the explosives regulations, have facilitated their effective loss or stealing, shall be punished with imprisonment of six months to three years, a fine of twelve to twenty- four months and special barring from public employment and office, profession or trade from six to twelve years.

3. In the cases defined in the preceding Sections, when a legal person is responsible for the acts pursuant to the terms established in Article 31 bis of this Code, the punishment of a fine from one to three years shall be imposed, except if, having proven the damage caused, the amount thereof were greater, in which case the fine shall be two to four times the amount of that damage.

Pursuant to the rules established in Article 66 bis, the Judges and Courts of Law may also impose the penalties established in Sub-Sections b) to g) of Section 7 of Article 33.

The penalties established in the preceding Sections shall be imposed in the upper half in the case of executives, directors or managers of the company, firm, organisation or operation.

4. Punishment by imprisonment of six months to one year, a fine from six to twelve months and special barring from public employment and office, profession or trade for a term of three to six years shall be imposed on the managers of factories, workshops, means of transport, depots and other establishments related to explosives that may cause criminal damage, when any one or number of the following conducts takes place:

a) Hindering inspection activity by the Authorities in matters of explosives safety;

b) Forging or concealing relevant information on compliance with mandatory safety measures related to explosives from the Authorities;

c) Disobeying specific orders by an Authority aimed at correcting serious anomalies detected in explosives safety matters.

Article 349

Those who breach the established safety measures in the handling, transport or possession of organisms, specifically endangering the life, physical integrity or health of persons or the environment, shall be punished with imprisonment of six months to two years, a fine from six to twelve months, and special barring from public employment and office, profession or trade for a term of three to six years.

Article 350

Without prejudice to what is set forth in Article 316, the penalties foreseen in the preceding Article shall be incurred by those who, when digging shafts or excavations, during construction or demolition of buildings, dams, channels or other similar works, or in their conservation, conditioning or maintenance, breach the established safety regulations, failure to comply with which may cause catastrophic results, and that specifically endanger the life, physical integrity of persons or the environment.

CHAPTER II

On fires

SUBCHAPTER 1. ON FELONIES OF ARSON

Article 351

Those who cause a fire involving threat to the life or physical integrity of persons, shall be punished with a sentence of imprisonment from ten to twenty years. The Judges or Courts of Law may impose the lower degree punishment in view of the lesser extent of the danger caused and the other circumstances of the fact.

When there is no danger to the life or physical integrity of persons, the acts shall be punished as damages as foreseen in Article 266 of this Code.

SUBCHAPTER 2. ON FOREST FIRES

Article 352

Whoever sets woods or forests on fire shall be punished with imprisonment from one to five years and a fine of twelve to eighteen months.

If this has endangered the life or physical integrity of persons, the act shall be punished as set forth in Article 351, imposing the punishment of a fine from twelve to twenty- four months in all cases.

Article 353

1. The penalties stated in the preceding Article shall be imposed in the upper half when the fire is especially serious, according to whether any of the following circumstances concur:

   1. When they cover a considerably large area;

   2. When they cause major or serious soil erosion effects;

   3. When they significantly alter the conditions of animal or plant life or affect any protected natural space;

   4. In all cases, when there is serious deterioration or destruction of the resources affected.

2. Those penalties shall also be imposed in the upper half when the principal acts to obtain economic profit from the effects arising from the fire.

Article 354

1. Whoever sets woods or forests on fire without the fire there spreading, shall be punished with a sentence of imprisonment of six months to one year and a fine from six to twelve months.

2. The conduct foreseen in the preceding Section shall be exempt of punishment if the fire is not propagated by the proactive, voluntary action of the principal.

Article 355

In all the cases foreseen in this Subchapter, the Judges or Courts of Law may order that zoning classification of the land in areas affected by a forest fire may not be changed for a term of up to thirty years. They may also order limitation or suppression of uses to which the areas affected by the fire have been put, as well as administrative seizure of the burned wood from the fire.

SUBCHAPTER 3. ON FIRES IN NON- FOREST AREAS

Article 356

Whoever sets fire to planted areas in non-forest areas, seriously damaging the environment, shall be punished with a sentence of imprisonment of six months to two years and a fine from six to twenty- four months.

SUBCHAPTER 4. ON ARSON OF OWN PROPERTY

Article 357

The arsonist of his own property shall be punished with a sentence of imprisonment of one to four years if fraud or damage to third parties is intended, if he has caused fraud or damage, if there is the hazard of propagation to a building, woods or plantations owned by others, or that may have seriously damaged the conditions of the wildlife, woods or natural environment.

SUBCHAPTER 5. COMMON PROVISION

Article 358

Whoever, due to serious negligence, were to cause any of the felonies of arson punished under the preceding Articles, shall be punished with the lower degree punishment, of those respectively foreseen for each case.

CHAPTER III

On felonies against public health

Article 359

Whoever, without being duly authorised, were to prepare substances that are harmful to health, or chemical products that may cause havoc, or who dispatches, supplies or trades in these, shall be punished with a sentence of imprisonment of six months to three years and a fine from six to twelve months, and special barring from profession or industry for a term of six months to two years.

Article 360

Whoever, being authorised to trade in the substances or products to which the preceding Article refers, dispatches or supplies them without complying with the formalities foreseen in the respective Laws and Regulations, shall be punished with the penalty of a fine from six to twelve months and barring from the profession or trade of six months to two years.

Article 361

Those who dispense or dispatch deteriorated or expired medicines, or who breach the technical demands related to their composition, stability and efficiency, or who replace one with another and thus endanger the life or health of persons shall be punished with imprisonment of six months to two years, a fine from six to eighteen months and special barring from profession or trade of six months to two years.

Article 361 bis

1. Those who, without therapeutic reason, prescribe, provide, dispense, supply, administer, offer or facilitate federated sportspersons who do not participate in competitions, non- federated sportspersons who perpetrate sport for leisure, or sportspersons who participate in competitions organised in Spain by sports organisations, prohibited substances or pharmaceutical groups, as well as non- regular methods, intended to increase their physical capacity or to modify the results of the competitions, that due to their content, repeated ingestion or other concurrent circumstances, endanger their life or health, shall be punished with imprisonment of six months to two years, a fine from six to eighteen months and special barring from public employment and office, profession or trade, from two to five years.

2. The penalties foreseen in the preceding Section shall be imposed in the upper half should the offence be committed when any of the following circumstances concur:

1. When the victim is a minor;

2. When deceit or intimidation are used;

3. When the offender has availed himself of his work or professional superiority.

Article 362

1. Punishment by imprisonment of six months to three years, a fine from six to eighteen months and special barring from profession or trade from one to three years shall apply to:

1. Whoever alters, at the time of manufacture or preparation, or at a subsequent moment, the quantity, the dosage or the genuine composition, as authorised or declared, of a medicine, fully or partially depriving it of its therapeutic effectiveness, and thus endangers the life or health of persons.

2. Whoever, in order to dispense or use them in any way, imitates or simulates medicines or substances that produce beneficial effects for health, making them appear to be real, and thus endangers the life or health of persons.

3. Whoever, being aware of their alteration and in order to dispense or assign them to use by other persons, stores on deposit, advertises or publicises, offers, displays, sells, facilitates or in any way uses the medicines stated, and thus endangers the life or health of persons.

2. The penalties of barring foreseen in this Article and in the previous ones shall be from three to six years when the acts are committed by pharmacists, or by the technical directors of legally authorised laboratories, in whose name and on behalf of whom they act.

3. In extremely serious cases, the Judges or Courts of Law, taking into account the personal circumstances of the principal and those of the act, may impose the penalties higher by one degree to those stated above.

Article 363

A sentence of imprisonment of one to four years, a fine from six to twelve months and special barring from profession, trade, industry or commerce for a term of three to six years shall be handed down to producers, distributors or traders who endanger the health of consumers:

1. Offering food products on the market with omission or alteration of the requisites established in the laws or regulations on expiry or composition;

2. Manufacturing or selling beverages or foodstuffs intended for public consumption that are damaging to health;

3. Trafficking with corrupted goods;

4. Preparing products whose use is not authorised and that are damaging to health, or trading with such;

5. Concealing or stealing items intended to be destroyed or disinfected, in order to trade with them.

Article 364

1. Whoever adulterates foodstuffs, substances or beverages intended for the food trade with additives or other unauthorised agents liable to cause damage to health of persons, shall be punished with the penalties of the preceding Article. If the convict is the owner or production manager of a food product factory, the punishment of special barring from profession, trade, industry or commerce from six to ten years shall also be imposed on him.

2. The same punishment shall be imposed on whoever carries out any of the following actions:

1. Administering prohibited substances that generate risk to the health of persons, or in higher doses, or for purposes other than those authorised, to animals whose meat or produce is intended for human consumption;

2. Slaughtering cattle or assigning the produce whereof to human consumption while being aware that they have been administered the substances mentioned in the preceding Section;

3. Slaughtering the cattle that has undergone therapeutic treatment with the substances mentioned in Section 1;

4. Dispatching slaughtered cattle meat or produce for public consumption without complying with the regulatory waiting periods foreseen.

Article 365

A sentence of imprisonment from two to six years shall be imposed on whoever poisons or adulterates the drinking water or foodstuffs intended for public use or consumption by a group of persons with infectious or other substances that may be seriously dangerous to health.

Article 366

In the case of the preceding Articles, the measure of closing the establishment, factory, laboratory or premises for a term of up to five years may be imposed, and in extremely serious cases, definitive closure may be ordered, as foreseen in Article 129.

Article 367

Should the acts foreseen in all the preceding Articles be perpetrated due to serious negligence, the respective lower degree penalties shall be imposed.

Article 368

Those who carry out acts of cultivation, preparation or trafficking, or who otherwise favour or facilitate the unlawful consumption of toxic drugs, narcotics or psychotropic substances, or who possess them for those purposes, shall be punished with imprisonment from three to six years and a fine of one to three times the value of the drug the offence concerns, if they are substances or products that cause serious damage to health, and of imprisonment from one to three years and a fine from one to two times the amount in the remaining cases.

Notwithstanding what is set forth in the preceding Paragraph, the Courts of Law may impose a lower degree punishment to those stated in view of the scarce importance of the facts and the offender's personal circumstances. This power may not be made use of if any of the circumstances referred to in Articles 369 bis and 370 concur.

Article 369

1. The penalties shall be imposed in one degree higher to those stated in the preceding Article, and a fine of one to four times the amount when any of the following circumstances concur:

   1. The offender is an authority, civil servant, medical practitioner, social worker, teacher or educator and acts while carrying out the duties of his office, profession or trade;

   2. The offender participates in other organised activities, or those whose carrying out is facilitated by committing the felony;

   3. The acts are perpetrated in establishments open to the public by those in charge or the employees thereof;

   4. The substances to which the preceding Article refers are provided to persons under the age of eighteen years, to the mentally disabled or to persons subject to detoxification or addiction treatment;

   5. The quantity of the substances the acts to which the preceding Article refers is notoriously large;

   6. Such substances are adulterated, manipulated or mixed together or with others, increasing possible damage to health;

   7. The actions described in the preceding Article take place at teaching centres, at military centres, establishments or units, within penitentiary institutions or at detoxification or addiction treatment centres, or in the surrounding areas thereof;

   8. The offender uses violence or displays or uses weapons to commit the offence

2. (Suppressed)

Article 369 bis

When the acts described in Article 368 have been carried out by those pertaining to a criminal organisation, prison sentences of nine to twelve years and a fine of one to four times the value of the drugs concerned shall be imposed, if they are substances and products that cause serious damage to health and of imprisonment for four years and six months to ten years and the same fine in the other cases.

The bosses, managers or directors of the organisation shall have the penalties higher by one degree to those stated in Section one imposed on them.

When, pursuant to the terms established in Article 31 bis, a legal person is responsible for the offences defined in the preceding two Articles, it shall have the following penalties imposed thereon:

   a) Fine from two to five years, or from three to five times the value of the drugs, when the resulting amount is higher, if the offence committed by a natural person has a punishment of imprisonment foreseen exceeding five years;

b) Fine from one to three years, or of two to four times the value of the drugs, when the resulting amount is higher, if the offence committed by a natural person has a punishment of imprisonment foreseen exceeding two years not included in the preceding Sub-Section.

Pursuant to the rules established in Article 66 bis, the Judges and Courts of Law may also impose the penalties established in Sub-Sections b) to g) of Section 7 of Article 33.

Article 370

The punishment imposed shall be higher by one or two degrees to that stated in Article 368 when:

1. Persons under the age of eighteen years or the mentally handicapped are used to commit those felonies;

2. They are the bosses, directors or managers of the organisations to whom circumstance 2 of Section 1 of Article 369 refers.

3. The actions described in Article 368 are extremely serious.

Extreme seriousness is understood to concur in cases in which the quantity of the substances to which Article 368 refers notably exceeds that deemed a notorious amount, or when using ships, vessels or aircraft as the specific means of transport, or when perpetrating the conduct stated simulating international trading operations between companies, or in the case of international networks dedicated to such activities, or when three or more of the circumstances foreseen in Article 369.1 concur simultaneously.

In the cases of the preceding Sub-Section 2 and 3 the offenders shall also have a fine of one to three times the value of the drugs the offence concerns imposed on them.

Article 371

1. Whoever manufactures, transports, distributes, trades or possesses equipment, materials or substances listed in Table I and Table II of the United Nations Convention, done at Vienna on 20th December 1988, against illegal traffic in narcotic drugs and psychotropic substances, and any other products added to the aforesaid Convention or that may be included in future Conventions ratified by Spain being aware that they shall be used for the unlawful cultivation, production or manufacture of toxic drugs, narcotics or psychotropic substances, or for those purposes, shall be punished with a sentence of imprisonment from three to six years and a fine of one to three times the value of the goods or items concerned.

2. The punishment stated shall be imposed in the upper half when the persons who perpetrate the acts described in preceding Section while belonging to an organisation dedicated to the ends stated therein, and the higher degree punishment in the case of bosses, directors or managers of those organisations or partnerships.

In such cases, the Judges or Courts of Law shall impose, in addition to the relevant penalties, that of special barring of the convict from practising his profession or industry for a term of three to six years, and the other measures foreseen in Article 369.2.

Article 372

Should the acts foreseen in this Chapter be perpetrated by an entrepreneur, broker in the financial sector, medical practitioner, civil servant, social worker, teacher or educator, in the exercise of his office, profession or trade, in addition to the relevant punishment, he shall be handed down that of special barring from public employment and office, profession or trade, industry or commerce, of three to ten years. The punishment shall be imposed of absolute barring from ten to twenty years when such acts are perpetrated by an authority or agent thereof, while carrying out the duties of his office. For these purposes, medical practitioners are construed to be doctors, psychologists, persons who hold higher educational health and veterinary qualifications, pharmacists and the employees thereof.

Article 373

Provocation, conspiracy and solicitation to commit the felonies foreseen in Articles 368 to 372 shall be punished with the penalty lower by one or two degrees to the relevant one, respectively, for the acts foreseen in the preceding provisions.

Article 374

1. The felonies foreseen in Articles 301.1, Section two, and 368 to 372, in addition to the relevant penalties to be imposed for the offence committed, shall give rise to seizure of the toxic drugs, narcotics or psychotropic substances, the equipment, materials and substances mentioned in Article 371, as well the goods, means, instruments and gains therefrom, subject to what is set forth in Article 127 of this Code and the following special rules:

1. The drugs, narcotics and psychotropic substances shall be destroyed by the administrative authority entrusted with their custody, once the appropriate analytical reports have been carried out and sufficient samples thereof stored, except if the competent judicial authority has ordered them to be conserved intact. Once the judgement is final, destruction of the samples provided shall be carried out, or destruction of all the substances confiscated, should the competent judicial body have ordered their conservation.

2. In order to guarantee the effectiveness of the confiscation, the assets, means, instruments and gains may be apprehended or seized and placed in deposit by the judicial authority from the moment of the first diligences.

3. The judicial authority may order that, with due guarantees for their conservation and while substantiating the proceedings, the objects seized, if of lawful commerce, may provisionally be used by the Judicial Police charged with suppression of illegal drug trafficking.

4. If it were not possible to seize the goods and items stated in the preceding Sub- Section for any reason, seizure of others of an equivalent value may be ordered.

5. When the goods, means, instruments and gains from the offence have disappeared from the assets of those presumed to be responsible, seizure of their value from other different goods, even if lawful in origin, pertaining to those responsible, may be ordered.

2. The goods seized may be disposed of, without waiting for the final judgement to be handed down, in the following cases:

a) When the owner specifically abandons them;

b) When their conservation may be hazardous to public health or safety, or may give rise to an important decrease in their value, or seriously affect their normal use and operation. This shall be construed to include those that, without suffering material deterioration, depreciate over time.

When these cases arise, the judicial authority shall order the disposal thereof, either on its own motion, or at the request of the Public Prosecutor, the State Attorney or the procedural representation of the Autonomous Communities, local entities or other public entities, and following hearing of the party concerned.

The proceeds of the disposal, which shall be carried out by any of the manners legally foreseen, shall be held on deposit whilst awaiting the result of the relevant legal proceedings, after expenses of any kind that have arisen have been deducted.

3. In the offences described in the preceding Sections, the Judges and Courts of Law that hear the cause may declare the nullity of the legal acts or transactions by virtue of which they have been conveyed, encumbered or the ownership or rights on to the assets and items stated in the preceding Sub-Sections have been changed.

4. The goods, means, instruments and gains definitively confiscated by judgement, not applied to settlement of the civil liabilities arising from the offence or the procedural costs, shall be fully awarded to the State.

Article 375

Convictions by foreign Judges or Courts of Law for offences of the same kind as foreseen in Articles 368 to 372 of this Chapter shall have the effects of recidivism, except if the criminal record has been cancelled, or might be under Spanish Law.

Article 376

In the cases foreseen in Articles 368 to 372, the Judges or Courts of Law, giving the reasons in their judgement, may impose a lower punishment by one or two degrees to that stated by the law for the offence concerned, as long as the subject has voluntarily abandoned his criminal activities and has actively collaborated with the authorities or their agents either to prevent the offence from taking place, or to obtain decisive proof for identification of capture of others who are responsible or to prevent actions or the furtherance of the organisations or assemblies to which they have belonged or with which they may have collaborated.

Likewise, in the cases foreseen in Articles 368 to 372, the Judges or Courts of Law may impose the punishment lower by one or two degrees upon the convict who, being addicted to drugs at the moment of committing the acts, sufficiently accredits that he has successfully completed detoxification treatment, as long as the quantity of toxic drugs, narcotics or psychotropic substances was not of notorious importance or extreme seriousness.

Article 377

In order to determine the amount of the fines imposed pursuant to Articles 368 to 372, the value of the drugs the felony involves, or the goods or items seized shall be the end price of the product or, as appropriate, the profit or gains obtained by the convict, or that he might have obtained.

Article 378

The payments made by the convict for in relation to one or several of the felonies to which Articles 368 to 372 refer shall be applied in the following order:

1. To repairing the damage caused and compensation of damage;

2. To compensating the State for the amount of expenses it has incurred on account of the case;

3. To the fine;

4. To the costs of the specific or private prosecutor, when the judgement orders their payment;

5. To the other procedural costs, even those of defending the accused, without preference among the parties concerned.

CHAPTER IV

On felonies against road safety

Article 379

1. Whoever drives a motor vehicle or a moped at a speed that exceeds the speed permitted by law by sixty kilometres per hour in urban streets, or by eighty kilometres per hour on non-urban roads, shall be punished with a sentence of imprisonment from three to six months, or with that of a fine from six to twelve months, or with that of community service from thirty one to ninety days, and, in all cases, with that of deprivation of the right to drive motor vehicles and mopeds for a term exceeding one and up to four years.

2. The same penalties shall be applied to whoever drives a motor vehicle or moped under the influence of toxic drugs, narcotics, psychotropic substances or alcoholic beverages. In all cases, whoever drives with a rate of alcohol in expired air exceeding 0.60 milligrams per litre, or a rate of alcohol in the blood exceeding 1.2 grams per litre, shall be sentenced to those penalties.

Article 380

1. Whoever drives a motor vehicle or a moped with manifest recklessness and specifically endangers the life or integrity of persons shall be punished with imprisonment of six months to two years and deprivation of the right to drive motor vehicles and mopeds for a term exceeding one and up to six years.

2. For the purposes this provision, driving under the circumstances foreseen in Sections 1 and in the second sentence of Section 2 of the preceding Article shall be deemed manifestly reckless.

Article 381

1. Punishment by imprisonment from two to five years, a fine of twelve to twenty- four months and deprivation of the right to drive motor vehicles and mopeds during a period from six to ten years shall be handed down to whoever, manifestly disregarding the life of others, behaves as described in the preceding Article.

2. When the life or integrity of persons has not been specifically placed in danger, the penalties shall be of imprisonment from one to two years, a fine from six to twelve months and deprivation of the right to drive motor vehicles and mopeds for the term foreseen in the preceding Section.

3. (Suppressed)

Article 382

When through the acts penalised in Articles 379, 380 and 381, the doer were to cause, in addition to the risk prevented, a result amounting to a felony, whatever its seriousness, the Judges or Courts of Law shall only consider the most seriously penalised felony, applying the punishment in its upper half and, in all cases, ordering compensation of the civil liability that has been incurred.

Article 383

The driver who, when required to by a law-enforcement officer, refuses to submit to the legally established alcohol level tests, and those for the presence of toxic drugs, narcotics and psychotropic substances referred to in the preceding Articles, shall be punished with imprisonment of six months to one year and deprivation of the right to drive motor vehicles and mopeds for a term exceeding one and up to four years.

Article 384

Whoever drives a motor vehicle or moped in the cases loss of validity of his driving licence or permit due to loss of all the points legally assigned, shall be punished with a sentence of imprisonment from three to six months, or with that of a fine from twelve to twenty- four months, or with that of community service of thirty one to ninety days.

The same punishment shall be imposed on whoever drives after precautionary or final removal of his driving licence or permit by court decision, and whoever drives a motor vehicle or moped without ever having obtained a driving licence or permit.

Article 385

Whoever causes a serious risk to traffic in any of the following manners shall be punished with a sentence of imprisonment of six months to two years or a fine of twelve to twenty- four months and community service from ten to forty days:

1. Placing unforeseeable obstacles on the roadway, spilling slippery or flammable substances or changing, stealing or cancelling out signs or by any other means;

2. Not re-establishing road safety when obliged to do so.

Article 385 bis

The motor vehicle or moped used in the acts foreseen in this Chapter shall be deemed an instrument of the offence for the purposes of Articles 127 and 128.

Article 385 ter

In the felonies foreseen in Articles 379, 383, 384 and 385, the Judge or Court of Law, may hand down a reasoned judgement that may lower a sentence of imprisonment by one degree in view of the lower extent of the risk caused and the other circumstances of fact.

TITLE XVIII

On forgery

CHAPTER I

On forgery of currency and tax stamps

Article 386

A sentence of imprisonment from eight to twelve years and a fine from one to ten times the apparent monetary value shall be handed down to:

1. Whoever alters the legal tender or forges money;

2. Whoever brings forged or altered money into the country or exports it;

3. Whoever transports, issues or distributes false or altered money in collusion with a forger, counterfeiter, introducer or exporter.

Possessing forged currency for its issue or distribution shall be punished with the penalty lower by one or two degrees, in view of its value and the degree of collusion with the principals mentioned in the preceding Sub-Sections. The same punishment shall be imposed on whoever acquires forged currency in order to put it into circulation, knowing it to be false.

Whoever, having received forged money in good faith, spends or passes it on after having realised it is forged shall be punished with a sentence of imprisonment from three to six months or a fine from six to twenty- four months, if the apparent value of the money exceeds four hundred euros.

Should the offender belong to a company, organisation or assembly, even if transitory in nature, dedicated to perpetrating such activities, the Judge or Court of Law may hand down any or several of the consequences foreseen in Article 129 of this Code.

Article 387

For the purposes of the preceding Article, money is construed to be the coinage and paper money of legal tender. The national currency of other countries of the European Union and foreign currencies shall be equally considered.

Article 388

Judgement by a foreign court, handed down for an offence of the same kind as those included in this Chapter, shall be equivalent to sentences by Spanish Judges or Courts of Law for the purposes of recidivism, except if the criminal record has been cancelled, or might have been pursuant to Spanish Law.

Article 389

Whoever forges or issues postal stamps or tax stamps in collusion with a forger, or imports them to Spain while aware of they are false, shall be punished with a sentence of imprisonment of six months to three years.

The acquirer in good faith of postal stamps or tax stamps who, aware that they are false, distributes or uses them in an amount exceeding four hundred euros shall be punished with a sentence of imprisonment from three to six months or a fine from six to twenty- four months.

CHAPTER II

On documentary forgery

SUBCHAPTER 1. ON FORGERY OF PUBLIC, OFFICIAL AND BUSINESS DOCUMENTS AND OF THE DISPATCHES TRANSMITTED BY TELECOMMUNICATIONS SERVICES

Article 390

1. Punishment by imprisonment from three to six years, a fine from six to twenty- four months and special barring for a term from two to six years, shall be handed down to the authority or public officer who, while carrying out the duties of office, commits forgery:

  1. By altering any of the essential elements or requisites of a document;

  2. Simulating all or part of a document, so as to lead to error concerning its authenticity;

  3. Claiming intervention in an act by persons who were not party to it, or attributing those who intervened declarations or statements other than those they made;

  4. Untruthful narration of the facts.

2. The same penalties as stated in the preceding Section shall apply to whoever is a responsible person in any religious confession and commits any of the conducts described in the preceding Section, regarding acts and documents that may have an effect on the status of persons or the civil order.

Article 391

The authority or public officer who, due to serious negligence, were to incur any of the forgeries described in the preceding Article or who causes another to commit them, shall be punished with the penalty of a fine from six to twelve months and suspension from public employment and office for a term of six months to one year.

Article 392

1. The private individual who were to commit any forgery described in the first Sub-Section of Section 1 of Article 390 shall be punished with imprisonment of six months to three years and a fine from six to twelve months.

2. The same penalties shall be imposed upon whoever, without having intervened in the forgery, were to trade in any way with a false identity document. A sentence of imprisonment shall be handed down of six months to one year and a fine of three to six months, to whoever knowingly uses a forged identity document.

This provision is applicable even when the forged identity document appears to belong to another State of the European Union or a third country, or that has been forged or acquired in another State of the European Union or in a third country, if it is used or traded in Spain.

Article 393

Whoever uses a forged document of the types described in the preceding Articles in a trial, or to harm another, knowing it is forged, shall be punished with the degree of punishment below that provided for forgers.

Article 394

1. The authority or public officer entrusted with the telecommunications service who supposes or forges a telegraphic dispatch, or another inherent to such services, shall incur a sentence of imprisonment of six months to three years and special barring for a term from two to six years.

2. Whoever, knowing it is forged, makes use of a false dispatch to damage another, shall be punished with the lower degree punishment to that set for forgers.

SUBCHAPTER 2. ON FORGERY OF PRIVATE DOCUMENTS

Article 395

Whoever, to damage another, were to commit any of the forgeries foreseen in the first three Sub-Sections of Section of Article 390, shall be punished with a sentence of imprisonment of six months to two years.

Article 396

Whoever, knowing that it is false, were to produce or make use of a false document of those described in the preceding Article in a trial, or to damage another, shall incur the lower degree punishment to that set for the forgers.

SUBCHAPTER 3. ON FORGERY OF CERTIFICATES

Article 397

A medical practitioner who issues a forged certificate shall be punished with the penalty of a fine from three to twelve months.

Article 398[12]

Any public authority or civil servant who issues false certification that is of limited importance in terms of legally recognised instruments shall be punished with a suspension of between six months and two years.

This rule does not apply to certificates relating to social security and the treasury.

[12] Amended by single art. 11 of Organic Law 7/2012 of 27 December

Article 399

1. Whoever forges a certificate of those described in the preceding Articles shall be punished with the penalty of a fine from three to six months.

2. That same punishment shall be imposed on whoever knowingly uses the certification, as well as whoever, without having intervened in its forgery, trades with it in any way.

3. This provision is applicable even when the forged certificate appears to belong to another State of the European Union or a third country, or that has been forged or acquired in another State of the European Union or in a third country, if it is used in Spain.

SUBCHAPTER 4: ON FORGERY OF CREDIT AND DEBIT CARDS AND TRAVELLERS' CHEQUES

Article 399 bis

1. Whoever alters, copies, reproduces or in any other way forges credit or debit cards or travellers' cheques, shall be punished with a sentence of imprisonment from four to eight years. The punishment shall be imposed in the upper half when the forged items affect persons at large, or when the acts are committed within the set of a criminal organisation dedicated to such activities.

When, pursuant to the terms established in Article 31 bis, a legal person is responsible for the above offences, the punishment of a fine from two to five years shall be imposed.

Pursuant to the rules established in Article 66 bis, the Judges and Courts of Law may also impose the penalties established in Sub-Sections b) to g) of Section 7 of Article 33.

2. Possessing forged credit or debit cards or travellers' cheques intended for distribution or trade shall be punished with the penalty set for forgery.

3. Whoever, without having intervened in the forgery, were to use forged credit or debit cards or travellers' cheques, to the detriment of another and being aware they are forged, shall be punished with a sentence of imprisonment from two to five years.

CHAPTER III

General provisions

Article 400

Manufacturing or possessing tools, materials, instruments, substances, machinery, computer programs or appliances specifically used to commit the offences described in the preceding Chapters, shall be punished with the penalty stated in each case for the principals.

Article 400 bis

In the cases described in Articles 392, 393, 394, 396 and 399 of this Code, use of a forged document, dispatch, certification or identity document shall also be construed as the use of the relevant authentic documents, dispatches, certificates or identity documents when carried out by whoever is not authorised to do so.

CHAPTER IV

On identity fraud

Article 401

Whoever usurps the identity of another shall be punished with a sentence of imprisonment of six months to three years.

CHAPTER V

On impersonation of a public officer and unlawful practice of a profession

Article 402

Whoever unlawfully carries out acts inherent to the duties of an authority or public officer, attributing himself official status, shall be punished with a sentence of imprisonment from one to three years.

Article 403

Whoever perpetrates acts inherent to a profession without holding the relevant academic qualification issued or recognised in Spain under the laws in force, shall incur the punishment of a fine from six to twelve months. Should the professional activity carried out require an official qualification that accredits the necessary skills and legally entitle the person to practice, and he not hold that qualification, the punishment of a fine from three to five months shall be imposed.

Should the offender also publicly claim the professional status covered by such qualification, a sentence of imprisonment of six months to two years shall be handed down.

TITLE XIX

On felonies against the public administration

CHAPTER I

Perverting the course of justice by civil servants and other injustice in their conduct

Article 404

The authority or public officer who, being aware of the injustice thereof, were to hand down an arbitrary resolution in an administrative matter, shall be penalised with the punishment of special barring from public employment and office for a term of seven to ten years.

Article 405

The authority or public officer who, in exercise of his duties of office, and being aware of the unlawfulness thereof, were to propose, appoint or grant possession to hold office in a specific public post to any person without him fulfilling the legal requisites established for such purpose, shall be punished with the penalties of a fine of three to eight months and suspension from public employment and office for a term of six months to two years.

Article 406

The same punishment of a fine shall be imposed on whoever accepts the proposal, appointment or the taking possession mentioned in the preceding Section, knowing the person lacks the legally established requisites.

CHAPTER II

On abandoning one's post and omission of the duty to pursue felonies

Article 407

1. The authority or public officer who abandons his post in order not to prevent or not to pursue any of the felonies included in Titles XXI, XXII, XXIII and XXIV shall be punished with a sentence of imprisonment of one to four years and absolute barring from public employment and office for a term from six to ten years. If he abandoned in order not to prevent or not to pursue any other offence, the punishment of special barring from public employment and office for a term from one to three years shall be imposed on him.

2. The same penalties shall be imposed, respectively, when the abandonment is intended so as not to execute the relevant penalties for those felonies imposed by the competent judicial authority.

Article 408

The authority or public officer who, failing in the obligations of his office, were to intentionally cease to promote persecution of the felonies that he or his officers obtain knowledge of, shall incur the punishment of special barring from public employment and office for a term of six months to two years.

Article 409

Authorities or civil servants who promote, direct or organise collective, manifestly unlawful abandonment of a public service, shall be penalised with the punishment of a fine from eight to twelve months and suspension from public employment and office for a term of six months to two years.

Authorities or civil servants who merely take part in collective or manifestly illegal abandonment of an essential public service, with serious damage to it or to the community, shall be punished with the penalty of a fine from eight to twelve months.

CHAPTER III

On disobedience and failure to provide assistance

Article 410

1. Authorities or civil servants who openly refuse to duly fulfil court resolutions, decisions or orders of a higher authority, handed down within the scope of their respective powers and complying with the legal formalities, shall be punished with a fine from three to twelve months and special barring from public employment and office

2. Notwithstanding what is set forth in preceding Section, no criminal liability shall be incurred by authorities or public officers due to not fulfilling an order that constitutes a manifest, clear and absolute breach of a provision of an Act of Parliament or of any other general provision.

Article 411

The authority or public officer who, having suspended execution of orders by his superiors for any reason other than that stated in Section 2 of the preceding Article, were to disobey them after the latter have not approved the suspension, shall incur the penalties of a fine of twelve to twenty- four months and special barring from public employment and office for a term from one to three years.

Article 412

1. The civil servant who, when required to by the competent authority, does not provide due assistance to the Judicial Administration or another public service, shall incur the penalties of a fine from three to twelve months, and suspension from public employment and office for a term of six months to two years.

2. If the person ordered is an authority, head or commander of a public force or a law enforcement officer, the penalties of a fine of twelve to eighteen months and suspension from public employment and office for a term of two to three years shall be imposed.

3. The authority or public officer who, when called on by a private individual to provide any assistance he is obliged to provide due to his office to prevent a felony against the life of persons, abstains from providing it, shall be punished with the penalty of a fine from eighteen to twenty- four months and special barring from public employment and office for a term of three to six years.

If it is a felony against the integrity, sexual freedom, health or liberty of persons, he shall be punished with the penalty of a fine from twelve to eighteen months and suspension from public employment and office from one to three years.

Should that call be to prevent any other felony or another harm, he shall be punished with the penalty of a fine from three to twelve months and suspension from public employment and office for a term of six months to two years.

CHAPTER IV

On disloyalty in the custody of documents and on disclosing secrets

Article 413

The authority or public officer who knowingly steals, destroys, full or partially cancels or conceals documents the custody of which is entrusted to him due to his office, shall incur a prison sentence of one to four years, a fine for seven to twenty- four months, and special barring from public employment and office for a term of three to six years.

Article 414

1. The authority or public officer who, due to his office, is entrusted the custody of documents to which the competent authority has restricted access, and who knowingly destroys or deactivates the means provided to prevent such access or consents their destruction or deactivation, shall incur a sentence of imprisonment of six months to one year or fine from six to twenty- four months and, in all cases, special barring from public employment and office for a term from one to three years.

2. The individual who destroys or deactivates the means referred to in the preceding Section shall be punished with the penalty of a fine from six to eighteen months.

Article 415

The authority or public officer not included in preceding Section who, knowingly and without due authorisation, accesses or permits access to secret documents the custody of which is entrusted to him due to his office, shall incur the punishment of a fine from six to twelve months, and special barring from public employment and office for a term from one to three years.

Article 416

Punishment by imprisonment or fine immediately below the ones respectively stated in the preceding three Articles shall be imposed on private individuals circumstantially charged with dispatch or custody of documents, commissioned by the Government or the authorities or civil servants to whom they have been entrusted due to their office, who behave as described therein.

Article 417

1. The authority or public officer who reveals secrets or information that come to his knowledge due to his position or office and that should not be disclosed, shall incur the punishment of a fine from twelve to eighteen months and special barring from public employment and office for a term from one to three years.

Should the disclosure referred to in the preceding Section cause serious damage to the public interest or to a third party, the punishment shall be imprisonment from one to three years, and special barring from public employment and office for a term of three to five years.

2. If the secrets of a private individual are involved, the penalties shall been those of imprisonment from two to four years, a fine of twelve to eighteen months, and suspension from public employment and office for a term from one to three years.

Article 418

The private individual who takes advantage of the inside information he may obtain from a civil servant or authority for himself or for a third party shall be punished with a fine of one to three times the profit obtained or facilitated. Should serious damage to the public interest or to a third party be caused, the punishment shall be imprisonment from one to six years.

CHAPTER V

On corruption

Article 419

The authority or public officer who, to his own advantage or that of a third party, were to receive or solicit, personally or through an intermediary, handouts, favours or remunerations of any kind, or who were to accept an offer or promise to do, while carrying out the duties of his office, in order to carry out an act contrary to the duties inherent thereto, or not to carry out these, or to unfairly delay those he must carry out, shall incur a sentence of imprisonment from three to six years, a fine of twelve to twenty- four months and special barring from public employment and office for a term of seven to twelve years, without prejudice to the relevant punishment for the act perpetrated, omitted or delayed due to the remuneration or promise, if that constitutes a felony.

Article 420

The authority or public officer who, to his own advantage or that of a third party, were to receive or solicit, personally or through an intermediary, handouts, favours or remuneration of any kind, or who were to accept an offer or promise to carry out an act inherent to his office, shall incur a sentence of imprisonment of two to four years, a fine of twelve to twenty- four months and special barring from public employment and office for a term of three to seven years.

Article 421

The penalties stated in the preceding Articles shall also be imposed when the handout, favour or remuneration were received or solicited by the authority or public officer, in the respective cases, as a reward for the conduct described in those Articles.

Article 422

The authority or public officer who, to his own advantage or that of a third party, were to accept, personally or through an intermediary, a handout or gift offered to him in view of his office or duty, shall incur a sentence of imprisonment of six months to one year and suspension from public employment and office from one to three years.

Article 423

The terms set forth in the preceding Articles shall also be applicable to juries, arbitrators, experts, administrators or receivers appointed by the court, or any others acting to carry out a public duty.

Article 424

1. The private individual who offers or delivers a handout or remuneration of any kind to an authority, civil servant or person who participates in the exercise of public duties in order for the latter to perpetrate an act that is against the duties inherent to his office, or an act inherent to his office, or in order for him not to carry out, or to delay what he should carry out, or in consideration of his office or duty, shall be punished in the respective cases, with the same prison sentences and fine as the corrupt authority, officer or person.

2. Should a private individual deliver the handout or remuneration following solicitation by the authority, civil servant or person who participates in exercise of public duties, the same prison sentences and fine shall be imposed on him as on the former.

3. Should the action achieved or intended by the authority or officer be related to contracting proceedings, subsidies or auctions called by public administrations or entities, penalties shall be handed down to the natural persons and, when appropriate, the company, partnership or organisation concerned, of barring to obtain public subsidies and aid, to enter contracts with public sector institutions, entities or bodies and to enjoy tax and Social Security benefits or incentives for a term from three to seven years.

Article 425

When bribery takes place in a criminal case in favour of the accused, perpetrated by the spouse or other person bound by a similar stable emotional relation, or by any ascendant, descendent, biological or adopted sibling or similar of the same degree, the briber shall be subject to a sentence of imprisonment of six months to one year.

Article 426

Should a natural person who has coincidentally obtained a handout or other remuneration made by an authority or public officer report the fact to the authority whose duty is of proceeding to investigate the matter, before proceedings commence, as long as no more than two months have elapsed from the date of the events, he shall be exempt of punishment for the felony of corruption.

Article 427

1. The terms set forth preceding Articles shall also be applicable when charges are brought against, or the acts concerned affect officers of the European Union or civil servants who are nationals of another Member State of the Union. To these ends, an officer of the European Union shall be construed to be:

1. All persons who have civil servant status or that of a hired agent pursuant to the European Community Officers' Statute, or regime applicable to other agents of the European Union.

2. All persons seconded to the European Union by the Member States, or by any public or private body exercising the equivalent functions carried out by civil servants or other agents of the European Union.

3. The members of bodies created pursuant to the European Union Constituting Treaties, as well as the staff of such bodies, to the extent that the European Union Officers' Statute or regime to which other agents of the European Union are subject is not applicable to them.

A national officer of another Member State of the Union shall also be construed as one with that status for the purposes of application of the criminal laws of that Member State.

2. When, pursuant to the terms established in Article 31 bis, a legal person is responsible for the felonies defined in this Chapter, it shall have the following penalties imposed thereon:

a) Fine from two to five years, or from three to five times the profit obtained when the resulting amount is higher, if the offence committed by a natural person has a punishment of imprisonment foreseen exceeding five years;

b) Fine from one to three years, or of two to four times the profit obtained when the resulting amount is higher, if the offence committed by a natural person has a punishment foreseen of more than two years custodial sentence not included in the preceding Section;

c) Fine of six months to two years, or of two to three times the profit obtained if the resulting amount is higher, in the rest of the cases.

Pursuant to the rules established in Article 66 bis, the Judges and Courts of Law may also impose the penalties established in Sub-Sections b) to g) of Section 7 of Article 33.

CHAPTER VI

On influence peddling

Article 428

A civil servant or authority who influences another public officer or authority, availing himself of the powers of his office or any other situation arising from his personal or hierarchical relation with the latter, or with any other officer or authority to attain a resolution that may directly or indirectly generate a financial benefit for himself or a third party, shall incur imprisonment of six months to two years, a fine of one to two times the benefit intended or obtained and special barring from public employment and office for a term of three to six years. If the intended benefit were obtained, these penalties shall be imposed in the upper half.

Article 429

Whoever influences a civil servant or authority taking advantage of any situation arising from his personal relation with him or with another public officer or authority to obtain a resolution that may directly or indirectly generate a financial benefit for him or for a third party, shall be punished with imprisonment of six months to two years and a fine of one to two times the benefit intended or obtained. If the intended benefit were obtained, these penalties shall be imposed in the upper half.

Article 430

Those who, offering to behave in the manner described in the preceding Articles, request handouts, presents or any other remuneration from third parties, or accept offers or promises, shall be punished with a sentence of imprisonment of six months to one year.

When, pursuant to the terms established in Article 31 bis of this Code, a legal person is responsible for the offences defined in this Chapter, the punishment of a fine from six months to two years shall be imposed.

Pursuant to the rules established in Article 66 bis, the Judges and Courts of Law may also impose the penalties established in Sub-Sections b) to g) of Section 7 of Article 33

Article 431

In all the cases foreseen in this Chapter and in the previous one, the handouts, presents or gifts shall be confiscated.

CHAPTER VII

On embezzlement

Article 432

1. The authority or public officer who, for profit, steals or allows a third party, with the same intention, to steal public funds or property he has under his charge due to his duties, shall incur a sentence of imprisonment from three to six years and absolute barring for a term from six to ten years.

2. A sentence of imprisonment shall be imposed from four to eight years and that of absolute barring for a term of ten to twenty years, if the embezzlement is especially serious, in view of the value of the sums embezzled and the damage or hindrance caused to the public service. The same penalties shall be applied if the items misappropriated are listed due to their heritage or artistic value, or if they are goods assigned to public catastrophe relief.

3. When the amount embezzled does not reach the sum of 4,000 euros, the penalties imposed shall be a fine exceeding two and up to four months, imprisonment from six months to three years and suspension from public employment and office for a term of up to three years.

Article 433

The authority or public officer who puts the funds or assets placed under his charge due to his duties to other uses shall incur the punishment of a fine from six to twelve months, and suspension from public employment and office for a term of six months to three years.

Should the offender not reimburse the amount embezzled within ten days following that of the proceedings being brought, the penalties of the preceding Article shall be imposed on him.

Article 433 bis[13]

1. Any public authority or civil servant who, intending to cause financial harm to the public entity by which he is employed, falsifies its accounts, the documents that should reflect its financial situation or the information contained

---
[13] Added by single art. 12 of Organic Law 7/2012 of 27 December.

in them, shall be punished with specific disqualification from public employment or office for a period of between one and ten years and a fine of between twelve and twenty-four months.

2. Any public authority or civil servant who, intending to cause financial harm to the public entity by which he is employed, provides third parties with untruthful information relating to its financial situation or any of the documents or information referred to in the preceding section shall be punished with the same sentences.

3. If the entity is caused financial harm, prison sentences of between one and four years, specific disqualification from public employment or office for a period of between three and ten years and a fine of between twelve and twenty-four months shall be imposed.

Article 434

The authority or public officer who, for his own benefit or that of others, and causing serious damage to the public interest, puts the real or personal properties pertaining to any administration or entity of the State, Autonomous Communities, Local Councils or bodies dependent on any of them, shall incur imprisonment from one to three years and special barring from public employment and office for a term of three to six years.

Article 435

The provisions of this Chapter cover:

1. Those who are in charge of funds, revenue or assets of the Public Administrations for any reason;

2. Natural persons legally appointed as custodians of public funds or property;

3. The administrators or custodians of money or assets, embargoed, seized or deposited by the public authority, even though they belong to private owners.

CHAPTER VIII

On fraud and illegal taxation

Article 436

The authority or public officer who, acting due to his office in any act of the modes of public contracting, or in settlement of public properties or credit, comes to an arrangement with the parties concerned or schemes in any other way to defraud any public institution, shall incur imprisonment from one to three years and special barring from public employment and office for a term from six to ten years. The private individual who has schemed with the authority or public officer shall have the same punishment of imprisonment imposed on him as the latter, as well as that of barring to obtain public subsidies and aid, for contracting with institutions, bodies or entities that form part of the public sector, and to take advantage of tax and Social Security rebates for a term from two to five years.

Article 437

The authority or public officer who directly or indirectly demands undue fees, tariffs or fees, or those in an amount exceeding those legally set, shall be punished, without prejudice to the reimbursement he is obliged to carry out, with the penalties of a fine from six to twenty- four months and suspension from public employment and office for a term of six months to four years.

Article 438

The authority or public officer who, abusing his office, were to commit any offence of swindling or misappropriation, shall incur the penalties respectively stated for these, in the upper half, and special barring from public employment and office for a term from two to six years.

CHAPTER IX

On prohibited negotiations and activities for civil servants and on abuse when carrying out their official duties

Article 439

The authority or public officer who, having to intervene, due to his office, in any kind of contract, matter, operation or activity, takes advantage of that circumstance to force or facilitate any kind of participation, either direct or by intermediary, in such transactions or actions, shall incur a sentence of imprisonment of six months to two years, a fine of twelve to twenty- four months and special barring from public employment and office for a term of one to four years.

Article 440

Experts, arbitrators and executors who behave in the manner foreseen in the preceding Article, regarding assets and items in the appraisal, distribution or award of which they have intervened, and guardians, carers or executors in relation to the properties of their pupils or the heirs to the estate, shall be punished with the penalty of a fine from twelve to twenty- four months and special barring from public employment and office, profession or trade, safekeeping, guardianship or care, as appropriate, for a term of three to six years.

Article 441

The authority or public officer who, outside the cases allowed by the Laws or Regulations, personally or through an intermediary, carries out a professional activity or permanent or occasional advice, dependent on or in the service of private concerns or individuals, in matters in which he must intervene or has intervened in due to his office, or in those that are processed, reported or resolved at the office or management centre where he is assigned or to which he reports, shall incur the penalties of a fine from six to twelve months, and suspension from public employment and office for a term from one to three years.

Article 442

The authority or public officer who makes use of a secret he has knowledge of due to his position or office, or of inside information, in order to obtain financial benefit for himself or for a third party, shall incur the penalties of a fine of one to three times the benefit intended, obtained or facilitated and special barring from public employment and office for a term of two to four years. If he obtains the intended benefit, the penalties shall be imposed in the upper half.

If serious damage to the public interests or to a third party is caused, the punishment shall be imprisonment from one to six years, and special barring from public employment and office for a term of seven to ten years. For the purposes of this Article, inside information is construed to be all information of a specific nature that is obtained exclusively due to the position or public office, and that has not been notified, published or disclosed.

Article 443

1. The authority or public officer who solicits the sexual services of a person, for himself or spouse, or for another person with whom he is bound by a stable relation of a similar emotional nature, ascendant, descendant, biological or adopted sibling, or in-laws of the same degree, who has claims pending resolution by that officer, or concerning which the latter must issue a report or make query to his superior, shall be punished with a sentence of imprisonment from one to two years and absolute barring for a term from six to twelve years.

2. The officer of Penitentiary Institutions or correctional or protection centres for minors who solicits the sexual services of a person in his safekeeping shall be punished with a sentence of imprisonment of one to four years and absolute barring for a term from six to twelve years.

3. The same penalties shall be incurred when the person solicited is an ascendant, descendent, biological or adoptive sibling, or in-laws of the same degree of the person under his safekeeping. He shall also incur these penalties when the person solicited is the spouse of a person he has under his safekeeping or who is linked thereto in a stable manner by a similar emotional relationship.

Article 444

The penalties foreseen in the preceding Article shall be imposed without prejudice to the relevant one for the felonies against sexual freedom effectively committed.

CHAPTER X

On felonies of corruption in international commercial transactions

Article 445

1. Those who by offering, promising or granting any undue pecuniary or other kind of benefit, corrupt or attempt to corrupt foreign civil servants or international organisations, personally or through an intermediary, for their own benefit or that of a third party, or who attend to requests in that regard, in order for them to act or abstain from acting in relation to exercise of public functions to obtain or conserve a contract, or another irregular benefit in carrying out international economic activities, shall be punished with imprisonment from two to six years and a fine of twelve to twenty- four months, except if the profit obtained exceeds the resulting sum, in which case the fine shall be from one to two times the amount of such profit.

In addition to the penalties stated, the offender shall be handed down the punishment of prohibition to enter into public sector contracts, as well as loss of the possibility of obtaining public subsidies or aid and the right to enjoy tax and Social Security benefits or incentives, and the prohibition to intervene in commercial transactions of public transcendence for a period from seven to twelve years.

The penalties foreseen in the preceding Sections shall be imposed in the upper half if the object of the business concerns humanitarian assets or services or any others of basic need.

2. When, pursuant to the terms established in Article 31 bis of this Code a legal person is responsible for this felony the punishment of a fine from two to five years, or from three to five times the profit obtained if the resulting amount is higher shall be imposed thereon.

Pursuant to the rules established in Article 66 bis, the Judges and Courts of Law may also impose the penalties established in Sub-Sections b) to g) of Section 7 of Article 33.

3. For the purposes of this Article a foreign civil servant is construed to be:

a) Any person who holds a legislative, administrative or judicial office in a foreign country, both by appointment or by election;

b) Any person who exercises a public duty for a foreign country, including a public body or a public company;

c) Any officer or agent of an international public organisation.

TITLE XIX BIS
(Suppressed)

Article 445 bis

(Suppressed)

TITLE XX

On felonies against the Judicial Power

CHAPTER I

On perverting the course of justice

Article 446

A Judge or Magistrate who knowingly hands down an unfair judgement or ruling shall be punished:

1. With a sentence of imprisonment of one to four years if an unjust judgement against the accused in a criminal case if the sentence has not yet been executed, and with the same punishment in its upper half and a fine of twelve to twenty- four months if it has been executed. In both cases, the punishment of absolute barring for a term of ten to twenty years shall also be imposed.

2. With the punishment of a fine from six to twelve months and special barring from public employment and office for a term from six to ten years, if an unfair sentence against an accused person is handed down in misdemeanour proceedings.

3. With the punishment of a fine from twelve to twenty- four months and special barring from public employment and office for a term of ten to twenty years, when any other unfair judgement or ruling is handed down.

Article 447

A Judge or Magistrate who, due to serious negligence or inexcusable ignorance, hands down a manifestly unjust judgement or ruling shall incur the punishment of special barring from public employment and office for a term from two to six years.

Article 448

A Judge or Magistrate who refuses to judge, without alleging a legal reason, or under the pretext of obscurity, insufficiency or silence of the Law, shall be punished with the penalty of special barring from public employment and office for a term of six months to four years.

Article 449

1. The same punishment stated in the preceding Article shall be incurred by the Judge, Magistrate or Court Clerk found guilty of malicious delay in administering justice. Malicious delay shall be construed as that caused to achieve any unlawful end.

2. When the delay is due to an officer other than those mentioned in the preceding Section, the lower half of the punishment stated shall be imposed on him.

CHAPTER II

On omission of the duties to prevent felonies or to promote their persecution

Article 450

1. Whoever is able, by his immediate intervention and without risk to himself or another, and does not prevent a felony being committed that affects the life, integrity or health, freedom or sexual freedom of persons, shall be punished with a sentence of imprisonment of six months to two years if the offence is against life, and that of a fine from six to twenty- four months in the other cases, except if the offence not prevented is subject to an equal or lower punishment, in which case a lower degree punishment than that for the actual felony shall be imposed.

2. The same penalties shall be incurred by whoever, being able to do so, does not resort to the authority or its agents in order for them to prevent a felony of those foreseen in the preceding Section when informed that it is about to be, or is being committed.

CHAPTER III

On covering up

Article 451

Whoever has knowledge of a felony committed and, without having intervened in it as a principal, subsequently intervenes in its execution, in any of the following manners, shall be punished with a sentence of imprisonment of six months to three years:

1. Aiding the principals or accomplices to benefit from the gains, product or price of the offence, without intending personal profit;

2. Hiding, altering or destroying the evidence, effects or instruments of an offence, to prevent it being discovered;

3. Aiding the suspected criminals to avoid investigation by the authority or its agents, or to escape search or capture, whenever any of the following circumstances concur:

   a) That the act covered up amounts to treason, regicide, the homicide of any of the King's ascendants or descendents, of the Queen Consort or the Consort of the Queen, the Regent or any other member of the Regency, of the Heir to the Throne, genocide, crimes against humanity, crimes against protected persons and assets in the event of armed conflict, rebellion, terrorism, homicide, piracy, trafficking in human beings or trafficking in human organs;

   b) When the person abetting has acted in abuse of his public functions. In this case, in addition to the punishment of custodial sentence, that of special barring from public employment and office for a term of two to four years shall be imposed if the felony concealed is less serious, and of absolute barring for a term from six to twelve years if it is serious.

Article 452

Under no circumstances whatsoever may a sentence of imprisonment be handed down that exceeds that set for the felony covered up. Should the latter be subject to a punishment of another nature, the sentence of imprisonment shall be substituted by that of a fine from six to twenty-four months, except if the felony concealed is assigned a punishment equal to or lower than this, in which case the offender shall have the punishment for the felony in its lower half imposed.

Article 453

The provisions of this Chapter shall be applied even when the principal thereof covered up cannot be held accountable or is personally exempt from punishment.

Article 454

If the accessory after the fact is the spouse or person to whom the offender is bound by a stable emotional relation of a similar nature, his ascendants, descendents, biological or adoptive siblings, or in-laws of the same degree, with the sole exception accessories after the fact included in Sub-Section 1 of Article 451 are exempt from the imposition of penalties.

CHAPTER IV

On arbitrary enforcement of one's own right

Article 455

1. Whoever, in order to enforce his own right, acting outside the legal channels, were to use violence, intimidation or force in matters, shall be punished with the penalty of a fine from six to twelve months.

2. A punishment higher in one degree shall be imposed if weapons or dangerous objects are used to threaten or commit violence.

CHAPTER V

On false accusation and reports and simulating offences

Article 456

1. Those who, with knowledge of their false nature or reckless disregard for the truth, accuse any person of acts that, were they true, would constitute a felony or misdemeanour, if that accusation is made before an officer of the court or administration who has the duty to proceed to investigate, shall be penalised:

1. With a sentence of imprisonment of six months to two years and a fine of twelve to twenty-four months, if the accusation is of a serious felony;

2. With the punishment of a fine from twelve to twenty-four months, if the accusation is of a less serious felony;

3. With the punishment of a fine from three to six months, if the accusation is of a misdemeanour.

2. Proceedings may not be brought against the person reporting or accusing other than after a final judgement, or also a final ruling, of dismissal or setting aside by the Judge or Court of Law that heard the arraignment. These shall act on their own motion against the reporter or accuser, as long as there is sufficient prima facie evidence in the main case of falsity of the accusation, without prejudice to the fact that they may also be prosecuted when reported by the victim thereof.

Article 457

Whoever pretends, before any of the officers stated in the preceding Section, that he is responsible for or the victim of a felony or misdemeanour or reports a non-existent one, causing procedural action, shall be punished with a fine from six to twelve months.

CHAPTER VI

On perjury

Article 458

1. A witness who does not tell the truth in his deposition in a court case shall be punished with imprisonment of six months to two years and a fine of three to six months.

2. If perjury is committed against the accused in a criminal case, the penalties shall be of imprisonment from one to three years and a fine from six to twelve months. If a conviction is handed down due to that deposition, the higher degree penalties shall be imposed.

3. The same penalties shall be imposed if the perjury takes place before International Courts of Law that, by virtue of treaties duly ratified under the Spanish Constitution, exercise powers deriving therefrom, or when committed in Spain on declaring by virtue of letters rogatory issued by a foreign court.

Article 459

The penalties set forth in the preceding Articles shall be imposed in the upper half on experts or interpreters who maliciously misconstrue the truth in their opinion or translation, who shall also be punished with the penalty of special barring from profession or trade, public employment and office, for a term from six to twelve years.

Article 460

Should the witness, expert or interpreter, without substantially misconstruing the truth, alter it with hesitation, inexactness or by silencing relevant facts or data known to him, he shall be punished with the penalty of a fine from six to twelve months and, when appropriate, suspension from public employment and office, profession or trade, of six months to three years.

Article 461

1. Whoever were to knowingly produce false witnesses or misleading experts or interpreters, shall be punished with the same penalties as those established for them in the preceding Articles.

2. Should the offender of such a felony be a solicitor, barrister, chartered labour consultant or representative of the Public Prosecutor, in their professional practice or duties of office, in each case the punishment in its upper half and that of special barring from public employment and office, profession or trade, for a term of two to four years, shall be imposed.

Article 462

Whoever, having committed perjury in a criminal case, retracts in a timely, due manner, declaring the truth in order for it to take effect before judgement is handed down in the proceedings concerned, shall be exempt of punishment. If a custodial sentence has been enforced as a consequence of the perjury, the lower degree penalties shall be imposed.

CHAPTER VII

On obstruction of justice and professional disloyalty

Article 463

1. Whoever, when summoned in the legal manner, voluntarily fails to appear, without a just cause, before a court or tribunal in criminal proceedings with the accused in preventive custody, causing suspension of the oral trial, shall be punished with a sentence of imprisonment from three to six months or a fine from six to twenty- four months. The punishment of a fine from six to ten months shall be incurred by whoever, having been warned, does so for a second time in a criminal cause without the accused being in prison, whether or not a suspension has been caused.

2. Should the offender in this offence be a solicitor, barrister or representative of the Public Prosecutor, in professional practice or in the duties of his office, the punishment in the upper half and that of special barring from public employment and office, profession or trade, for a term of two to four years, shall be imposed on him.

3. If the suspension takes place in the case of Section 1 of this Article, as a consequence of the judge, a member of the court or whoever is acting as court clerk, failing to appear, a sentence of imprisonment from three to six months or a fine from six to twenty- four months shall be imposed and, in all cases, special barring for a term of two to four years.

Article 464

1. Whoever, by means of violence or intimidation directly or indirectly attempts to influence the accuser, a party or the accused, solicitor, barrister, expert, interpreter or witness in proceedings, in order for him to change his behaviour in the proceedings, shall be punished with a sentence of imprisonment of one to four years and a fine from six to twenty- four months.

Should the principal thereof achieve his objective, the punishment shall be imposed in its upper half.

2. The same penalties shall be imposed on whoever commits any act contrary to life, integrity, liberty, sexual freedom or assets, in retaliation against the persons mentioned in the preceding Section, due to their action in the judicial proceedings, without prejudice to the relevant punishment for the offence to which these amount.

Article 465

1. Whoever, when intervening in proceedings as a solicitor or barrister, abusing his duties, destroys, makes void or conceals documents or proceedings notified to him in that capacity shall be punished with a sentence of imprisonment of six months to two years, a fine for seven to twelve months and special barring from his profession, public employment and office of three to six years.

2. Should the acts described in Section one of this Article be perpetrated by a private individual, the punishment shall be a fine of three to six months.

Article 466

1. A solicitor or barrister who discloses procedural actions declared secret by the judicial authority shall be punished with the penalties of fine of twelve to twenty- four months and special barring from employment, public office profession or trade for one to four years.

2. Should the disclosure of the proceedings declared secret be perpetrated by the Judge or a member of the Court of Law, representative of the Public Prosecutor, Court Clerk or any officer in the service of the Judicial Administration, the penalties foreseen in Article 417 in the upper half shall be imposed on him.

3. Should the conduct described in Section 1 be perpetrated by any other individual who has intervened in the proceedings the punishment shall be imposed in their lower half.

Article 467

1. A solicitor or barrister who, having advised, defended or represented a person, defends or represents whoever has contrary interests in the same matter, without the consent of the former, shall be punished with the penalty of a fine from six to twelve months and special barring from his profession of two to four years.

2. A solicitor or barrister who, by action or omission, manifestly damages the interests entrusted to him shall be punished with the penalties of a fine of twelve to twenty- four months and special barring from public employment or office, profession or trade of one to four years.

Should the acts be perpetrated due to serious negligence, the penalties shall be imposed of a fine from six to twelve months and special barring from his profession of six months to two years.

CHAPTER VIII

On breach of sentence

Article 468

1. Those who breach their conviction, security measure, imprisonment, precautionary measure, driving ban or custody, shall be punished with a sentence of imprisonment of six months to one year if in custody, and with the punishment of a fine from twelve to twenty- four months in the other cases.

2. In all cases, a sentence of imprisonment of six months to one year, shall be imposed on those who breach a punishment of those set forth in Article 48 of this Code or a precautionary or security measure of the same kind imposed in criminal proceedings in which the victim is one of the persons referred to in Article 173.2, as well as those who breach probation measures.

Article 469

Convicts or prisoners who escape from the place where they are interned, using violence or intimidation against persons, force against property or taking part in an uprising, shall be punished with a sentence of imprisonment of six months to four years.

Article 470

1. The private individual who aids and abets escape by a convict, prisoner or detainee, either from the place where he is in custody, or in transport, shall be punished with a sentence of imprisonment of six months to one year and a fine of twelve to twenty- four months.

2. If violence or intimidation against persons, force against property or bribery are used for the purpose, the punishment shall be imprisonment from six months to four years.

3. If committed by any of the persons mentioned in Article 454, they shall be penalised with the punishment of a fine from three to six months, in which case the Judge or Court of Law may impose only the relevant penalties for the damage caused or the intimidation or violence exercised.

Article 471

A punishment higher in one degree shall be imposed, in the respective cases, if the offender is an officer in charge of driving or of the custody of the convict, prisoner or detainee. The officer shall also be punished with the penalty of special barring from public employment and office from six to ten years if the fugitive is convicted by final judgement, and with special barring from public employment and office of three to six years in the other cases.

CHAPTER IX

On felonies against the Judicial Administration of the International Criminal Court

Article 471 bis

1. A witness who intentionally commits perjury in his deposition before the International Criminal Court, being bound to tell the truth pursuant to the rules and regulations of procedure and evidence of that Court, shall be punished with imprisonment from six months to two years. Should the perjury be committed against the accused, the punishment shall be imprisonment from two to four years. Should a conviction be handed down as a consequence of the witness statement, the punishment of imprisonment from four to five years shall be imposed.

2. Whoever presents evidence before the International Criminal Court knowing that it is false or has been forged shall be punished with the penalties stated in the preceding Section of this Article.

3. Whoever intentionally destroys or alters evidence, or interferes with the procedures for giving evidence before the International Criminal Court, shall be punished with a sentence of imprisonment of six months to two years and a fine for seven to twelve months.

4. Whoever bribes a witness, obstructs his appearance or deposition before the International Criminal or interferes with them, shall be punished with a sentence of imprisonment of one to four years and a fine from six to twenty- four months.

5. Whoever obstructs an officer of the Court, bribes or intimidates him, to oblige or induce him not to carry out his duties or to do so unduly, shall be punished with imprisonment from one to four years and a fine from six to twenty- four months.

6. Whoever retaliates against an officer of the International Criminal Court due to the duties he or another officer has carried out shall be punished with a sentence of imprisonment of one to four years and a fine from six to twenty- four months.

The same punishment shall be incurred by whoever retaliates against a witness for his deposition before the Court.

7. Whoever solicits or accepts a bribe as an officer of the Court of Law and in relation to his official duties shall incur a sentence of imprisonment from two to five years and a fine of one to three times the value of the handout solicited or accepted.

TITLE XXI

On felonies against the Constitution

CHAPTER I

Rebellion

Article 472

A conviction for the offence of rebellion shall be handed down to those who violently and publicly rise up for any of the following purposes:

1. To fully or partially repeal, suspend or amend the Constitution;

2. To fully or partially strip the King, the Regent or members of the Regency of all or part of their prerogatives and powers, or to oblige them to execute an act contrary to their will;

3. To prevent freely holding elections to public offices;

4. To dissolve the *Cortes*, the Congress of Deputies, the Senate or any Legislative Assembly of an Autonomous Community, to prevent them from meeting, discussing or resolving, to force them to pass any resolution, or to strip them of any of their attributions or powers.

5. To declare the independence of any part of the national territory;

6. To replace the Government of the Nation or the Governing Council of an Autonomous Community with another, or to use or exercise oneself, or to strip the Government or Governing Council of an Autonomous Community, or any of its members, of their powers, or to prevent or limit the free exercise thereof, or to force any of them to carry out acts against their will;

7. To disaffect from obedience to the Government any armed force.

Article 473

1. Those who, inducing the rebels, have promoted or sustain the rebellion, and its ringleaders, shall be punished with a sentence of imprisonment from fifteen to twenty- five years and absolute barring for the same time; those who act as subaltern commanders, with that of imprisonment from ten to fifteen years and absolute barring from ten to fifteen years, and mere participants, with that of imprisonment from five to ten years and special barring from public employment and office for a term from six to ten years.

2. If weapons have been used, or if there has been combat between the rebellious force and the sectors loyal to the lawful authority, or when the rebellion has caused criminal damage to publicly or privately owned property, cutting off telegraphic and telephone lines, the airwaves, railways or any other kind of communications, with serious violence against persons, demanding contributions or diverting the public funds from their lawful investment, imprisonment shall be handed down, respectively, of twenty- five to thirty years for the former and from fifteen to twenty- five years for the second, and from ten to fifteen years for the latter.

Article 474

When the rebellion has not been organised by known leaders, the persons assumed to be such shall be those who direct others or speak on their behalf, or those who sign documents issued on their behalf, or who perpetrate other similar acts of command or representation.

Article 475

Those who persuade or lead troops or any other kind of armed force to commit the offence of rebellion shall be convicted as rebels and punished with a sentence of imprisonment from five to ten years and absolute barring for a term from six to twelve years.

Should the rebellion take place, they shall be deemed promoters and shall suffer the punishment stated in Article 473.

Article 476

1. A serviceperson who does not use the means available to him to contain a rebellion by the forces under his command shall be punished with imprisonment from two to five years and absolute barring from six to ten years.

2. Servicepersons who, having knowledge of an attempt to commit a felony of rebellion and do not immediately report this to their superiors, or authorities or officers who, due to his office, are obliged to pursue the felony shall be punished with the same penalties foreseen in the preceding Section in their lower half.

Article 477

Provocation, conspiracy and solicitation to commit rebellion shall be punished, in addition to the barring foreseen in the preceding Articles, with a sentence of imprisonment lower by one or two degrees to that of the relevant offence.

Article 478

Should whoever commits any of the felonies foreseen in this Chapter be an authority, the punishment of barring foreseen in each case shall be substituted by that of absolute barring for a term from fifteen to twenty years, except if that circumstance is specifically included in the criminal classification concerned.

Article 479

After the rebellion becomes apparent, the governmental authority shall call on the rebels to immediately disperse and withdraw.

Should the rebels not immediately desist in their attitude immediately after being called to do so, the authority shall apply the force available to it to disperse them.

No call shall be required from the moment the rebels open fire.

Article 480

1. Whoever, being involved in an offence of rebellion, discloses it in time to be able to avoid its consequences, shall be exempt of the punishment for it.

2. Those who are merely instrumental, who lay down their weapons before having used them, submitting to the lawful authorities, shall be subject to the lower degree sentence of imprisonment. The same punishment shall be imposed if the rebels disperse or submit to the lawful authority prior to the call or due to it.

Article 481

The specific felonies committed in a rebellion or due to it shall be punished, respectively, pursuant to the provisions of this Code.

Article 482

Authorities who have not resisted the rebellion shall be punished with the penalty of absolute barring from twelve to twenty years.

Article 483

Civil servants who continue to carry out their duties of office under the command of the rebels or who, failing acceptance of the resignation they may have tendered, abandon their post when there is the danger of rebellion, shall incur the punishment of special barring from public employment and office from six to twelve years.

Article 484

Those who accept employment from the rebels shall be punished with the penalty of absolute barring from six to twelve years.

CHAPTER II

On felonies against the Crown

Article 485

1. Whoever kills the King, or any of his ascendants or descendents, the Queen consort or the Queen's Consort, the Regent or any member of the Regency, or the Heir to the Crown, shall be punished with a sentence of imprisonment from twenty a twenty- five years.

2. Attempt to commit the same felony shall be punished with the penalty lower by one degree.

3. Should two or more aggravating circumstances concur in the felony, a sentence of imprisonment from twenty-five to thirty years shall be imposed.

Article 486

1. Whoever were to cause the King, or any of his ascendants or descendents, the Queen Consort or the Queen's Consort, the Regent or any member of the Regency, or the Heir to the Throne, injuries of those foreseen in Article 149, shall be punished with a sentence of imprisonment from fifteen to twenty years.

If any of the injuries foreseen in Article 150, this shall be punished with a sentence of imprisonment from eight to fifteen years.

2. Whoever were to cause them any other injury shall be punished with a sentence of imprisonment from four to eight years.

Article 487

Whoever deprives the King, or any of his ascendants or descendents, the Queen Consort or the Queen's Consort, the Regent or any member of the Regency, or the Heir to the Throne, of their personal liberty shall be punished with a sentence of imprisonment from fifteen to twenty years, except if the acts are punished with a greater punishment in other provisions of this Code.

Article 488

Provocation, conspiracy and solicitation to commit the felonies foreseen in the preceding Articles shall be punished with the penalty lower by one or two degrees to those respectively foreseen.

Article 489

Whoever, by serious violence or intimidation, forces the persons mentioned in the preceding Articles to act against their will, shall be punished with a sentence of imprisonment from eight to twelve years.

In the case foreseen in the preceding Paragraph, if the violence or intimidation were not serious, the punishment imposed shall be lower by one degree.

Article 490

1. Whoever, by means of violence or intimidation, were to trespass on the dwelling of any of the persons mentioned in the preceding Articles shall be punished with a sentence of imprisonment from three to six years. If there is no violence or intimidation, the punishment shall be from two to four years.

2. Whoever seriously intimidates any of the persons mentioned in the preceding Section shall be punished with a sentence of imprisonment from three to six years, and with a sentence of imprisonment from one to three years if the threat is minor.

3. Whoever commits slander or defamation against the King or any of his ascendants or descendents, the Queen Consort or the Queen's Consort, the Regent or any member of the Regency, or the Heir to the Throne, while carrying out the duties of office or due to or on occasion thereof, shall be punished with a sentence of imprisonment of six months to two years if the slander or defamation are serious and with that of a fine of six to twelve months if not.

Article 491

1. Slander and defamations against any of the persons mentioned in the preceding Article, and outside the cases foreseen therein, shall be punished with the penalty of a fine from four to twenty months.

2. The punishment shall be imposed of a fine from six to twenty-four months upon whoever uses the image of the King or of any of his ascendants or descendents, or of the Queen Consort or the Queen's Consort, or the Regent or any member of the Regency, or Heir to the Throne, in any way that may damage the prestige of the Crown.

CHAPTER III

On felonies against the Institutions of the State and the division of powers

SUBCHAPTER 1. FELONIES AGAINST THE INSTITUTIONS OF THE STATE

Article 492

Those who, on vacancy of the Throne or when the Incumbent is unable to exercise his authority, prevent the Cortes from meeting to appoint the Regency or guardian to the minor Incumbent, shall been punished with a sentence of imprisonment from ten to fifteen years and absolute barring for a term of ten to fifteen years, without prejudice to the punishment to which they may be subject for committing other more serious offences.

Article 493

Those who, without public uprising, forcibly trespass on, use violence or intimidation at the seats of the Congress of Deputies, the Senate or at a Legislative Assembly of an Autonomous Community, it they are in session, shall be punished with a sentence of imprisonment of three to five years.

Article 494

Those who promote, direct or lead demonstrations or other kinds of meetings before the seats of the Congress of Deputies, of the Senate or a Legislative Assembly of an Autonomous Community, when in session, altering their normal operation, shall incur a sentence of imprisonment of six months to one year or a fine of twelve to twenty- four months.

Article 495

1. Those who, without public uprising, bearing weapons or other dangerous instruments, attempt to enter the seats of the Congress of Deputies, the Senate or the Legislative Assembly of an Autonomous Community, to lodge personal or group petitions there, shall incur a sentence of imprisonment of three to five years.

2. The punishment foreseen in the preceding Section shall be applied in its upper half to whoever promotes, directs or leads the group.

Article 496

Whoever commits serious defamation against Parliament or a Legislative Assembly of an Autonomous Community, while in session, or any of its Commissions, in the public acts in which they represent these, shall be punished with the penalty of a fine from twelve to eighteen months.

Those charged with the defamations described in the preceding Section shall be exempt of punishment if the circumstances foreseen in Article 210 concur.

Article 497

1. Whoever, without being a member of the Congress of Deputies, the Senate or Legislative Assembly of an Autonomous Community, seriously disturbs the order of its sessions, shall incur a sentence of imprisonment of six months to one year.

2 When disturbance of the order of the sessions referred to in the preceding Section is not serious, the punishment of a fine from six to twelve months shall be imposed.

Article 498

Those who use force, violence, minor or serious intimidation of prevent a member of the Congress of Deputies, the Senate or of a Legislative Assembly of an Autonomous Community from attending its meetings, or by the same means limits free expression of his opinions or casting his vote, shall be punished with a sentence of imprisonment of three to five years.

Article 499

The authority or public officer who infringes the inviolability of Parliament or a Legislative Assembly of an Autonomous Community shall be punished with the penalties of special barring from public employment and office for a term of ten to twenty years, without prejudice to those that may befall him if the act constitutes another more serious offence.

Article 500

The authority or public officer who detains a Member of the Congress of Deputies or of the Senate or of a Legislative Assembly of an Autonomous Community outside the cases or without the requisites established by the laws in force, shall incur, as appropriate, the penalties foreseen in this Code, imposed in the upper half, and also that of special barring from public employment and office from six to twelve years.

Article 501

The judicial authority who indicts or prosecutes a member of the Cortes or of a Legislative Assembly of an Autonomous Community without the requisites established by the laws in force shall be punished with the penalty of special barring from public employment and office of ten to twenty years.

Article 502

1. Those who, having been summoned in the legal manner and under admonition, fail to appear before an investigation committee of Parliament or a Legislative Assembly of an Autonomous Community shall be convicted and punished as felons of disobedience. Should the accused be an authority or public officer, the punishment of suspension from public employment and office for a term of six months to two years shall also be imposed on him.

2. The same penalties shall be incurred by the authority or officer who hinders an investigation by the Ombudsman, Court of Auditors or equivalent bodies of the Autonomous Communities, refusing or unduly delaying submission of the reports they request or hindering their access to the administrative files or documentation required for that investigation.

3. Whoever is called before a parliamentary investigation commission and commits perjury under oath shall be punished with a sentence of imprisonment of six months to one year or fine from twelve to twenty- four months.

Article 503

A sentence of imprisonment of two to four years shall be incurred by:

1. Those who violently or threateningly trespass on the premises where the Council of Ministers or Governing Council of an Autonomous Community is in session;

2. Those who interfere or in any way hinder the liberty of the Government convened in Council, or of the members of a Government of an Autonomous Community, convening in Council, except if the acts constitute another more serious offence.

Article 504

1. The punishment of a fine from twelve to eighteen months shall be incurred by those who seriously slander, defame or threaten the Government of the Nation, the General Council of the Judiciary, the Constitutional Court, the Supreme Court, or the Governing Council or High Court of Justice of an Autonomous Community.

Whoever is found guilty of slander or defamation as set forth in the preceding Section shall be exempt of punishment if the circumstances foreseen, respectively, in Articles 207 and 210 of this Code concur.

A sentence of imprisonment shall be imposed of three to five years on those who use force, violence or intimidation to prevent the members of those bodies from attending their respective meetings.

2. Those who seriously defame or threaten the Armed Forces, Classes or the Police and Security Forces, shall be punished with the penalty of a fine from twelve to eighteen months.

Whoever is found guilty of the defamations foreseen in the preceding Section shall be exempt of punishment if the circumstances described in Article 210 of this Code concur.

Article 505

1. Whoever, without being a member of the council of a local corporation, seriously disturbs the order of its plenary meetings, prevent access thereto, impede conducting the agenda foreseen, the passing of resolutions, or who

cause disorders aimed at expressing support for armed gangs, terrorist organisations or groups, shall incur a sentence of imprisonment of six months to one year.

2. Whoever, availing himself of the existence of armed gangs, terrorist organisations or groups, commits slander, defamation, coercion or intimidation against the members of a local corporation shall be punished with the higher degree punishment than the relevant one for the felony committed.

SUBCHAPTER 2. ON USURPATION OF ATTRIBUTIONS

Article 506

The authority or public officer who, lacking the power to do so, hands down a general provision or suspends execution thereof, shall be punished with a sentence of imprisonment from one to three years, a fine from six to twelve months and special barring from public employment and office for a term from six to twelve years.

Article 506 bis

(Suppressed)

Article 507

A Judge or Magistrate who claims for himself administrative powers that he lacks, or prevents lawful exercise thereof by whoever holds them, shall be punished with a sentence of imprisonment of six months to one year, a fine of three to six months and suspension from public employment and office for a term from one to three years.

Article 508

1. The authority or public officer who claims judicial powers for himself or prevents enforcement of a ruling handed down by the competent judicial authority shall be punished with imprisonment of six months to one year, a fine of three to eight months and suspension from public employment and office for a term from one to three years.

2. The administrative authority or officer or serviceperson who acts against the independence of Judges or Magistrates guaranteed by the Constitution, issuing them instructions, orders or demands related to cases or actions that are being heard by them, shall be punished with a sentence of imprisonment from one to two years, a fine from four to ten months and special barring from public employment and office for a term from two to six years.

Article 509

A Judge or Magistrate, authority or civil servant who, being legally required to inhibit himself, continues to proceed, without awaiting decision on the relevant jurisdictional conflict, except in the cases allowed by the Law, shall be punished with the penalty of a fine from three to ten months and special barring from public employment and office for a term of six months to one year.

CHAPTER IV

On felonies related to the exercise of fundamental public rights and liberties.

SUBCHAPTER 1. ON THE FELONIES COMMITTED WHEN EXERCISING THE FUNDAMENTAL RIGHTS AND PUBLIC LIBERTIES GUARANTEED BY THE CONSTITUTION

Article 510

1. Those who provoke discrimination, hate or violence against groups or associations due to racist, anti-Semitic reasons or any other related to ideology, religion or belief, family situation, belonging to an ethnic group or race, national origin, gender, sexual preference, illness or handicap, shall be punished with a sentence of imprisonment from one to three years and a fine from six to twelve months.

2. Those who, with knowledge of its falseness or reckless disregard for the truth, were to distribute defamatory information on groups or associations in relation to their ideology, religion or belief, belonging an ethnic group or race, national origin, gender sex, sexual preference, illness or handicap shall be punished with the same penalty.

Article 511

1. A sentence of imprisonment of six months to two years and a fine of twelve to twenty- four months and special barring from public employment and office for a term from one to three years shall be incurred by private individuals in charge of a public service who refuse a person a service to which he is entitled due to his ideology, religion or belief, belonging to an ethnic group or race, national origin, gender, sexual preference, family situation, illness or handicap.

2. The same penalties shall be applicable when the acts are committed against an association, foundation, society or corporation, or against its members due to their ideology, religion or belief, belonging all or some of its members to an ethnic group or race, national origin, gender, sexual preference, family situation, illness or handicap.

3. Civil servants who commit any of the acts foreseen in this Article shall incur the same penalties in the upper half and that of special barring from public employment and office for a term of two to four years.

Article 512

Those who, in the exercise of their professional or business activities, were to deny a person a service to which he is entitled due to his ideology, religion or belief, his belonging to an ethnic group, race or nation, his gender, sexual preference, family situation, illness or handicap, shall incur the punishment of special barring from exercise of profession, trade, industry or commerce, for a term of one to four years.

Article 513

Unlawful assemblies or demonstrations are punishable and those deemed to be such are:

1. Those held in order to commit an offence;

2. Those attended by persons bearing weapons, explosive devices, blunt objects or any other dangerous item;

Article 514

1. The promoters or directors of any assembly or demonstration described under Section 1 of the preceding Article and those who, in relation to Section 2 thereof, have not attempted to prevent the circumstances mentioned therein

by all the means available to them shall incur imprisonment from one to three years and a fine of twelve to twenty-four months. To these ends, the directors or promoters of an assembly or demonstration shall be deemed to be those who call or lead them.

2. Those attending an assembly or demonstration bearing weapons or other equally dangerous items shall be punished with a sentence of imprisonment from one to two years and a fine from six to twelve months. The Judges or Courts of Law, in view of the criminal records of the subject, circumstances of the case and characteristics of the weapon or instrument borne, may lower the punishment stated by one degree.

3. Persons who commit acts of violence when an assembly or demonstration is held, against the authorities, their agents, persons or public or private properties, shall be punished with the penalty to which the relevant offence is subject, in its upper half.

4. Those who prevent the lawful exercise of the freedom to assemble or demonstrate, or who seriously disturb the proceedings of a lawful assembly or demonstration shall be punished with a sentence of imprisonment of two to three years if the acts are perpetrated with violence, and with a sentence of imprisonment from three to six months or a fine from six to twelve months if committed by imposition or any other unlawful procedure.

5. The promoters or directors of any assembly or demonstration who again call, hold or attempt to hold any assembly or demonstration that had previously been suspended or prohibited, provided they intend to subvert the constitutional order or to seriously alter the public peace, shall be punished with imprisonment of six months to one year and a fine from six to twelve months, without prejudice to the punishment to which they may be subject as appropriate, pursuant to the preceding Sections.

Article 515

Unlawful associations shall be punishable, the following being deemed so:

1. Those whose purpose is to commit any offence or that, having been constituted, encourage commission thereof, as well as those with the object of committing or promoting commission of offences in an organised, co- ordinated, reiterated manner;

2. (Suppressed)

3. Those that, even having a lawful end as their object, use violent means or alteration or control of personality to achieve these;

4. Organisations of a paramilitary nature;

5. Those that promote discrimination, hate or violence against persons, groups or associations due to their ideology, religion or belief, their members or any of them belonging to an ethnic group, race or nation, their gender, sexual preference, family situation, illness or handicap, or incite to do so.

Article 516

(Suppressed)

Article 517

In the cases foreseen in Sections 1 and 3 to 6 of Article 515 the following penalties shall be imposed:

1. The founders, directors and chairpersons of associations, those of imprisonment from two to four years, a fine of twelve to twenty- four months and special barring from public employment and office for a term from six to twelve years.

2. Active members, those of imprisonment of one to three years and a fine of twelve to twenty- four months.

Article 518

Those who, through their financial aid or any other kind of aid, if important, favour the founding, organisation or activity of the associations described in Sections 1 and 3 to 6 of Article 515, shall incur a sentence of imprisonment from one to three years, a fine of twelve to twenty- four months, and barring from public employment and office for a term of one to four years.

Article 519

Provocation, conspiracy and solicitation to commit the offence of criminal association shall be punished with the penalty lower by one or two degrees to the relevant one, respectively, for the acts foreseen in the preceding Articles.

Article 520

The Judges or Courts of Law, in the cases foreseen in Article 515, shall order dissolution of the criminal association and, when appropriate, any other of the accessory consequences of Article 129 of this Code.

Article 521

In the felony of criminal association, if the accused is an authority, agent thereof or public officer, in addition to the penalties stated, absolute barring from ten to fifteen years shall be imposed on him.

Article 521 bis

(Suppressed)

SUBCHAPTER 2. ON FELONIES AGAINST FREEDOM OF CONSCIENCE, RELIGIOUS FEELINGS AND RESPECT FOR THE DEAD

Article 522

The punishment of a fine from four to ten months shall be incurred by:

1. Those who, by means of violence, intimidation, force or any other unlawful imposition, prevent a member or members of a religious confession from carrying out the acts inherent to the belief they profess, or from attending these.

2. Those who, by the same means, force another or others to practice or to attend to acts of worship or rites, or to carry out acts that reveal whether or not they profess a religion, or to change the religion they profess.

Article 523

Whoever, by violence, intimidation, tumultuous action or by imposition, were to prevent, interrupt or disturb the acts, functions, ceremonies or manifestations of religious confessions registered on the relevant public register at the Ministry of Justice and Internal Affairs, shall be punished with a sentence of imprisonment of six months to six years, if the act was committed at the place of worship, and with that of a fine from four to ten months if perpetrated anywhere else.

Article 524

Whoever perpetrates profane acts that offend the feelings of a legally protected religious confession in a temple or place of worship, or at religious ceremonies, shall be punished with a sentence of imprisonment of six months to one year or a fine from twelve to twenty- four months.

Article 525

1. Whoever, in order to offend the feelings of the members of a religious confession, publicly disparages their dogmas, beliefs, rites or ceremonies in public, verbally or in writing, or insult, also publicly, those who profess or practice these, shall incur the punishment of a fine from eight to twelve months.

2. The same penalties shall be incurred by those who publicly disparage, verbally or in writing, those who do not profess any religion or belief whatsoever.

Article 526

Whoever, lacking due respect for the memory of the dead, breaches tombs or sepulchres, desecrate a corpse or its ashes or, in order to outrage destroys, alters or damages the funerary urns, pantheons, headstones or niches, shall be punished with a sentence of imprisonment of three to five months or a fine from six to ten months.

SUBCHAPTER 3. ON FELONIES AGAINST THE DUTY TO SERVE SUBSTITUTE SOCIAL SERVICE
(Suppressed)

Article 527

(Without content)

Article 528

(Repealed)

CHAPTER V

On felonies committed by civil servants against constitutional guarantees

SUBCHAPTER 1. ON FELONIES COMMITTED BY CIVIL SERVANTS AGAINST INDIVIDUAL LIBERTIES

Article 529

1. A Judge or Magistrate who delivers a criminal case to another authority or officer, either military or administrative, that unlawfully clams it, shall be punished with the penalty of special barring from public employment and office for a term of six months to two years.

2. If a detained person is also handed over, the higher degree punishment shall be imposed on him.

Article 530

The authority or public officer who, in the course of criminal proceedings, were to order, enforce or prolong any deprivation of freedom of a detainee, prisoner or convict, with breach of the terms or other constitutional or legal guarantees, shall be punished with the penalty of special barring from public employment and office for a term from four to eight years.

Article 531

The authority or public officer who, in the course of criminal proceedings, were to order, enforce or prolong the solitary confinement of a detainee, prisoner or convict, with breach of the terms or other constitutional or legal guarantees, shall be punished with the penalty of special barring from public employment and office for a term from two to six years.

Article 532

Should the acts described in the preceding two Articles be committed due to serious negligence, they shall be punished with the penalty of suspension from public employment and office for a term of six months to two years.

Article 533

Officers of penitentiary, correctional or protection centres for minors who impose undue punishment or privations on the detainees or inmates, or who treat them with unnecessary strictness, shall be punished with the penalty of special barring from public employment and office for a term from two to six years.

SUBCHAPTER 2. ON FELONIES COMMITTED BY CIVIL SERVANTS AGAINST THE INVIOLABILITY OF THE HOME AND OTHER GUARANTEES OF PRIVACY

Article 534

1. An authority or public officer who acts as follows, in the course of criminal proceedings and without respecting the constitutional or legal guarantees, shall be punished with the penalties of a fine from six to twelve months and special barring from public employment and office from two to six years:

   1. Who enters a dwelling without the consent of the dweller;

   2. Who searches the papers or documents of a person or belongings found in his dwelling, unless the owner has freely provided his consent.

If he does not return the papers, documents and belongings searched to their owner immediately after the search, the penalties shall be those of special barring from public employment and office from six to twelve years and a fine of twelve to twenty- four months, without prejudice to the punishment to which he may be subject for misappropriation.

2. The authority or public officer who, when lawfully searching papers, documents or belongings of a person, commits any unlawful humiliation or unnecessary damage to his belonging, shall be punished with the penalties foreseen for these acts, imposed in the upper half, and also with the punishment of special barring from public employment and office for a term from two to six years.

Article 535

The authority or public officer who, in the course of criminal proceedings, intercepts any kind of private postal or telegraphic correspondence, in breach of the constitutional or legal guarantees, shall incur the punishment of special barring from public employment and office from two to six years.

Should he disclose or reveal the information obtained, the punishment shall be imposed of special barring, in its upper half, and also a fine from six to eighteen months.

Article 536

Such an authority, civil servant or agent thereof who, tin the course of criminal proceedings, intercepts telecommunications or uses technical tapping devices to listen, transmit, record or play sound, image or any other communication signal, in breach of the constitutional or legal guarantees, shall incur the punishment of special barring from public employment and office for two to six years.

Should he disclose or reveal the information obtained, the penalties of special barring, in the upper half and also a fine from six to eighteen months shall be imposed.

SUBCHAPTER 3. ON FELONIES COMMITTED BY CIVIL SERVANTS AGAINST OTHER INDIVIDUAL RIGHTS

Article 537

The authority or public officer who prevents or hinders a detainee or prisoner in the exercise of his right to legal counsel, who attempts or favours his renunciation to such counsel, or does not immediately inform him of his rights and of the reasons for his arrest in an understandable way, shall be punished with the penalty of a fine from four to ten months and special barring from public employment and office of two to four years.

Article 538

The authority or public officer who establishes prior censorship or, outside the cases permitted by the Constitution and the Laws, seizes editions of books or newspapers or suspends their publication or the broadcast of any radio or television programme, shall incur the punishment of absolute barring from six to ten years.

Article 539

The authority or public officer who dissolves or suspends the activities of a legally constituted association without prior court order, or without a lawful cause to prevent it from holding its sessions, shall be punished with the penalty of special barring from public employment and office from eight to twelve years and a fine from six to twelve months.

Article 540

The authority or public officer who prohibits a peaceful meeting or dissolves it outside the cases specifically allowed by the laws shall be punished with the penalty of special barring from public employment and office from four to eight years and a fine from six to nine months.

Article 541

The authority or public officer who confiscates personal property outside the cases permitted and without fulfilling the legal requisites, shall incur the penalties and special barring from public employment and office of one to four years and a fine from six to twelve months.

Article 542

The authority or civil servant who knowingly prevents a person from exercising other civil rights recognised by the Constitution and the Laws shall incur the punishment of special barring from public employment and office for a term of one to four years.

CHAPTER VI

On offending Spain

Article 543

Verbal or written offences or outrages, or those by action, against Spain, its Autonomous Communities or the symbols or emblems thereof, perpetrated with publicly, shall be punished with the penalty of a fine for seven to twelve months.

TITLE XXII

Felonies against public order

CHAPTER I

Sedition

Article 544

Conviction for sedition shall befall those who, without being included in the felony of rebellion, public and tumultuously rise up to prevent, by force or outside the legal channels, application of the laws, or any authority, official corporation or public officer from lawful exercise of the duties thereof or implementation of the resolutions thereof, or of administrative or judicial resolutions.

Article 545

1. Those who have induced, sustained or directed the sedition or who appear as the main doers thereof, shall be punished with a sentence of imprisonment from eight to ten years, and with that ten to fifteen years if they are persons with the status of an authority. In both cases, absolute barring for the same term shall also be imposed.

2. Apart from those cases, a punishment from four to eight years imprisonment and of special barring from public employment and office for a term from four to eight years shall be imposed.

Article 546

The terms set forth in Article 474 are applicable to the case of sedition when this has not been organised with known leaders.

Article 547

In the event of the sedition not having managed to seriously interfere with exercise of the public authority nor having caused commission of another felony for which the Law prescribes serious penalties, the Judges or Courts of Law shall lower the penalties stated in this Chapter by one or two degrees.

Article 548

Provocation, conspiracy and solicitation of sedition shall be punished with the penalties lower by one or two degrees to those respectively foreseen, except if the sedition takes place, in which case it shall be punished with the penalty set forth in Section 1 of Article 545, and its principals shall be deemed promoters.

Article 549

The provisions contained in Articles 479 to 484 are also applicable to the offence of sedition.

CHAPTER II

On assaults on the authority, its agents and civil servants, and on resistance and disobedience

Article 550

Conviction for assault shall befall those who attack the authority, its agents or civil servants, or use force against them, seriously threaten or actively resist them, when they are carrying out their duties of office, or on occasion thereof.

Article 551

1. The attacks included in the preceding Article shall be punished with imprisonment of two to four years and a fine of three to six months if the assault is against an authority and of imprisonment from one to three years in the other cases.

2. Notwithstanding what is foreseen in the preceding Section, if the authority against whom the assault is committed is a member of the Cabinet, of the Government Councils of the Autonomous Communities, of the Congress of Deputies, the Senate or the Legislative Assemblies of the Autonomous Communities, of the Local Corporations, of the General Council of the Judiciary or Magistrate of the Constitutional Court, a sentence of imprisonment shall be imposed from four to six years and a fine from six to twelve months.

Article 552

The penalties shall be imposed higher by one degree to those respectively foreseen in the preceding Article when any of the following circumstances concur in the assault:

1. If the aggression is perpetrated with weapons or by other dangerous means;

2. If the principal takes advantage of his condition as an authority, agent or public officer thereof.

Article 553

Provocation, conspiracy and solicitation of any of the felonies foreseen in the preceding Articles shall be punished with the penalty lower by one or two degrees to that for the relevant offence.

Article 554

1. Whoever physically abuses or actively resists an armed force that is carrying out its duties of office or on occasion thereof, shall be punished with the penalties established in Articles 551 and 552, in the respective cases.

2. To these ends, an armed force shall be construed to be soldiers who, wearing uniform, are providing a service that is legally entrusted to the Armed Forces and that they have been duly ordered to carry out.

Article 555

The penalties foreseen in Articles 551 and 552 shall be imposed with a lower degree, in the respective cases, on those who assault or threaten the persons who come to the aid of the authority, its agents or officers.

Article 556

Those who, without being included under Article 550, resist the authority or its agents, or seriously disobey them, while carrying out the duties of office, shall be punished with a sentence of imprisonment of six months to one year.

CHAPTER III

On public disorders

Article 557

1. Those who, acting as a group and in order to disturb the public peace, alter public order causing injury to persons, damaging property, blocking the public thoroughfares or access to these in a way that endangers those travelling along them, or trespassing on premises or buildings, shall be punished with a sentence of imprisonment of six months to three years, without prejudice to the penalties to which they may be subject under other provisions of this Code.

2. A punishment higher in one degree to those foreseen in the preceding Section shall be imposed on principals of the acts described therein who perpetrate these when events or shows are held at which a large number of individuals gather. The same punishment shall be applied to whoever acts inside premises where such events are held to alter the public order by conducts that cause or are liable to cause a situation of danger to part of or all those attending. In these cases, the punishment of barring to attend events or shows of the same kind for a term of up to three years longer than a sentence of imprisonment imposed may be handed down.

Article 558

Those who seriously disturb order at the hearing of a court or tribunal, at public acts inherent to any authority or corporation, of an electoral college, public office or establishment, educational centre, or when sports or cultural events are held, shall be punished with a sentence of imprisonment from three to six months or a fine from six to twelve months. In these cases, the punishment of barring to attend places, events or shows of the same kind for a term up to three years longer than a sentence of imprisonment imposed may be handed down.

Article 559

Those who seriously disturb the public order in order to prevent any person from exercising his civil rights shall be punished with the penalties of a fine of three to twelve months and special barring from the right of passive suffrage for a term from two to six years.

Article 560

1. Those who were to cause damage that interrupts, obstructs or destroys telecommunications lines or installations or postal correspondence, shall be punished with a sentence of imprisonment from one to five years.

2. The same punishment shall be incurred those who cause damage to railways or cause serious damage to railway traffic in any of the manners foreseen in Article 382.

3. The same punishment shall be imposed on those who damage the water, gas or electricity pipes or lines to inhabited areas, interrupting or seriously altering the supply or service thereof.

Article 561

Whoever, intending to attack the public peace, falsely affirms the existence of explosive devices or any others that may cause the same effect, or of chemical, biological or toxic substances that might cause damage to health, shall be punished with a sentence of imprisonment of six months to one year or a fine from twelve to twenty- four months, in view of the alarm or alteration of order effectively caused.

CHAPTER IV

Common provision to the preceding Chapters

Article 562

Should the person committing any of the felonies stated in the preceding Chapters of this Title be an established authority, the punishment of barring that is foreseen in each case shall be substituted by that of absolute barring for a term of ten to fifteen years, except if that circumstance is specifically considered in the criminal definition concerned.

CHAPTER V

On owning, trafficking and deposit of weapons, ammunition or explosives

Article 563

Possessing prohibited weapons and those obtained by substantial alteration of the manufacturing features of regulated firearms shall be punished with a sentence of imprisonment from one to three years.

Article 564

1. Possessing regulated firearms while lacking the necessary licences or permits shall be punished:

   1. With a sentence of imprisonment from one to two years for handguns;

   2. With a sentence of imprisonment of six months to one year for long firearms;

2. The felonies defined in the preceding Section shall be punished, respectively, by prison sentences of two to three years and from one to two years, when any of the following circumstances concurs:

   1. When the weapons lack factory marks or serial numbers, or have these altered or obliterated;

   2. Which have been unlawfully imported into Spain;

   3. Which have been transformed, modifying their original characteristics.

Article 565

The Judges or Courts of Law may lower the penalties stated in the preceding Articles by one degree, as long as the circumstances of the fact and of the offender prove the lack of intention to use the weapons for unlawful purposes.

Article 566

1. Those who manufacture or market arms or ammunition or set up depots for these that are not authorised by law or the competent authority shall be punished:

1. In the case of weapons or ammunition for warfare or chemical or biological weapons or anti-personnel mines or cluster munitions, with a sentence of imprisonment from five to ten years for the promoters and organisers, and with imprisonment from three to five years for those who have co-operated in forming them;

2. In the case of regulated firearms or the ammunition for these, with a sentence of imprisonment of two to four years for the promoters and organisers, and with imprisonment from six months to two years for those who have co-operated in forming them.

3. The same penalties shall be applied, in the respective cases, to trafficking in weapons and ammunition for war or defence, in chemical or biological weapons or anti-personnel mines or cluster munitions.

2. The penalties set forth in Sub-Section 1 of the preceding Section shall be imposed on those who develop or use chemical or biological weapons or anti-personnel mines or cluster munitions, who commence military preparations to use them, or do not destroy them in breach of the international treaties or conventions to which Spain is a party.

Article 567

1. A depot of weapons for war is deemed to include manufacturing, trafficking or possession of such weapons, regardless of their model or class, even when they are in disassembled components. A depot of chemical or biological weapons or anti-personnel mines or cluster munitions shall be deemed to include manufacturing, trafficking or possession thereof.

The firearms depot, in its aspect of trafficking, includes both acquisition as well as disposal.

2. Arms for warfare are deemed to be those determined as such in the provisions regulating national defence. Chemical or biological weapons, anti-personnel mines or cluster munitions are deemed to be those defined as such in the international treaties or conventions to which Spain is a party.

Development of chemical or biological weapons, anti-personnel mines or cluster munitions is construed to be any activity consisting of research or study of a scientific or technical nature aimed at creation of a new chemical or biological weapon, anti-personnel mine or cluster munitions or modification of existing ones.

3. A depot of regulated firearms is deemed to include manufacturing, trading or gathering five or more of those weapons, even when they are in disassembled components.

4. Regarding ammunition, the Judges and Courts of Law, taking into account the quantity and class thereof, shall declare whether or not they constitute a depot for the purposes of this Chapter.

Article 568

Possession or having a depot of explosive, flammable, incendiary or asphyxiating substances or devices, as well as their manufacturing, trafficking or transport, or supply in any way not authorised by the laws or the competent authority, shall be punished with a sentence of imprisonment from four to eight years, for their promoters and organisers, and with a sentence of imprisonment of three to five years for those who have co-operated in forming them.

Article 569

Depots of arms, munitions or explosives established in name or on behalf of an assembly with criminal purposes shall lead to it being declared unlawful by the court and to its consequential dissolution.

Article 570

1. In the cases foreseen in this Chapter, the punishment of deprivation of the right to own and carry weapons for a term exceeding three years may be handed down in a sentence of imprisonment imposed.

2. Likewise, should the convict be authorised to manufacture or trade in any one or number of substances, arms and ammunition mentioned therein, in addition to the penalties stated, he shall also suffer special barring from exercise of his industry or trade for a term of twelve to twenty years.

CHAPTER VI

On criminal organisations and groups

Article 570 bis

1. Whoever promotes, constitutes, organises, co-ordinates or directs a criminal organisation shall be punished with a sentence of imprisonment from four to eight years, if it has the purpose or object of committing serious felonies, and with a sentence of imprisonment from three to six years in other cases; and whoever actively participates in the organisation, forms part thereof or co-operates financially or in any other way therein, shall be punished with imprisonment from two to five years if its purpose is to commit serious felonies, and with a sentence of imprisonment from one to three years in other cases.

For the purposes of this Code, a criminal organisation is construed to be a stable group formed by one or more persons, for an indefinite term, in collusion and co-ordination to distribute diverse tasks or duties in order to commit felonies, as well as to carry out reiterated commission of misdemeanours.

2. The penalties foreseen in the preceding Section shall be imposed in the upper half when the organisation:

a) is formed by a large number of persons;

b) possesses weapons or dangerous instruments;

c) has advanced technological resources for communication or transport that, due to their characteristics, are especially fit to facilitate commission of the offences or the impunity of the offenders.

Should two or more of those circumstances concur, the higher degree penalties shall be imposed.

3. The upper half of the penalties respectively foreseen in this Article shall be imposed if the offences are against the life or integrity of persons, liberty, sexual freedom and indemnity, or involve trafficking in human beings.

Article 570 ter

1. Whoever constitutes, finances or forms a criminal group shall be punished:

a) If the purpose of the group is to commit the felonies mentioned in Section 3 of the preceding Article, with the punishment of two to four years imprisonment for one or more serious felonies and with that of one to three years imprisonment for less serious felonies;

b) With the punishment of six months to two years imprisonment if the purpose of the group is to commit any other serious felony;

c) With the punishment from three months to a year of imprisonment when the aim is to commit one or several less serious felonies not included in Section a) or reiterated commission of misdemeanours, in the latter case the punishment must be imposed in the lower half, except if the purpose of the group is reiterated perpetration of the misdemeanour defined in Section 1 of Article 623, in which case the full punishment may be handed down.

For the purposes of this Code, a criminal group shall be construed as the collusion of more than two persons who, without fulfilling any or a number of the characteristics of a criminal organisation defined in the preceding Section, has the purpose or object of perpetrating felonies in collusion, or co-ordinated, reiterated commission of misdemeanours.

2. The penalties foreseen in the preceding Section shall be imposed in the upper half when the group:

a) is formed by a large number of persons;

b) has weapons or dangerous instruments;

c) has advanced technological resources for communication or transport that, due to their characteristics, are especially fit to facilitate commission of the offences or the impunity of the offenders.

If two or more of those circumstances concur, the higher degree penalties shall be imposed.

Article 570 quater

1. In the cases foreseen in this Chapter and the following one, the Judges and Courts of Law shall order dissolution of the organisation or group and, when appropriate, any other of the consequences of Articles 33.7 and 129 of this Code.

2. Those responsible for the conduct described in the preceding two Articles, in addition to the penalties foreseen therein, shall be subject to that of special barring from all economic activities or legal transactions related to the activity of the criminal organisation or group, or to their action within these, for a time exceeding that of the term of the custodial sentence imposed by six to twenty years, as appropriate, proportionally to the seriousness of the offence, the number of those committed and the circumstances of the criminal.

In all cases, when the conduct foreseen in those Articles is included under another provision of this Code, the terms set forth in rule 4 of Article 8 shall apply.

3. The provisions of this Chapter shall be applicable to all criminal organisations or groups that perpetrate any criminally relevant act in Spain, even if they have been formed, are based or perpetrate their activity abroad.

4. The Judges or Courts of Law, giving the reasons in their judgement, may impose a lower punishment by one or two degrees on the person responsible for any of the felonies foreseen in this Chapter, as long as the subject has voluntarily quit his criminal activities and has actively collaborated with the authorities or their agents either to obtain decisive evidence for the identification or capture of others who are responsible or to prevent the activities or furtherance of the organisations or groups to which they have belonged or to prevent a felony being committed within or through those organisations or groups.

CHAPTER VII

On terrorist organisations and groups and on felonies of terrorism

SUBCHAPTER 1: ON TERRORIST ORGANISATIONS AND GROUPS

Article 571

1. Whoever promotes, forms, organises or directs a terrorist organisation or group shall be punished with imprisonment from eight to fourteen years and special barring from public employment and office for a term from eight to fifteen years.

2. Whoever actively participate in the organisation or group, or forms part thereof, shall be punished with imprisonment from six to twelve years and special barring from public employment and office for a term from six to fourteen.

3. For the purposes of this Code, terrorist organisations or groups shall be deemed to be those groups that, fulfilling the characteristics respectively established in Sub-Section 2 of Section 1 of Article 570 bis) and in Sub-Section 2 of

Section 1 of Article 570 ter, have the purpose or object of subverting the constitutional order or seriously altering the public peace by committing any of the felonies foreseen in the following Subchapter.

SUBCHAPTER 2: ON FELONIES OF TERRORISM

Article 572

1. Those who, while pertaining to, acting in the service of, or collaborating with terrorist organisations or groups, commit the felonies of havoc or arson defined in Articles 346 and 351, respectively, shall be punished with a sentence of imprisonment from fifteen to twenty years, without prejudice to the punishment to which they may be subject if they cause loss of life or injury to the physical integrity or health of persons.

2. Those who, while pertaining to, acting in the service of, or collaborating with terrorist organisations or groups commit attacks against persons, shall incur:

  1. Sentence of imprisonment from twenty to thirty years if they cause the death of a person;

  2. Sentence of imprisonment from fifteen to twenty years if they cause injuries of the kind foreseen in Articles 149 and 150 or kidnap a person;

  3. Sentence of imprisonment from ten to fifteen years if they cause any other injury or unlawfully detain, intimidate or coerce a person.

3. If the acts are perpetrated against the persons mentioned in Section 2 of Article 551 or against members of the Armed Forces, of the State Police and Security Forces, the Police Forces of the Autonomous Communities or those of the local corporations, the punishment shall be imposed in its upper half.

Article 573

Depots of arms or ammunition or possession or storage of explosive, flammable, incendiary or asphyxiating substances or devices, or of their components, as well as their manufacture, trafficking, transport or supply in any way, and merely placing or using those substances or the appropriate means or devices, shall be punished with a sentence of imprisonment from six to ten years when those acts are committed by whoever belongs to, acts in the service or collaborates with armed gangs, terrorist organisations or groups described in the preceding Articles.

Article 574

Those who, while pertaining to, acting in the service of, or collaborating with terrorist organisations or groups, commit any other felony or misdemeanour for any of the purposes stated in Section 3 of Article 571, shall be punished with the penalty set for the felony or misdemeanour, in its upper half.

Article 575

Those who, in order to provide funds to armed gangs, terrorist organisations or groups aforementioned, or in order to favour their activities, attack property, shall be punished with the higher degree punishment that would be applicable for the felony committed, without prejudice to the appropriate ones that would be imposed pursuant to what is set forth in the following Article for acts of collaboration.

Article 576

1. Punishment by imprisonment from five to ten years and a fine of eighteen to twenty- four months shall be handed down to whoever carries out, procures or facilitates any act of collaboration with the activities or purposes of a terrorist organisation or group.

2. Acts of collaboration include information on or surveillance of persons, property or installations; construction, conditioning, assignment or use of accommodation or storage facilities; concealment or transport of individuals related to terrorist organisations or groups; organisation of training practices or attending them and, in general, any other equivalent form of co-operation, aid or mediation, economic or of any other kind whatsoever, with the activities of those terrorist organisations or groups.

When the information or surveillance of persons mentioned in the preceding Paragraph endangers the life, physical integrity, liberty or property thereof, the punishment shall be imposed as foreseen in Section 1, in the upper half. Should the risk foreseen concur, the act shall be punished as co-perpetration or complicity, as appropriate.

3. The same penalties foreseen in Section 1 of this Article shall be imposed on whoever carries out any activity to recruit, indoctrinate, train or induct, aimed at having others join a terrorist organisation or group, or at committing any of the offences foreseen in this Chapter.

Article 576 bis

1. Whoever by any means, directly or indirectly provides or collects funds intending them to be used, or knowing they shall be used, fully or partially to commit any of the felonies included in this Chapter or to deliver them to a terrorist organisation or group, shall be punished with prison sentences of five to ten years and a fine of eighteen to twenty- four months.

Should the funds eventually be used to execute specific acts of terrorism, this shall be punished as co-perpetration or complicity, as appropriate, provided this involves a higher penalty.

2. Whoever, being specifically obliged by law to collaborate with the authorities in the prevention of terrorism financing activities, gives rise, due to serious negligence in the fulfilment of those obligations, to any of the conducts described in Section one of this Article not being detected or prevented, shall be punished with the penalty lower by one or two degrees to that foreseen herein.

3. When, pursuant to the terms established in Article 31 bis of this Code, a legal person is responsible for the offences defined in this Article, it shall have the following penalties imposed thereon:

a) Fine from two to five years, if the offence committed by a natural person has a punishment of imprisonment foreseen exceeding five years;

b) Fine from one to three years, if the offence committed by a natural person has a punishment foreseen of more than two years custodial sentence not included in the preceding Sub-Section.

Pursuant to the rules established in Article 66 bis of this Code, the Judges and Courts of Law may also impose the penalties established in Sub-Sections b) to g) of Section 7 of Article 33.

Article 577

Those who, without pertaining to an armed gang, terrorist organisation or group, and with in order to subvert the constitutional order or seriously alter the public peace, or to contribute to those ends by terrorising the inhabitants of a town or the members of a social, political or professional group, were to commit homicides, injuries of the kind defined under Articles 147 to 150, illegal detentions, kidnappings, intimidations or coercion against persons, or who carry out any felonies of arson, havoc, damages defined under Articles 263 to 266, 323 or 560, or possession, manufacturing, storage, trafficking, transport or supply of arms, ammunition or explosive, flammable, incendiary or asphyxiating substances or devices, or components thereof, shall be punished with the relevant punishment for the act committed, in the upper half.

Article 578

Apologism or justification by means of public expression or diffusion of the felonies included in Articles 571 to 577 of this Code, or of anybody who has participated in commission thereof, or in perpetrating acts that involve discredit, disdain or humiliation of the victims of terrorist offences or their relatives shall be punished with a sentence of imprisonment from one to two years. In the judgement, the Judge may also order any one or number of the prohibitions foreseen in Article 57 of this Code for the term he may set.

Article 579

1. Provocation, conspiracy and solicitation to commit the offences foreseen in Articles 571 to 578 shall be punished with the penalty lower by one or two degrees to the relevant one, respectively, for the acts foreseen in the preceding Articles.

Provided it is not included in the preceding Section or another provision of this Code with a higher penalty, distribution or public diffusion by any means of messages or slogans aimed at provoking, encouraging or favouring commission of any of the felonies foreseen in this Chapter, generating or increasing the risk of them effectively being committed, shall be punished with the penalty of six months to two years imprisonment.

2. Those responsible for the felonies foreseen in this Chapter, without prejudice to the relevant penalties under the preceding Articles, shall also be punished with the penalty of absolute barring for a time exceeding that of the term of the sentence custodial sentence duly imposed in the sentence by six to twenty years, proportionally in view of the seriousness of the felonies, the number committed and the circumstances of the criminal.

3. Those convicted to serious custodial sentences for one or more felonies included in this Chapter shall also have a measure of probation from five to ten years imposed, and one to five years if the sentence of imprisonment is less serious. Notwithstanding the foregoing, in the case of a single offence that is not serious committed by a first time offender, the Court of Law may hand down the probation measure or not, in view of the lesser or greater dangerousness of the principal.

4. In the felonies foreseen in this Subchapter, the Judges and Courts of Law may impose, giving the reasons in the judgement, a punishment lower by one or two degrees to that stated by the Law for the felony concerned, when the subject has voluntarily quit his criminal activities and has appeared before the authorities to confess the acts in which he has participated and has also collaborated actively with the authorities to prevent the felony taking place or effectively aids the obtaining of decisive evidence to identify or capture the others who are responsible, or to prevent the action or development of the terrorist organisations or groups to which he has belonged, or with which he has collaborated.

Article 580

In all felonies related to the activity of armed gangs, terrorist organisations or groups, conviction by a foreign Judge or Court of Law shall be equivalent to judgements by Spanish Judges or Courts of Law for the purposes of application of the aggravating circumstance of recidivism.

TITLE XXIII

On felonies of treason and against the peace or independence of the Stateand those referring to National Defence

CHAPTER I

Felonies of treason

Article 581

A Spaniard who induces a foreign power to declare war on Spain, or who makes arrangements with it to the same end, shall be punished with a sentence of imprisonment from fifteen to twenty years.

Article 582

A sentence of imprisonment from twelve to twenty years shall be handed down to:

1. Spaniards who facilitate the entry of the enemy to Spain, the taking of a town, military post, ship or aircraft of the State or quartermasters' or arms warehouses or depots;

2. Spaniards who persuade or encourage Spanish troops, or those serving Spain, to join the enemy ranks, or to desert from their flags while on campaign;

3. Spaniards who recruit persons or supply weapons or other means that are effective to wage war on Spain, under enemy flags.

Article 583

A sentence of imprisonment from twelve to twenty years shall be handed down to:

1. Spaniards who take up arms against their Fatherland under enemy flags. Whoever acts as a leader or promoter, or who has any command or established authority, shall have the higher degree punishment imposed.

2. A Spaniard who supplies enemy troops funds, weapons, vessels, aircraft, assets or intendancy munitions or weaponry, or other direct means that are effective to wage hostilities against Spain, or who favours progress by the armed forces in a manner not included in the preceding Article;

3. A Spaniard who supplies the enemy with plans of fortresses, buildings or land, documents or news that lead directly to the same end of hostilities against Spain, or to favour progress by the enemy forces;

4. Spaniards who, in wartime, prevent Spanish troops receiving the aid stated in Sub-Section 2 or the data and news indicated in Sub-Section 3 of this Article.

Article 584

A Spaniard who, in order to favour a foreign power, association or international organisation, obtains, forges, deactivates or discloses information classified as reserved or secret, liable to damage national security or national defence, shall be punished, as a traitor, with a sentence of imprisonment from six to twelve years.

Article 585

Provocation, conspiracy and solicitation for any of the felonies foreseen in the preceding Articles of this Chapter shall be punished with a sentence of imprisonment lower by one or two degrees to that for the relevant offence.

Article 586

An alien resident in Spain who were to commit any of the offences included in this Chapter shall be punished with the lower degree punishment to that set for them, except as established in Treaties or by International Law with reference to the staff of diplomatic missions, consular posts and international organisations.

Article 587

The penalties stated in the preceding Articles of this Chapter are applicable to those who commit the felonies defined therein against a power allied to Spain, in the event of campaigning against a common enemy.

Article 588

A sentence of imprisonment from fifteen to twenty years shall be handed down to members of the Government who, without complying what is set forth in the Constitution, declare war or sign a peace agreement.

CHAPTER II

Felonies that compromise the peace or independence of the State

Article 589

Whoever publishes or executes any order, provision or document in Spain of a foreign Government that attacks the independence or security of the State, that opposes obeying its laws or causes them to be breached, shall be punished with a sentence of imprisonment from one to three years.

Article 590

1. Whoever, by unlawful acts or those that are not duly authorised, provokes or gives rise to a declaration of war against Spain by another power, or exposes Spaniards to abuse or retaliation against their persons or assets, shall be punished with a sentence of imprisonment from eight to fifteen years if an authority or officer, and from four to eight if not.

2. Should war not be declared, nor the abuse or retaliation take place, the respective punishment immediately below that set shall be imposed.

Article 591

Whoever, during a war in which Spain does not intervene, perpetrates any act that compromises the neutrality of the State or breaches the provisions published by the Government to maintain such neutrality, shall be punished with the same penalties as those stated in the preceding Article.

Article 592

1. Those who, in order to damage the authority of the State or compromise the dignity or vital interests of Spain, maintain intelligence or relations of any kind with foreign governments, with their agents, or with foreign or international groups, bodies or associations, shall be punished with a sentence of imprisonment from four to eight years.

2. Whoever perpetrates the acts listed in the preceding Section with the intention of provoking a war or rebellion shall be punished pursuant to Articles 581, 473 or 475 of this Code as appropriate.

Article 593

A sentence of imprisonment shall be imposed from eight to fifteen years upon whoever breaches a truce or armistice agreed between the Spanish Nation and another enemy one, or between their armed forces.

Article 594

1. A Spaniard who, in time of war, were to communicate or circulate false news or rumours aimed at damaging the prestige of the State or the interests of the Nation, shall be punished with imprisonment of six months to two years.

2. The same penalties shall be incurred by any alien who perpetrates any of the acts included in the preceding Section in Spanish territory.

Article 595

Whoever, without a legally granted authorisation, raises up troops in Spain to serve a foreign power, whatever the object proposed or the nation hostilities are intended against, shall be punished with a sentence of imprisonment from four to eight years.

Article 596

1. Whoever, in time of war and in order to compromise the peace, security or the independence of the State, were to correspond with an enemy country or one occupied by its troops, when the Government has prohibited this, shall be punished with a sentence of imprisonment from one to five years. If the correspondence provides warnings or news that may be taken advantage of by the enemy, a sentence of imprisonment from eight to fifteen years shall be imposed.

2. The same penalties shall be incurred by whoever commits the felonies included in this Article, even though addressing the correspondence through a friendly or neutral country to circumvent the Law.

3. Should the accused aim to serve the enemy with his warnings or news, he shall be deemed to fall under Sub-Sections 3 or 4 of Article 583.

Article 597

A Spaniard or alien who, being present in Spain, enters, or attempts to enter a foreign country when this has been prohibited by the Government, shall be punished with the penalty of a fine from six to twelve months.

CHAPTER III

On disclosure and revealing secrets and information on National Defence

SUBCHAPTER 1. ON DISCLOSURE AND REVEALING SECRETS AND INFORMATION ON NATIONAL DEFENCE
(Suppressed)

Article 598

Whoever, without intending to favour a foreign power, obtains, reveals, forges or erases information legally classified as reserved or secret, related to national security or national defence, or on the technical means or systems used by the Armed Forces or industries of military interest, shall be punished with a sentence of imprisonment of one to four years.

Article 599

The punishment established in the preceding Section shall be applied in the upper half when any of the following circumstances concurs:

1. When the doer is the custodian or has knowledge of the secret or information due to his office or post;

2. When the disclosure consists of publicising the secret or information in any social media or in a way that ensures its diffusion.

Article 600

1. Whoever, without specific authorisation, were to produce plans or documentation related to military zones, installations or materials that have restricted access and the knowledge of which is protected and reserved by information with the legal classification of reserved or secret, shall be punished with a sentence of imprisonment of six months to three years.

2. The same punishment shall apply to whoever has objects, information legally classified as reserved, or secret in his possession, related to national security or defence, without complying with the provisions established in the laws in force.

Article 601

Whoever, due to his office, commission or service, has in his possession or has official knowledge of objects or information legally classified as reserved or secret, or of military interest, related to national security or national defence and, due to serious negligence, gives rise to these becoming known to an unauthorised person or divulged, published or made void, shall be punished with a sentence of imprisonment of six months to one year.

Article 602

Whoever discovers, infringes, reveals, steals or uses information legally classified as reserved or secret related to nuclear energy, shall be punished with a sentence of imprisonment of six months to three years, except if the act has a more serious punishment set for it by Law.

Article 603

Whoever destroys, makes void, forges or opens correspondence or documentation legally classified as reserved or secret without authorisation, related to national defence and that he has in his possession due to his office or post, shall be punished with a sentence of imprisonment from two to five years and special barring from public employment and office for a term of three to six years.

SUBCHAPTER 2. ON FELONIES AGAINST THE DUTY TO PERPETRATE MILITARY SERVICE
(Suppressed)

Article 604

(Without content)

TITLE XXIV

Crimes against the International Community

CHAPTER I

Crimes against International Law

Article 605

1. Whoever kills a foreign Head of State, or another person internationally protected by a Treaty who is in Spain, shall be punished with a sentence of imprisonment from twenty to twenty- five years. Should two or more aggravating circumstances concur in the crime, a sentence of imprisonment from twenty- five to thirty years shall be imposed.

2. Whoever were to cause the injuries defined in Article 149 to the persons mentioned in the preceding Section, shall be punished with a sentence of imprisonment from fifteen to twenty years.

If any of the injuries foreseen in Article 150 are caused, he shall be punished with a sentence of imprisonment from eight to fifteen years, and from four to eight years if any other injury.

3. Any other crime committed against persons mentioned in the preceding Sections, or against local officers, the private residence or the means of transport of those persons, shall be punished with the penalties established in this Code for the respective offences, in the upper half.

Article 606

1. Whoever violates the personal immunity of the Head of State of another country, or that of another person internationally protected by a Treaty, shall be punished with a sentence of imprisonment of six months to three years.

2 When the felonies included in this Article and the previous one do not have a reciprocal punishment established in the laws of the country of origin of the persons offended, the offender shall have the punishment to which the crime is subject imposed, pursuant to the provisions of this Code, as if the person offended does not have the official status mentioned in the preceding Section.

CHAPTER II

Crimes of genocide

Article 607

1. Those who, aiming to fully or partially exterminate a national, ethnic, racial, religious or specific group determined by the disability of its members, commit any of the following acts, shall be punished:

   1. With a sentence of imprisonment from fifteen to twenty years, if they were to kill any of its members. If two or more aggravating circumstances were to concur in the act, the higher degree punishment shall be imposed;

   2. With imprisonment from fifteen to twenty years, if they were to sexually assault any of its members or cause any of the injuries foreseen in Article 149;

   3. With imprisonment from eight to fifteen years, if they were to subject the group or any of its members to conditions of existence that endanger their life or seriously affect their health, or when any of the injuries foreseen in Article 150 are caused;

   4. With the same punishment, if forcible transportation of the group or its members are carried out, if they adopt any measure aimed at preventing their lifestyle or procreation, or if they forcibly transfer individuals from one group to another;

   5. With imprisonment from four to eight years, if they were to cause any injury other than that stated in Sub-Sections 2 and 3 of this Section.

2. Diffusion by any means of ideas or doctrines that deny or justify the crimes defined in the preceding Section of this Article, or that aim to reinstate regimes or institutions that protect practices that generate these shall be punished with a sentence of imprisonment from one to two years.

CHAPTER II BIS

On crimes against humanity

Article 607 bis

1. Conviction for crimes against humanity shall befall whoever commits the acts foreseen in the following Section as part of a widespread or systematic attack on the civil population or against part thereof.

In all cases, committing such acts shall be deemed a crime against humanity when:

1. Due to the victim pertaining to a group or community persecuted for political, racial, national, ethnic, cultural, religious or another kind of reasons, disability, or other motives universally recognised as unacceptable under International Law;

2. In the context of an institutionalised regime of systematic oppression and domination of a racial group over one or more racial groups and with the intention of maintaining such a regime.

2. Those convicted of crimes against humanity shall be punished:

1. With a sentence of imprisonment from fifteen to twenty years if they cause the death of any person. A punishment higher in one degree shall be imposed if any of the circumstances foreseen in Article 139 concur;

2. With a sentence of imprisonment from twelve to fifteen years if they commit rape, and from four to six years imprisonment if the act were to consist of any other type of sexual assault;

3. With a sentence of imprisonment from twelve to fifteen years if any of the injuries of Article 149 were to take place and from eight to twelve years imprisonment if persons are subjected to conditions of existence that endanger their life or seriously affect their health, or when they are caused any of the injuries foreseen in Article 150. A sentence of imprisonment from four to eight years shall be applied if they commit any of the injuries of Article 147;

4. With a sentence of imprisonment from eight to twelve years if they deport or forcibly transport one or more persons from one State or place to another, by expulsion or other acts of coercion without authorised reasons;

5. With a sentence of imprisonment from six to eight years if they were to forcibly make pregnant any woman in order to modify the ethnic composition of the population, without prejudice to the relevant punishment, as appropriate, for other felonies;

6. With a sentence of imprisonment from twelve to fifteen years when they detain any person and refuse to recognise that custodial sentence or to report on the situation or whereabouts of the person arrested;

7. With a sentence of imprisonment from eight to twelve years if they were to arrest a person, depriving him of his liberty, with breach of the international rules on arrest.

    The punishment shall be imposed at a lower degree when the arrest lasts less than fifteen days;

8. With the punishment from four to eight years imprisonment if they commit serious torture of persons they have under their custody or control and of imprisonment from two to six years if less serious. For the purposes of this Article, torture shall be construed as submitting a person to physical or mental suffering. The punishment foreseen in this Sub-Section shall be imposed without prejudice to the relevant penalties, as appropriate, for the violations of other rights of the victim;

9. With a sentence of imprisonment from four to eight years if they commit any of the conducts related to prostitution defined in Article 187.1, and with that of six to eight years in the cases foreseen in Article 188.1. The punishment shall be imposed from six to eight years on whoever transports persons from one place to another with the intent to sexually exploit them, using violence, intimidation or deceit, or abusing a situation of superiority or need or the vulnerability of the victim. When the conduct foreseen in the preceding Section and in Article 188.1 is committed against minors or the incapacitated, the higher degree penalties shall be imposed;

10. With a sentence of imprisonment from four to eight years if any person is subjected to slavery or kept in servitude. The punishment shall be applied without prejudice to the appropriate ones for the specific violations committed against the rights of persons. Slavery shall be construed as the situation of a person over whom another exercises, albeit *de facto*, all and some of the attributes of the right of property, such as buying, selling, lending or exchanging such person.

CHAPTER III

On crimes against protected persons and assets in the event of armed conflict

Article 608

For the purposes of this Chapter, the following are intended as protected persons:

1. The wounded, the sick or shipwrecked, and the medical or religious personnel protected by the First and Second Geneva Conventions dated on 12th August 1949, or the First Additional Protocol dated on 8th June 1977;

2. Prisoners of war protected by the Third Geneva Convention dated on 12th August 1949 or the First Additional Protocol dated on 8th June 1977;

3. The civilian population and individual civilian protected by the Fourth Geneva Convention dated on 12th August 1949 and by the First Additional Protocol dated on 8th June 1977;

4. Non-combatants and the personnel of the Protecting Power and its Substitute protected by the Geneva Conventions dated on 12th August 1949 or by the First Additional Protocol dated on 8th June 1977.

5. Parliamentarians and the persons accompanying them, protected by the Second Convention of The Hague dated on 29th July 1899;

6. The United Nations and associated personnel, protected by the Convention on the Safety of United Nations and Associated Personnel, dated on 9th December 1994;

7. Any others with that status by virtue of the Second Additional Protocol dated 8th June 1977, or any other international treaties to which Spain is a party.

Article 609

Whoever, during an armed conflict, physically abuses or seriously endangers the life, health or integrity of any protected persona, subjects him to torture or inhumane treatment, including biological experiments, causes him serious suffering or subjects him to any medical act that is not in keeping with his state of health, nor according to the generally recognised medical standards that the Party responsible would apply to its own nationals not detained under similar medical circumstances, shall be punished with a sentence of imprisonment from four to eight years, without prejudice to the punishment that might be appropriate for the damaging results caused.

Article 610

Whoever, during an armed conflict, uses or orders methods or means of combat that are prohibited or intended to cause unnecessary suffering or superfluous harm, as well as those conceived to cause, or that can be reasonably be expected to cause extensive, lasting and serious damage to the natural environment, compromising the health or survival of the population, or who orders all-out war, shall be punished with a sentence of imprisonment from ten to fifteen years, without prejudice to the relevant punishment for the results caused.

Article 611

Whoever perpetrates the following acts during an armed conflict shall be punished with a sentence of imprisonment from ten to fifteen years, without prejudice to the relevant punishment for the results caused:

1. Conducts or orders indiscriminate or excessive attacks or makes the civil population the target of attacks, retaliation or acts or threats of violence, the main purpose of which is to strike fear therein;.

2. Destroys or damages, breaching the rules of International Law applicable to armed conflicts, the non-military ships or aircraft of an adversary or neutral party, unnecessarily and without allowing time or without adopting the necessary measures to provide for the safety of persons and conservation of the ship's papers;

3. Forces a prisoner of war or a civilian to serve, in any way, in the Armed Forces of the adversary, or deprives him of his right to a due and impartial process of law;

4. Deports, forcibly transports, takes hostage or unlawfully detains or confines any protected person or uses him to protect certain military locations, zones or forces from an attack by the adversary;

5. Transports and settles population from the side occupying, directly or indirectly, in the occupied territory, to reside there permanently;

6. Perpetrates, orders the carrying out or maintains, with regard to any protected person, practices of racial segregation and other inhumane and degrading practices based on other distinctions of an unfavourable nature, that amount to an outrage against personal dignity;

7. Prevents or delays, without reason, the release or repatriation of prisoners of war or civilians;

8. Declares the rights and actions by the nationals of the adversary to be abolished, suspended or inadmissible before a Judge or Court of Law;

9. Attacks the sexual freedom of a protected person by committing acts of rape, sexual slavery, induced or forced prostitution, forced pregnancy, forced sterilisation or any other kind of sexual assault.

Article 612

Whoever perpetrates the following acts during an armed conflict shall be punished with a sentence of imprisonment of three to seven years, without prejudice to the relevant punishment for the results caused:

1. Knowingly violates the protection due to hospitals, installations, materiel, units and means for health transport, prisoner camps, sanitary and safety zones and locations, neutralised zones, locations for internment of the civil population, undefended locations and demilitarised zones, made known by the appropriate and distinctive signs;

2. Acts with violence against the medical or religious staff or those forming medical missions or aid organisations, or against the personnel authorised to use then signs and distinctive signals, established by the Geneva Conventions, pursuant to International Law;

3. Severely abuses, deprives or does not ensure the essential food or necessary medical assistance to any protected person, or subjects him to humiliating or degrading treatment, fails to inform him of his situation without justified delay, and in a comprehensible manner, imposes collective punishment for individual acts, or infringes the requisites for accommodation of women and families, or for special of women and children established in the international treaties to which Spain is a party, and in particular, who recruits or enrols persons under the age of eighteen or uses them to participate directly in the hostilities;

4. Unduly uses the protective or distinctive signs, emblems or signals established and recognised in the international treaties to which Spain is a party, especially the distinctive signs of the Red Cross, of the Red Crescent and the Red Crystal.

5. Unduly or perfidiously uses a flag, uniform, insignia or distinctive emblem of neutral States, of the United Nations or other States that are not parties to the conflict, or of the adversaries, during attacks or to cover, favour, protect or hinder military operations, except in the cases specifically foreseen in the international treaties to which Spain is a party;

6. Unduly or perfidiously uses the flag of parley or surrender to attack the inviolability or unduly retain the negotiator or any of the persons accompanying him, personnel of the Protecting Power or its Substitute, or a member of an International Fact Finding Commission;

7. Strips a corpse, the wounded, sick, shipwrecked, prisoner of war or interned civilian of his belongings;

8. Intentionally starves the civilian population as a means of warfare, depriving it of the indispensable resources for survival, including the act of randomly obstructing aid supplies conducted pursuant to the Geneva Conventions and its Additional Protocols;

9. Violates a ceasefire, armistice, capitulation or another arrangement made with the adversary;

10. Intentionally attacks any member of the United Nations and associated personnel, or that participating in a peace or humanitarian aid mission pursuant to the United Nations Charter, as long as they are entitled to the protection granted to civilians or civil objects, pursuant to International Law on armed conflicts, or threaten them with such an attack to oblige a natural or legal person to carry out or abstain from carrying out any act.

Article 613

1. Whoever perpetrates or orders any of the following actions during an armed conflict shall be punished with a sentence of imprisonment from four to six years:

   a) Attacks or targets cultural property or places of worship that are the cultural or spiritual heritage of persons as an object of reprisals or acts of hostility, as long as those assets or locations are not in the immediate vicinity of a military objective and are not used to support the military effort by the adversary and are duly marked;

   b) Makes undue use of the cultural property or places of worship referred to in Sub-Section a) to support military action;

   c) Appropriates on a large scale, robs, sacks or perpetrates acts of vandalism against the cultural property or places of worship referred to in Sub-Section a);

   d) Attacks or makes assets of a civil nature of the adversary a target for reprisals or acts of hostility, when this does not provide, under the circumstances of the case, a defined military advantage, or when those assets do not contribute effectively to the military action of the adversary;

   e) Attacks, destroys, removes or puts assets that are indispensable for survival of the civilian population out of service, except if the adversary uses those assets to directly support military action, or exclusively as a means of subsistence for members of its armed forces;

   f) Attacks or makes works or facilities that contain hazardous substances or energy the target of reprisals when such attacks might cause those substances to be released and thus cause major damage to the civilian population, except if those works or installations are used to support in a regular, significant and direct way military operations and those attacks are the only feasible way to end that support;

   g) Destroys, damages or seizes, without military need, items that do not belong to him, obliging another to hand them over or perpetrating any other acts of pillage;

   h) Unduly or unnecessarily confiscates moveable personal or real property in the occupied territory or destroys non- military ships or aircraft and their cargo, of an adversary or neutral party, or captures them in breach of the applicable international provisions on armed conflicts at sea;

   i) Attacks or carries out acts of hostility against installations, material, units, private residences or vehicles of any member of the personnel stated in Section 10 of Article 612, or threatens to carry out such attacks or acts of hostility to oblige a natural or legal person to carry out or to abstain from carrying out any act.

2. When the reprisal, act of hostility or undue use targets cultural property or places of worship under special protection, or those granted protection by virtue of special agreements, or buildings that are cultural property or places of worship under reinforced protection, or their immediate surroundings, the higher degree punishment may be handed down.

In the other cases foreseen in the preceding Section of this Article, the higher degree punishment may be imposed when extensive, major destruction is caused to assets, works or facilities covered by these, or in cases of extreme severity.

Article 614

Whoever, during an armed conflict, perpetrates or orders any other violations or acts contrary to the provisions of the international treaties to which Spain is a party and related to how hostilities are conducted, regulation of the means and methods of combat, protection of the wounded, the sick and shipwrecked, due treatment of prisoners of war, protection of civilians and protection of cultural property in the case of armed conflict, shall be punished with a sentence of imprisonment of six months to two years.

Article 614 bis

When any of the conducts set forth in this Chapter form part of a plan or policy or are committed on a major scale, the upper half of the respective penalties shall be applied.

CHAPTER IV

Common provisions

Article 615

Provocation, conspiracy and solicitation to commit the crimes foreseen in the preceding Chapters of this Title shall be punished with the penalty lower by one or two degrees to which the actual crime is subject.

Article 615 bis

1. The military authority or commanding officer, or whoever acts as such, who does not take the measures available to him to prevent the forces under his effective command or control committing any of the crimes included in Chapters II, II bis and III of this Title, shall be punished with the same penalty as the principals.

2. Should the above conduct take place due to serious negligence, the punishment shall be the lower one by one or two degrees.

3. The military authority or commanding officer, or whoever acts as such, who does not take the measures available to him to pursue the crimes included in Chapters II, II bis and III of this Title committed by persons under his effective command or control shall be punished with the penalty lower by two degrees to that of the principals.

4. The superior not included in the preceding Sections who, within the scope of his competence, does not adopt the measures available to him to avoid his subordinates committing any of the crimes included in Chapters II, II bis and III of this Title shall be punished with the same penalty as the principals.

5. The superior who does not adopt the measures available to him for prosecution of the crimes included in Chapters II, II bis and III of this Title committed by his subordinates shall be punished with the penalty lower by two degrees to that of the principals.

6. The civil servant or authority who, without behaving as foreseen in the preceding Sections, and failing in the duties of his office, ceases to promote prosecution of any of the crimes included in Chapters II, II bis and III of this Title that come to his notice shall be punished with the penalty of special barring from public employment and office for a term from two to six years.

Article 616

Should any of the crimes included in the previous Chapters of this Title, except those foreseen in Article 614 and in Sections 2 and 6 of 615 bis, and in the preceding Title be committed by an authority or civil servant, in addition to the penalties stated therein, absolute barring for a term of ten to twenty years shall be imposed on him; if a private individual, the Judges and Courts of Law may order that of special barring from public employment and office for a term from one to ten years.

Article 616 bis

The terms set forth Article 20.7 of this Code shall not be applicable under any circumstance whatsoever to whoever obeys orders to commit or participate in the acts included in Chapters II and II bis of this Title.

CHAPTER V

Crime of piracy

Article 616 ter

Whoever, by violence, intimidation or deceit, seizes, damages or destroys an aircraft, ship or another kind of vessel or platform in the sea, or attacks persons, cargo or property found on board thereof, shall be convicted of the crime of piracy with a sentence of imprisonment from ten to fifteen years.

In all cases, the punishment foreseen in this Article shall be imposed without prejudice to the relevant ones for the felonies committed.

Article 616 quater.

1. Whoever, in the prevention or persecution of the acts foreseen in the preceding Article, resists or disobeys a warship or military aircraft or another ship or aircraft bearing clear signs that is identifiable as a ship or aircraft in the service of the Spanish State and that is authorised for such purposes, shall be punished with a sentence of imprisonment from one to three years.

2. Should force or violence be used in the conduct described above, the punishment of ten to fifteen years imprisonment shall be imposed.

3. In all cases, the penalties foreseen in this Article shall be imposed without prejudice to the relevant ones for the felonies committed.

BOOK III

On misdemeanours and their penalties

TITLE I

Misdemeanours against persons

Article 617

1. Whoever, by any means or procedure, were to cause another an injury not defined as a felony in this Code shall be punished with the penalty of permanent traceability from six to twelve days or a fine of one to two months.

2. Whoever were to assault or physically abuse another without causing him injury shall be punished with the penalty of permanent traceability from two to six days or a fine of ten to thirty days.

Article 618

1. Those who, having found an abandoned minor or incapacitated person do not hand him over to the authorities or his family, or do not provide him the appropriate aid as the circumstances require, shall be punished with the penalty of permanent traceability from six to twelve days or a fine from twelve to twenty- four days.

2. Whoever breaches the family obligations established in a judicially approved convention or court ruling in cases of legal separation, divorce, declaration of nullity of marriage, filiation process or maintenance allowance proceedings in favour of his offspring, provided it does not constitute a felony, shall be punished with the penalty of a fine from ten days to two months or community service from one to 30 days.

Article 619

Those who cease to provide assistance or, as appropriate, the aid the circumstances require, to an elderly or handicapped person who is unable and depends on their care, shall be punished with the penalty of a fine from ten to twenty days.

Article 620

The following shall be punished with the penalty of a fine from ten to twenty days:

1. Those who slightly threaten another with weapons or other dangerous instruments, or take these out during a brawl, unless in legitimate defence, except if the act constitutes a felony.

2. Those who intimidate, coerce, defame or unfairly abuse lightly another except if the act constitutes a felony.

The acts described in the preceding two Sections shall only be pursuable when reported by the person offended or his legal representative.

In the cases to which Section 2 of this Article refers, when the victim is any of the persons referred to in Article 173.2, the punishment shall be that of permanent traceability from four to eight days, always at a different dwelling far from that of the victim, or community service from five to ten days. In these cases, the report referred to in the preceding Paragraph of this Article shall not be required, except for persecution of defamation.

Article 621

1. Those who due to serious negligence were to cause any of the injuries foreseen in Section 2 of Article 147, shall be punished with the penalty of a fine from one to two months.

2. Those who, due to slight negligence, were to cause the death of another person, shall be punished with the penalty of a fine from one to two months.

3. Those who, due to slight negligence, cause an injury that would constitute a felony shall be punished with a punishment of a fine from ten to thirty days.

4. Should the act be committed with a motor vehicle or moped, he may also be sentenced the punishment of deprivation of the right to drive motor vehicles and mopeds for a term from three months to a year.

5. Should the act be committed with a weapon, he may also be sentenced to deprivation of the right to own and carry weapons for a term from three months to a year.

6. Misdemeanours penalised under this Article shall only be pursuable when reported by the person offended or his legal representative.

Article 622

Parents who, without actually committing a felony against relatives or, as appropriate, of disobedience, breach the custody regime of their minor children established by a judicial or administrative authority, shall be punished with the penalty of a fine from one to two months.

TITLE II

Misdemeanours against property

Article 623

The following shall be punished with permanent traceability from four to twelve days, or a fine of one to two months:

1. Those who commit larceny, if the value of what is stolen does not exceed four hundred euros. In cases of repeated perpetration of this misdemeanour, the punishment of permanent traceability shall be imposed in all cases. In the latter case, the Judge may provide in the sentence that the permanent traceability be served on Saturdays, Sundays and holidays at the penitentiary centre nearest to the convict's dwelling, pursuant to the terms set forth in Section 2 of Article 37.1.

    The reiteration shall be appraised on the basis of the number of misdemeanours committed, whether judged or not, and how near in time they are.

2. Those who behave as described in Article 236, as long as the value of the item concerned does not exceed four hundred euros.

3. Those who take or use a motor vehicle or moped pertaining to another without due authorisation, without the will to appropriate it, should the value of the vehicle used not exceed four hundred euros.

    If the act is perpetrated using force against property, the punishment shall be imposed in the upper half. If perpetrated by means of violence or intimidation of persons, it shall be penalised pursuant to the terms set forth in Article 244.

4. Those who commit swindling, misappropriation, or fraud related to electricity, gas, water or any other element, energy or fluid, on telecommunications terminal equipment, in amounts not exceeding four hundred euros.

5. Those who perpetrate the acts described in Section 2 of Articles 270.1 and 274.2, when the profit does not exceed four hundred euros, except if any of the circumstances foreseen in Articles 271 and 276, respectively, concurs.

Article 624

1. Whoever executes the acts included in Article 246 shall be punished with a fine of ten to thirty days if the utility does not exceed four hundred euros or if it cannot be estimated, as long as reported by the victim.

2. Whoever perpetrates the acts covered by Article 247 shall be punished with a fine of ten days to two months if the utility reported does not exceed four hundred euros.

Article 625

1. Those who intentionally cause damage in an amount not exceeding four hundred euros shall be punished with the penalty of permanent traceability of two to twelve days or a fine of ten to twenty days.

2. The punishment shall be imposed in the upper half if the damage is caused in places or to the properties to which Article 323 of this Code refers.

Article 626

Those who damage moveable assets or real estate that is public or privately owned, without due authorisation from the authorities or their owners, shall be punished with the penalty of permanent traceability from two to six days or three to nine days of community service.

Article 627[14]

(Repealed)

Article 628[15]

(Repealed)

TITLE III

Misdemeanours against the general interest

Article 629

The punishment of permanent traceability from two to eight days or a fine of twenty to sixty days shall be imposed on those who, having received counterfeit coins, notes, postal or fiscal stamps in good faith, pass them on in sums not exceeding four hundred euros once they know they are false.

---

[14] Repealed by single repealing provision 1 of Organic Law 7/2012 of 27 December
[15] Repealed by single repealing provision 1 of Organic Law 7/2012 of 27 December

Article 630

Those who abandon syringes, in all cases, or other dangerous instruments, in a manner and under circumstances that might cause damage to persons or spread diseases, or in places frequented by minors, shall be punished with the penalties of permanent traceability from six to ten days or a fine of one to two months.

Article 631

1. Owners or those charged with the custody of wild or harmful animals who let them loose or leave them under conditions in which they may cause harm shall be punished with the penalty of a fine from one to two months.

2. Whoever abandons a pet under conditions that endanger its life or integrity shall be punished with the penalty of a fine from fifteen days to two months.

Article 632

1. Whoever fells, burns, tears up, harvests any species or subspecies of endangered flora or its shoots, without serious damage to the environment, shall be punished with the penalty of a fine from ten to thirty days or community service from ten to twenty days.

2. Those who cruelly abuse pets or any other animals in legally unauthorised shows without incurring in the cases foreseen in Article 337 shall be punished with the penalty of a fine from twenty to sixty days or community service from twenty to thirty days.

TITLE IV

Misdemeanours against public order

Article 633

Those who slightly disturb the order at the hearing of a court or tribunal, at public acts, sports or cultural events, solemn ceremonies or large gatherings, shall be punished with the penalties of permanent traceability of two to twelve days and a fine of ten to thirty days.

Article 634

Those who show lack of due respect and consideration for the authority or its agents, or slightly disobey them, when perpetrating its functions, shall be punished with the penalty of a fine from ten to sixty days.

Article 635

Whoever remains on the premises of a public or private legal person, professional studio or office, or a commercial establishment or premises open to the public after the opening hours, against the will of the owner, shall be punished with the penalty of permanent traceability of two to ten days or a fine of one to two months.

Article 636

Those who carry out activities while lacking the mandatory civil liability insurance legally required to carry these out shall be punished with the penalty of a fine from one to two months.

The activities referred to in the preceding Section shall not include driving motor vehicles and mopeds.

Article 637

Whoever publicly and unduly uses an official uniform, suit, official insignia or decorations or who publicly claims professional status under an academic qualification he does not hold, shall be punished with the penalty of permanent traceability of two to ten days or a fine of ten to thirty days.

TITLE V

Common provisions for misdemeanours

Article 638

Judges and Courts of Law shall proceed to apply the penalties of this Book pursuant to their prudent criteria, within the limits of each one, in view of the circumstances of the case and of the offender, without being bound by the rules of Articles 61 to 72 of this Code.

Article 639

Misdemeanours that can only be prosecuted at the request of the person offended may also be reported by the Public Prosecutor if the victim is a minor, incapacitated or a handicapped person.

The absence of a report shall not stop preventive proceedings being conducted.

In these misdemeanours, forgiveness by the victim or his legal representative shall extinguish the criminal action or the punishment imposed, except as provided in Sub-Section Two of Section 4 of Article 130.

ADDITIONAL PROVISIONS

Additional Provision One

When a person is declared exempt of criminal accountability due to any of the causes foreseen in Sections 1 and 3 of Article 20 of this Code arising, the Public Prosecutor shall request, when appropriate, for declaration of incapacity before the Civil Jurisdiction, except if this has already been previously resolved and, when appropriate, internment pursuant to the civil legislation.

Additional Provision Two

When a governmental authority has knowledge of the existence of a minor or incapacitated person who is in a state of prostitution, whether voluntary or otherwise, but with the complicity of the persons exercising family, ethical-social or *de facto* authority over him, or who is lacking such, or should these have abandoned and not take charge of custody of him, it shall immediately report this to the public institution charged with protection of minors in the relevant territory, as well as to the Public Prosecutor, for them to act within their respective domains.

Likewise, in the cases in which the Judge or Court of Law orders special barring from the exercise of parental rights, fostership, safekeeping, guardianship or care, or deprivation of parental rights, this shall immediately be notified to the public institution charged with protection of minors in the relevant territory, as well as to the Public Prosecutor, for them to act within their respective domains.

Additional Provision Three

When, by report or claims by the offended part, criminal proceedings are commenced acts constituting felonies foreseen and punishable under Articles 267 and 621 of this Code, all other parties affected by those acts that consider themselves victims may appear in the criminal proceedings to be deemed a party thereto, whatever the amount of damages they claim.

TRANSITIONAL PROVISIONS

Transitional Provision One

The felonies and misdemeanours committed up to the day this Code came into force shall be judged pursuant to the legal text and other special criminal laws that are hereby repealed. Once this Code comes into force, should the provisions hereof be more favourable to the convict, these shall be applied.

Transitional Provision Two

In order to determine which law is most favourable, the relevant punishment for the act judged through application of the complete rules of one Code or another shall be taken into account. The provisions on redemption of penalties through work shall only be applicable to all convicts pursuant to the Code hereby repealed and they may not be taken advantage of by those to whom the provisions of this Code apply. The convict shall be heard in all cases.

Transitional Provision Three

Within the shortest possible time following publication of this new Criminal Code, the Directors of penitentiary establishments shall submit the Judges or Courts of Law dealing with the enforcement the list of convicts interned in the Centre they direct and the provisional settlement of the sentence being served, stating the days the convict has redeemed for work and those who may redeem them in the future, as appropriate, pursuant to Article 100 of the repealed Criminal Code and complementary provisions.

Transitional Provision Four

The Judges or Courts of Law mentioned in the preceding Provision shall proceed, once they have received the preceding settlement of conviction, to notify the Public Prosecutor, in order for him to report on whether it is appropriate to review the sentence and, in such an event, the terms of the review. Once the Public Prosecutor has given his report, they shall also proceed to hear the convict, notifying him of the terms of the review proposed, as well as informing the Solicitor who defended him at the trial, in order for him to state what he considers most favourable for the convict.

Transitional Provision Five

The General Council of the Judiciary, within the scope of the powers it is attributed by Article 98 of the Organic Act on the Judiciary, may appoint one or several of the Criminal Courts of Law or Sections of the High Provincial Courts exclusively to devote themselves to enforcement of criminal sentences to review the final judgements handed down before this Code came into force.

Those Judges or Courts of Law shall proceed to review final judgements and those sentences the convict is effectively serving, applying the most favourable provision construed strictly without taking into account judicial discretion possible in handing down sentence. In custodial sentences, this Code shall not be deemed more favourable when the term of the prior sentence imposed due to the act and its circumstances may also be imposed pursuant to this new Code. Exceptionally, if this Code establishes provisions for a non-custodial punishment for the same offence; in which case the sentence must be reviewed.

Sentences shall not be reviewed in which fulfilment of the punishment is suspended, without prejudice of doing so in the event of the suspension being revoked and prior to proceeding to effective fulfilment of the punishment suspended. The same rule shall be applied if the convict is on probation.

Nor shall sentences be reviewed in which, pursuant to the Code repealed and the new one, only the punishment of a fine is applicable.

Transitional Provision Six

Sentences shall not be reviewed in which the punishment has been executed or suspended, although other pronouncements of the ruling may be pending enforcement, as well as those that have been fully enforced, without prejudice to the fact that the Judge or Court of Law which has to take them into account in the future for the purposes of recidivism must previously examine whether the act penalised therein has ceased to be a felony or might attract a lower punishment than that imposed under this Code.

In cases of partial pardon, the sentences shall not be reviewed when the resulting punishment the convict is serving falls within a lower applicable framework established in this new Code.

Transitional Provision Seven

For the purposes of appreciating the aggravating circumstance of recidivism, the same Title of this Code shall be construed to include the felonies foreseen in the Code that is repealed and that have the same name and affect the legal right in the same way.

Transitional Provision Eight

In cases in which the punishment that may be applicable by application of this Code is one of weekend arrest, it shall be deemed, in order to value its comparative severity, that the duration of the custodial sentence be equivalent to two days for each weekend that is to be imposed. Should the punishment be one of a fine, it shall be deemed that each day of substitute detention that has been imposed, or that might be imposed by the Judge or Court of Law under the Code repealed shall be equivalent to two daily quotas of the fine under this Code.

Transitional Provision Nine

In the sentences handed down under the legislation repealed and that are not final due to an appeal being pending, the following rules shall be observed once the period of *vacatio legis* has elapsed:

a) In the case of appeal, the parties may invoke and the Court of Law shall apply the provisions of the new Code on its own motion, when they are more favourable to the convict;

b) In the case of a cassation appeal, even when not yet formalised, the appellant may define the legal offences based on the provisions of this new Code;

c) If, having filed the cassation appeal, this is being substantiated, this shall be returned to the appellant, on the Court's own motion or at the request of the party, for the term of eight days, in order to adapt the motives for cassation alleged to the provisions of this new Code, and the parties concerned, the Public Prosecutor and Magistrate presiding shall given time to scrutinise the appeal thus amended, continuing the formalities in the legal manner thereafter.

Transitional Provision Ten

Security measures that are under execution or pending, ordered pursuant to the Dangerousness and Social Reinstatement Act, or in application of Sections 1 and 3 of Article 8 or number 1 of Article 9 on the Criminal Code that is hereby repealed, shall be reviewed pursuant to the provisions of Title IV of Book I of this Code and the preceding rules.

In cases in which the maximum duration of the measure foreseen in this Code is lower than the time effectively served by those subject to it, the Judge or Court of Law shall declare that fulfilment completed and, if a custodial measure, order the inmate to be released immediately.

Transitional Provision Eleven

1. When special criminal or procedural laws are to be applied by the ordinary jurisdiction, the following substitutions are deemed to take place:

a) The punishment of major incarceration, for that of a custodial sentence from fifteen to twenty years, with the clause of this being raised to a sentence of imprisonment from twenty to twenty- five years when two or more aggravating circumstances concur with the offence.

b) The punishment of minor incarceration, for that of a custodial sentence from eight to fifteen years.

c) The punishment of major imprisonment, for that of a custodial sentence from three to eight years.

d) The punishment of minor imprisonment, for that of a custodial sentence from six months to three years.

e) The punishment of major detention, for that of detention from seven to fifteen weekends.

f) The punishment by fine imposed in an amount exceeding one hundred thousand pesetas set for acts punished as a felony, for that of fine of three to ten months.

g) The punishment by fine imposed in an amount less than one hundred thousand pesetas set for acts punished as a felony, for that of a fine from two to three months.

h) The punishment by fine imposed for criminal acts in an amount proportional to the gains obtained or the damage caused shall continue to be applied proportionally.

i) The punishment of minor detention, for that of detention from one to six weekends.

j) The punishment by fine set for acts defined as a misdemeanour, for a fine from one to sixty days.

k) The penalties depriving the convict of rights shall be imposed pursuant to the provisions and for the terms set in this Code.

l) Any other punishment included among those suppressed by this Code, for the punishment or security measure the Judge or Court of Law deems more similar and of equal or lower severity. Should such not exist, or if all are more serious, their imposition shall be lifted.

2. In the event of doubt, the convict shall be heard.

Transitional Provision Twelve

(Repealed)

REPEALING PROVISION

Sole Repealing Provision

1. The following are hereby repealed:

a) The consolidated text of the Criminal Code published by Decree 3096/1973, of 14th September, pursuant to the Act 44/1971, dated on 15th November, with its subsequent amendments, except for Articles 8.2, 9.3, Rule 1 of Article 20 with regard to Section 2 of Article 8, Section 2 of Article 22, 65, 417 bis and Additional Provisions One and Two of Organic Act 3/1989, dated 21st June;

b) The Act, dated 17th March 1908, on parole, with its subsequent amendments and complementary provisions;

c) Act 16/1970, dated 4th August, on Social Dangerousness and Reinstatement, with its subsequent amendments and complementary provisions;

d) The Act dated 26th July 1878, on prohibition of dangerous practices carried out by minors;

e) The substantive criminal provisions contained in the following special

laws: Act dated 19th September 1896, for protection of insectivorous birds;

Act dated 16th May 1902, on industrial property;

Act dated 23rd July 1903, on begging by minors;

Act dated 20th February 1942, on river fishing;

Act dated 31st December 1946, on fishing with explosives;

Act 1/1970, dated 4th April, on hunting. The felonies and misdemeanours foreseen in that Act, not contained in this Code, shall be deemed very serious administrative offences, being punished with a fine of fifty thousand to five hundred thousand pesetas and withdrawal of the hunting licence, or entitlement to obtain one, for a term from two to five years.

f) The following provisions:

Article 256 of the Penitentiary Regulations, approved by Royal Decree 1201/1981, of 8th May;

Articles 65 to 73 of the Prisons Services Regulations, approved by Decree of 2nd February 1956;

Articles 84 to 90 F) the Act 25/1964, dated 29th April, on Nuclear Energy;

Article 54 of Act 33/1971, dated 21st July, on Emigration;

Section 2 of Article 24 of Organic Act 2/1981, dated 6th April, on the Ombudsman;

Article 2 of Organic Act 8/1984, dated 26th December, on the regime of appeals in the case of conscientious objection and its penal regime;

Article 4 of Organic Act 5/1984, of 24th May, on Appearance before the Investigation Commissions of Congress of Deputies, the Senate or both Chambers;

Articles 29 and 49 of Act 209/1964, dated 24th December, Penal and Procedural on Aviation;

The terms "active and" of Article 137 of Organic Act 5/1985, dated 19th June, on the General Electoral Regime;

Article 6 of the Act 57/1968, dated 27th July, on Receipt of Moneys Advanced for the Building and Sale of Homes.

2. All provisions that are incompatible with the provisions of this Code are also hereby repealed.

FINAL PROVISIONS

Final Provision One

The Criminal Procedure Act is hereby amended and shall henceforth be drafted as follows:

"Article 14. Three. For the cognisance and resolution of trials over less serious felonies, as well as for misdemeanours, whether or not they are incidental, with which the principals of those felonies or others may be charged, when commission of the misdemeanour or its evidence is related thereto, the Penal Judge of the district where the felony was committed, or the Central Penal Judge where this falls within his remit."

"Article 779. Without prejudice to the terms established in the other special proceedings, the procedure regulated under this Title shall be applied to the judgement of felonies punished with a sentence of imprisonment not exceeding nine years, or by any other penalties of a different nature, whether unique, joint or alternative, whatever their amount or duration."

Final Provision Two

Section 2 of Article 1 of Organic Act 5/1995, on the Jury, hereby amended and shall henceforth be drafted as follows:

"2. Within the field of the judicial proceedings to which the preceding Section refers, a Jury shall be competent to consider and hand down a verdict in the felonies defined in the following provisions of the criminal code:

a) On unlawful killing (Articles 138 to 140);

b) On intimidation (Article 169.1);

c) On failure in the duty to assist (Articles 195 and 196);

d) On trespassing a dwelling (Articles 202 and 204);

e) On forest fires (Articles 352 to 354);

f) On disloyalty in the custody of documents (Articles 413 to 415);

g) On corruption (Article 419 to 426);

h) On influence peddling (Articles 428 to 430);

i) On embezzlement (Articles 432 to 434);

j) On fraud and illegal taxation (Articles 436 to 438);

k) On negotiations prohibited to civil servants (Articles 439 and 440);

l) On disloyalty in the custody of prisoners (Article 471)".

Final Provision Three

1. Chapter VI of Act 35/1988, dated 22nd November, on Assisted Reproduction Techniques, is hereby amended and shall henceforth be drafted as follows:

1. Letters a), k), l) and v) of Section 2.B) of Article 20 are suppressed;.

2. The text of Sub-Section r) of Section 2. b) shall be replaced with the following: "transfer of human gametes or pre-embryos in the uterus of another animal species, or the reverse operation, as well as unauthorised fecundation between human and animal gametes".

2. Article 21 of Chapter VII of Act 35/1988, on Assisted Reproduction Techniques, shall become Article 24.

Final Provision Four

Organic Act 1/1982, dated 5th May, on Protection of the Right to Honour, Personal and Family Privacy and Personal Image, is hereby amended and shall be drafted as follows:

"Article 1.

2. The criminal nature of the intrusion shall not prevent recourse to the judicial protection proceedings foreseen in Article 9 of this Act. In any event, the criteria of this Act shall be applicable to determine the civil liability arising from the felony"

"Article 7.

7. Charging with facts, or judgemental statements through actions or expressions that are in any way damaging to the dignity of another person, detracting from his fame or attacking his self-esteem."

Final Provision Five

Additional Provision Two of Organic Act 6/1995, dated 29th June, is hereby amended and shall be drafted as follows:

"The exemption from criminal accountability established in the second paragraphs of Articles 305, Section 4; 307, Section 3, and 308, Section 4, shall be equally applicable although the debts subject to regularisation are lower than the amounts established in those Articles."

Final Provision Six

Title V of Book I of this Code, Articles 193, 212, 233.3 and 272, as well as Additional Provisions One and Two, Transitional Provision Twelve and Final Provisions One and Three shall have the status of an ordinary Act of Parliament.

Final Provision Seven

This Code shall come into force six months after its full publication in the "Official State Gazette" and it shall be applied to all punishable acts committed after it coming into force.

Notwithstanding the foregoing, Article 19 hereof shall not be effective, until the act that regulates criminal accountability of minors to which such provision refers comes into force.

www.ingramcontent.com/pod-product-compliance
Lightning Source LLC
Chambersburg PA
CBHW082328220526

45470CB00008B/2432